FORGOTTEN MOVIE STARS OF THE 30's, 40's, and 50's

Motion Picture Stars of The Golden Age of Hollywood Who Are Virtually Unknown Today by Anyone under 40

By Gary Koca

This book is dedicated to the memory of my friend and fellow lover of classic movies, Oliver Gaddini. We would regularly get together for lunch or over the phone to discuss such things as:

1. Who was the better dancer, Fred Astaire or Gene Kelly? He liked Astaire, I liked Kelly.
2. Who was the better actor, Henry Fonda or James Stewart? We both agreed that Fonda was actually the better actor.
3. What was Gary Cooper's best performance? We both agreed on *High Noon*, although *Sergeant York* and *Pride of the Yankees* are in the team picture.
4. Are any of the modern day movie stars as beautiful as Gene Tierney? Simple answer – no.

I will miss him.

Copyright 2013 under the title *Forgotten Movie Stars of the 30's, 40's, and 50's.*

Table of Contents

Robert Taylor..1
Louis Hayward..20
Dana Andrews..40
Gene Tierney..58
Teresa Wright...72
Victor Mature...86
Paulette Goddard..102
Glenn Ford..117
Barbara Stanwyck 131
Ray Milland...153
Joseph Cotten..173
John Garfield...187
Susan Hayward..200
William Powell...213
Myrna Loy..228
Ronald Colman..239
Kathryn Grayson..252
Howard Keel...268
Tyrone Power..285
Jean Simmons..304
Jean Arthur...321

Gail Russell..341

Lizabeth Scott..353

Randolph Scott..368

Marlene Dietrich..388

Forgotten Movie Stars of the 30's, 40's, and 50's

By Gary Koca

Introduction – Who the Hell is Glenn Ford?

Picture this scene from the western film *3:10 to Yuma*. The central character – a bank robber and murderer named Ben Wade –has been caught and is being taken on a journey to catch a train that will take him to the Yuma prison. He has told his captor that he will never be put on that train, that his band of outlaws will rescue him well before he has to get on it. You are intrigued by this outlaw, because on the one hand he seems like such a compassionate and caring individual, asking how the hero's family is doing, while you know that he is a sadistic killer waiting for just the right opportunity to disarm his captor and grab his gun. As a result, you are spellbound by the actor playing the part – Russell Crowe. But wait a minute! It's not the Russell Crowe version, it's the superior 1957 version. And the part of Ben Wade is played by none other than Glenn Ford.

The day after movie star Glenn Ford died – August 31, 2006 – a local sports talk radio host – Mike North - was discussing what a huge western star Glenn Ford was, on his daily morning show. Half the callers were over 45 and calling him to agree, and the other half were people – mainly guys under 40 – calling in to ask him, "Who the hell is Glenn Ford?" That bit of information started me thinking that maybe it was time for a book on some of those old-time forgotten movie stars who made terrific contributions to film and should be remembered. Instead of Glenn Ford, it could easily have been people like Robert Taylor, Dana Andrews, John Garfield, Gene Tierney, Teresa Wright, Paulette Goddard, and a whole host of others.

It has become increasingly apparent to me that a number of movie stars whose careers blossomed in the 1930's, 1940's, and 1950's, are just not very well known by today's generation of movie fans. These are stars who were pretty big in their heyday, but are virtually unknown today by almost everyone under the age of 40 or 45. If you look on Turner Classic Movies, you will find one of their movies highlighted several nights a week, and fans of classic movies like myself enjoy these stars as much as the top stars of that era. Collectively, they simply made some great movies!

Now, I am not talking about the 50 or so stars from that era who are and continue to be well known to everyone – people like John Wayne, James Stewart, Bette Davis, Kathryn Hepburn, Joan Crawford, Cary Grant, Clark Gable, Errol Flynn, Henry Fonda, Marilyn Monroe, Burt Lancaster, Humphrey Bogart, James Cagney, and many other stars of that era. Instead, the focus of this book will be about those stars who, for whatever reason, just were not quite as big or whose legacy is just not that well known today as those mentioned above. Yet they made important contributions to movies in the era that began after silent films ended and when movies were still the major form of entertainment in this country – that is, before television really took off. This book will be a snapshot look at 25 of those individuals – 13 men and 12 women.

The criteria for inclusion in this book are four-fold:

1. The individual had to be a fairly big star in his/her time but not in that top group of 50 or so that people under the age of 40-45 still remember today.
2. They had to be what we would call leading men and women rather than character actors like Walter Brennan, Thomas Mitchell, or Claude Rains, for example.
3. The major portion of their careers had to be after the silent era but before 1960. Marlon Brando, for example, made his film debut in 1950 in *The Men*, but his major

timeframe was clearly in the late 1950's and later. While a great star, he does not qualify in the time period I am focusing on. Same with Sidney Poitier, who continued to work for 40+ years after that. Plus, neither would be in the forgotten star category as required by #1.
4. The individual had to be someone that I really enjoyed watching on screen – after all, it's my book and I decided to place whomever I wanted in it. Therefore, someone like Frederick March or George Brent, for example, would easily meet the first three criteria. However, if I was never a big fan of the individual, they will not be in this book. That explains why there are many well qualified stars who did not make it into the book.

For each of the 25 individuals listed, I will provide a brief summary of that person, followed by a biography of that individual, followed by any recognition (basically any awards) that they received in their career. Then I will take between 4-8 of their major films and discuss the plot plus the contribution of that individual to the film. Please remember that these are my favorite films of that particular individual and not necessarily the best films of that person. In most cases, the two are one in the same, but not in all cases. For example, *It Happens Every Spring*, with Ray Milland, is not necessarily one of Milland's best films, but since the background is baseball, it happens to be one of my favorites of his films.

Finally, the reader should understand that, as far as recognition is concerned, there were nowhere near the number of awards given in the 1930's through 1950's to actors and actresses as there are today. The Emmys and Golden Globes did not go into effect until the mid or late 1940's, and there were really no other awards given other than Oscars at that time. That will explain the lack of recognition for just about all of these individuals compared to the stars of today, who can be recognized by film festivals in half the cities in the U.S.

Hopefully, we can continue the legacies of these individuals as well as the 50 or so major stars from that era. After all, the films these individuals starred in 60 to 80 years ago are partially responsibility for continuing the movies that we are able to enjoy today. And who knows, maybe one day fifty years from now while people still remember Sandra Bullock, Angelina Jolie, Brad Pitt, and Johnny Depp, one of today's stars like a Mark Wahlberg, Matt Damon, or Charlize Theron will be a "forgotten star" who is worthy of remembering.

My Forgotten Stars for this book are the following. They are not listed in any particular order, although I will admit that the first ten happen to be real favorites of mine:

1. Robert Taylor
2. Louis Hayward
3. Dana Andrews
4. Gene Tierney
5. Teresa Wright
6. Victor Mature
7. Paulette Goddard
8. Glenn Ford
9. Barbara Stanwyck
10. Ray Milland
11. Joseph Cotten
12. John Garfield
13. Susan Hayward
14. William Powell
15. Myrna Loy
16. Ronald Colman
17. Kathryn Grayson
18. Howard Keel
19. Tyrone Power
20. Jean Simmons
21. Jean Arthur
22. Gail Russell
23. Lizabeth Scott
24. Randolph Scott
25. Marlene Dietrich

Robert Taylor – 1911-1968

Robert Taylor is probably the single best illustration of a forgotten star from the 1930's through 1950's. In his heyday, he was as popular as any male movie star of that era – including Cary Grant, Clark Gable, Henry Fonda, and others. Taylor was often identified as the handsomest movie star of that era because of his classic good looks. He became known as The Man with the Perfect Profile, in fact. Make no mistake about it – Robert Taylor was a classic star in the Golden Age of Hollywood.

Taylor made a number of important films in a variety of genres, including romantic comedies, swashbucklers, westerns, and historical fiction as well as adventure stories, and even a crime drama or two. In addition, he starred in television's *The Detectives* in the late 1950's and early 1960's.

FORGOTTEN MOVIE STARS OF THE 30's, 40's, and 50's

> Some of Taylor's Leading Ladies included the following:
>
> - Elizabeth Taylor
> - Greta Garbo
> - Joan Fontaine
> - Vivian Leigh
> - Deborah Kerr
> - Greer Garson
> - Lana Turner

I used to think that Robert Taylor was a rather wooden actor, and indeed he is in some films. But he displayed some range and was actually pretty capable in several others. My selections, therefore, include a typical Robert Taylor film, *Ivanhoe*, perhaps his best overall film, *Waterloo Bridge*, one where he was a downright villain, *The Last Hunt*, and a very little known but very enjoyable and somewhat moving film, *Devil's Doorway*.

My favorite Robert Taylor films include the following:

- *Ivanhoe*
- *Waterloo Bridge*
- *The Last Hunt*
- *Devil's Doorway*
- *Johnny Eager*
- *Quo Vadis*
- *The Law and Jake Wade*

By the way, Robert Taylor's real name cried out to be changed. Can you see this on a marquee – *Ivanhoe,* starring Spangler Arlington Brugh?

FORGOTTEN MOVIE STARS OF THE 30's, 40's, and 50's

Biography

Robert Taylor was considered by many the most handsome actor ever to grace the silver screen. Robert Taylor (actually, Spangler Arlington Brugh), was born in Filley, Nebraska on August 5, 1911, the only son of a farmer who worked in the grain business but turned doctor in order to find a cure for his wife's recurrent health problems.

Taylor grew up in a rural environment surrounded by open farmlands and developed a love for the outdoors that he treasured the rest of his life; no wonder he looked so natural in westerns like *The Last Hunt* and *The Law and Jake Wade*. He actually served as a physician's assistant – perhaps he invented this occupation? - to his father on visits to patients. He had an active high school resume, participating in track, playing cello in the school orchestra, and winning oratory awards, which contributed to his interest in acting rather than medicine.

From 1929 to 1931 he attended Doane College in Crete, Nebraska, where he established the dramatic group called The Doane Players. Taylor's first appearance on stage at Doane was on December 19, 1929 in the play "Helena Boys." Taylor won several oratorical contests at that time and was quite popular with his classmates and teachers.

In 1931 he moved to Claremont, California – perhaps because his cello teacher, whom he was close to, moved to the Pomona area and Taylor decided to follow him. There, he enrolled at Pomona College where he participated in various plays like "The Importance of Being Ernest" and "Camille." Because of his uncommonly good looks, Taylor was frequently given leading roles in productions. Remember that this was the very beginning of the sound era, and Hollywood was clearly starting to look for new talent.

FORGOTTEN MOVIE STARS OF THE 30's, 40's, and 50's

While performing "Journey's End" in 1932, Robert Taylor was discovered by MGM talent scout Ben Piazza, and was offered a screen test and dramatic instruction from dramatics coach Oliver Hindsdell at MGM Studios in Culver City. After he graduated from Pomona College, on February 6, 1934 he signed a seven year contract with MGM for $35.00 a week (perhaps the lowest-paid actor on record!) and his name was changed to Robert Taylor – big surprise.

Making his screen debut for 20th Century Fox, Taylor played a supporting role in *Handy Andy* (1934), which starred Will Rogers. After a few small parts he was loaned to Universal in 1935 to star in *Magnificent Obsession* (1935) with Irene Dunne. The movie was a big success, Taylor was excellent in his first leading man role, and his performance was praised by the critics, establishing him as a major star.

Extremely handsome, with good manners and disarming candor, Taylor was artfully groomed by MGM to become "The Heartthrob of the Nation." In a short time he became one of the most popular box-office stars of the period, especially after starring with Garbo in *Camille*, and even had a fan-mail base that exceeded Clark Gable's.

> With that in mind, you can clearly see why he is in this book. Clark Gable was the King of Hollywood, yet Taylor was more popular than Gable at times. Why is Taylor a forgotten star? Perhaps the quality of his movies were not as good as the quality of Gable's. And of course, Clark Gable had *Gone with the Wind*.

FORGOTTEN MOVIE STARS OF THE 30's, 40's, and 50's

In 1936 he met Barbara Stanwyck, and they began a well-publicized romance which had interesting results. The January 1939 *Photoplay* magazine published an article titled "Hollywood's Unmarried Husbands and Wives," condemning the relationships between Charles Chaplin and Paulette Goddard, Clark Gable and Carole Lombard, and Taylor and Barbara Stanwyck, among others. At that time, studio executives did not relish any negative publicity about their stars. So as in the case of Gable and Lombard, Louis B. Mayer encouraged Taylor to marry Barbara Stanwyck as quickly as possible in order to avoid public scandal. Marrying on May 14, 1939, Taylor's popularity only increased after filming *A Yank at Oxford* (1938), MGM's first British production.

> "Nobody survives the sort of publicity that he's had," said director George Cukor at that time. Cukor was wrong!

Taylor's range extended in the early 1940's into several genres and characters, playing an aristocratic British officer in the tragic love story of *Waterloo Bridge* (1940) – perhaps his best film - with Vivien Leigh, a despairing man trying to rescue his mother from a Nazi concentration camp in *Escape* (1940) with Norma Shearer, the impulsive outlaw William Bonney in *Billy the Kid* (1941), his first western and first color film, a cold-blooded racketeer in the impressive film noir *Johnny Eager* (1941) with Lana Turner and Oscar winner Van Heflin, and a tough no-nonsense sergeant in the war film *Bataan* (1943). He also proved to have a skillful sense of comic timing in movies like *Her Cardboard Lover* (1942), Norma Shearer's last picture, and *When Ladies Meet* (1941) with Joan Crawford and Greer Garson.

FORGOTTEN MOVIE STARS OF THE 30's, 40's, and 50's

> Westerns, war films, dramas, swashbucklers, gangster flicks, and comedies – you can't get much more diversified than that!

With the arrival of World War II, Taylor enlisted in the U.S. Navy where he served under his real name of Spangler Arlington Brugh as a flight instructor from 1943 to 1945. He also directed 17 Navy training films and was the narrator for the Academy Award winning documentary *The Fighting Lady* (1944). After the war ended, in 1947, he was subpoenaed to testify before the House Committee on Un-American Activities (HUAC) about alleged Communist infiltration of the motion picture industry.

On May 14, 1947 in a closed session at the Biltmore Hotel in California, Taylor stated that the government had pressed him to star in *Song of Russia* (1944). He asserted that he didn't want to do it because he thought it was definitely Communist propaganda. Louis B. Mayer denied Taylor's statement and in a public hearing held by the Committee in Washington D.C. on October 1947, Taylor retracted and declared that he was not forced to do the picture.

In his testimony, he also named Karen Morley, Howard Da Silva, and Lester Cole as disrupters within Screen Actors Guild meetings. Although these individuals were in fact members of the Communist Party, were previously investigated by the FBI, and were also named by other witnesses, the act of mentioning them at a public hearing affected Taylor's public image in the following years. As you may guess, Taylor was not held in the highest regard by the left-leaning Hollywood for calling fellow actors communists.

FORGOTTEN MOVIE STARS OF THE 30's, 40's, and 50's

Although a box-office flop, *Devil's Doorway* (1950) was a remarkable western ahead of its time in which Taylor portrays a Shoshone Indian who defends his land and his people against the contempt and the abuse of the white man. Taylor regained the top spot in the early 1950's when he landed the role of commander Marcus Vinicius in the epic *Quo Vadis* (1951), which became the biggest box-office draw of its time. However, during the filming, his marriage to Barbara Stanwyck ended in divorce after he had a very public affair with an Italian starlet in Rome. Other big, lavish and flamboyant productions followed; *Ivanhoe* (1952), *Knights of the Round Table* (1953), the first film made by MGM using the wide-screen process known as CinemaScope, and *Quentin Durward* (1955), all filmed in England, which made him the epitome of the "knight in shining armor."

Nevertheless, he gave his most notable performances playing harsh characters in other less popular titles. He was the rude, arrogant and misogynist but still good guy scout in William A. Wellman's *Westward the Women* (1951), the troubled man struggling between his duty and his conscience in *Above and Beyond* (1952), the hero of the biopic of Col. Paul Tibbets, about the man who commanded the mission that dropped the atomic bomb on Hiroshima in 1945, the violent and racist buffalo hunter in Richard Brooks's *The Last Hunt* (1956), and the cynical, crooked policeman in *Rogue Cop* (1954).

In April of 1952 he met German-born actress Ursula Thiess and married her two years later, becoming a father for the first time when his son Terry was born in 1955. His wife gave up her screen career in order to take care of the family and gave birth to his daughter Tessa in 1959, when Taylor purchased a large ranch in the Brentwood area of Los Angeles, afterward known as The Robert Taylor Ranch. There, the Taylors enjoyed a quiet life away from the limelight.

FORGOTTEN MOVIE STARS OF THE 30's, 40's, and 50's

Taylor turned successfully to television in 1959 after negotiating a new non-exclusive contract with MGM, starring in a crime series "The Detectives Starring Robert Taylor," featured on ABC-TV (1959-1961) and NBC-TV (1961-1962). In addition, he continued working in minor films and was host and occasional star of the television series "Death Valley Days" from 1966 until 1968 when he became too ill to continue working. A longtime smoker, he was diagnosed with lung cancer in April, 1968.

After a long struggle with the disease, Robert Taylor died on June 8, 1969 in St. John's Hospital in Santa Monica, California at the age of 57. Long-time best friend Ronald Reagan delivered the eulogy.

> During his 34-year career Taylor's friends always heard him say: "I really don't have any talent and won't last long. I'm a flash in the pan." He had enough talent to last for more than 30 years.

Recognition

Robert Taylor won a Golden Globe Award – Henrietta Award – as a World Film Favorite in 1954. Taylor was inducted into the Hall of Great Western Performers of the National Cowboy and Western Heritage Museum in 1970.

He has a star on the Hollywood Walk of Fame at 1500 Vine Street.

My Favorite Robert Taylor Films

FORGOTTEN MOVIE STARS OF THE 30's, 40's, and 50's

1. Ivanhoe – 1952

The unrelated Taylor's – Robert and Elizabeth – in *Ivanhoe*. He is Ivanhoe, and she is Rebecca, the woman he defends and fights for. In this scene, he vows to be her champion. Very noble indeed!

If you are looking for a Robert Taylor movie based on a work of historical fiction, look no further than *Ivanhoe*. Based on the classic novel by Sir Walter Scott, *Ivanhoe* is a classic historical fiction/costume drama that tells the tale of the disinherited knight who joins the likes of Robin Hood and others to rescue King Richard the Lionhearted from the clutches of his brother, the evil Prince John and his cronies. Ivanhoe returns from the Crusades to learn that King Richard is imprisoned for a huge ransom in Austria. His plan to pay the ransom falls on deaf ears - Prince John and his fellow Normans are certainly not going to help him - until the Jews in England assist him by raising most of the ransom money.

FORGOTTEN MOVIE STARS OF THE 30's, 40's, and 50's

After several thrilling adventures and villainous double-crosses, Rebecca, the beautiful daughter of his Jewish friend, is kidnapped and tried as a witch, and Ivanhoe volunteers to defend her honor as her champion in the final climatic scene. The film features several jousting tournaments and action galore, with Taylor turning in a rousing performance as Ivanhoe. This is a movie made in the days when there were clear heroes and villains, and Taylor was never more heroic than in the title character.

I really love this swashbuckler! The color, pageantry, and sets are first-rate, and there is just enough action to keep the involved plot interesting. When Ivanhoe rides in during a jousting tournament to defend the helpless Saxons from the awful Normans, a chill goes up my spine. Although Taylor is probably a bit too old to play Ivanhoe (he was 40 at the time), he nevertheless turns in a most convincing performance as the title character. He is completely believable as the disinherited knight, attempting to gain back the respect of his father, juggle the love of two women, and rescue England from sinister forces. The film also features, among others, Joan Fontaine as his love, Lady Rowena; Elizabeth Taylor as Rebecca, who loves him and whose honor Ivanhoe fights for in the closing conflict; and the always-good George Sanders as his enemy, Brian De Bois-Guilbert. Featured in a small role is Guy Rolfe as Prince John, along with Finlay Currie and Felix Aylmer as Isaac, the father of Rebecca.

This film was nominated for three Academy awards – Best Cinematography (not surprising), Best Music, and Best Picture.

> Personally, I cannot imagine anyone choosing Joan Fontaine (Rowena) over Elizabeth Taylor (Rebecca), but that is the novel's story line.

FORGOTTEN MOVIE STARS OF THE 30's, 40's, and 50's

2. Waterloo Bridge - 1940

A poster from *Waterloo Bridge* featuring star-crossed lovers Robert Taylor and Vivien Leigh.

Waterloo Bridge is told in a flashback format. On his way to France to fight in World War II, British Colonel Roy Cronin (Robert Taylor) stops his cab on London's Waterloo Bridge and reflects on the past: It is 1914 and air raid sirens screech. A young woman drops her purse and Roy helps its owner, Myra Lester (Vivien Leigh), a beautiful ballet dancer, to retrieve it. They seek shelter together and a whirlwind wartime courtship follows, resulting in Roy asking Myra to marry him. Before the ceremony can be performed, however, Roy is called to the front and Myra is fired by the troupe's tyrannical ballet mistress for missing a performance in order to see him off to war.

FORGOTTEN MOVIE STARS OF THE 30's, 40's, and 50's

Unable to find work in another ballet or show, Myra is broke and hungry. One afternoon, while waiting to meet Roy's aristocratic mother for the first time, Myra sees a notice about Roy's death in the newspaper and faints. When Lady Margaret arrives, Myra cannot tell her the terrible news, and her erratic behavior shocks and angers Roy's mother, who leaves in disgust. Myra then falls ill and lies close to death from grief. After recovering, she turns to a life of prostitution to make ends meet. One year later, Roy returns to London – he was in a German prison for a year - and the first sight that he sees upon getting off the train is Myra, who has come to pick up and "entertain" soldiers. He believes that she has come to meet him, and knowing nothing of her life in the past year, takes her home to his family estate in Scotland. Although Myra tries to convince herself that they can be happy, she soon realizes that her past will ruin Roy's life. After confessing all to his mother, she runs away. Roy follows, but she eludes him and commits suicide by throwing herself in front of an onrushing military truck on Waterloo Bridge. Now back in the present and holding the good luck charm that he had once given Myra, Roy leaves for the front.

This film – a real tear jerker – features two great performances by two great stars, Taylor and Leigh. The chemistry between them is terrific, and Taylor gives another first-rate performance as the British soldier. *Waterloo Bridge* may be his all-around best film. And it does not hurt that the two stars are among the most beautiful people in Hollywood, at that time or ever.

> As Robert Osborne of TCM said in his introduction to this film, "That's why people go to the movies – to see people that don't look like their neighbors."

FORGOTTEN MOVIE STARS OF THE 30's, 40's, and 50's

I really enjoy this movie because it tells such a great story and really gets one involved in caring about the two stars. From the beginning, you know the movie is not going to have a happy ending, but you are so interested in the story of these two individuals that you don't really mind it.

> *Waterloo Bridge* was Vivien Leigh's first film after another movie you may have heard of – as Scarlett O'Hara in *Gone with the Wind*.

3. The Last Hunt - 1956

The Last Hunt is an excellent western starring Robert Taylor and Stewart Granger as buffalo hunters. Set in the early 1880s, this is the story of one of the last buffalo hunts in the Northwest. Sandy McKenzie (Granger) is tired of hunting and killing defenseless buffalo (bison). His friend, Charley Gilson (Taylor), on the other hand, relishes the hunt and enjoys killing buffalo as well as Indians. When Charley kills an Indian raiding party, and takes their squaw as his own, tension develops between the two hunters, and matters will only be settled in the inevitable showdown. Taylor is subject to a "chilling" ending in the final scene of this movie.

The film features some beautiful scenery as well as a different type of role for Robert Taylor. He is clearly the villain in this movie. He hates Indians, he hates buffalo, he hates women, he probably even hates Santa Claus and the Easter Bunny. This film is quite a departure from Taylor's typical role as the hero, and he is excellent. I like the film because it gives Taylor a chance to play something besides the good guy and believe me, he is anything but that in this film. Plus, filmed on location in the West, the scenery is breathtaking.

FORGOTTEN MOVIE STARS OF THE 30's, 40's, and 50's

> Three years earlier, Taylor and Granger co-starred in a movie about ship captains and mutinous pirates called *All the Brothers Were Valiant*. As the title implies, they played brothers in this movie. But this time, Granger was the villain and Taylor the hero.

4. Devil's Doorway - 1950

In this black and white western, Robert Taylor plays Lance Poole, a Native American who won a Medal of Honor fighting at Gettysburg during the Civil War. He returns to his tribal lands intent on peaceful cattle ranching on lands that he owns. But white sheep farmers want his fertile grass range and manage to turn the ostensibly civilized white population against the Indians, with tragic results for everyone involved. Even when Poole enlists the aid of a local female attorney to assist him in fighting for the land that is rightfully his, he is not ultimately successful and must turn to violence to defend his land.

Devil's Doorway is unique for its refusal to fall back on the clichés of the genre. There is no romantic subplot to detract from the rising tension in the narrative and no "happy ending" for our hero either - the movie ends in genocide with the surviving Shoshone women and children being escorted by the cavalry to a reservation. Most unconventional of all is the introduction of a female lawyer (played by Paula Raymond) who defends Taylor. She seems like an anachronism in the frontier town of Medicine Bow. But, like Poole, she's an outsider in her own community who is further discredited for representing and defending a Shoshone Indian against the white sheep farmers and townspeople. While there is an undeniable attraction between Masters and Poole, they never acknowledge it directly.

FORGOTTEN MOVIE STARS OF THE 30's, 40's, and 50's

Devil's Doorway was made at the same time as another pro-Native American film, *Broken Arrow,* with Jeff Chandler. When *Broken Arrow* proved to be a box office hit, the studio released *Devil's Doorway* but it was largely ignored by critics and the public. The irony of all this is that, seen today, *Broken Arrow* seems preachy and patronizing whereas *Devil's Doorway*, directed by Anthony Mann, stands out as a much more realistic and grim depiction of how the West was really won – by massacring Native Americans and ignoring their legitimate claims for land.

Frankly, I had never heard of this movie until I watched it on Turner Classic Movies a while back. During the introduction before the movie, TCM host Robert Osborne asked his guest, a historian of Native American films and arts and himself a Native American, if the American Indians were upset that a white man was cast in this part. The guest said no, because Taylor did an excellent job in portraying Poole as a sympathetic figure in this film that showed the American Indian point of view very effectively.

5. Johnny Eager – 1942

Van Heflin, unidentified actress, and Robert Taylor in a scene from *Johnny Eager*.

FORGOTTEN MOVIE STARS OF THE 30's, 40's, and 50's

Robert Taylor plays an ex-con pretending to be a cabbie in order to satisfy his parole board. In reality, gangster Eager is up to old tricks, bankrolling a dog track and jockeying for the top spot in the local underworld. Into this scheme steps Lisabeth Bard (Lana Turner), a socialite sociologist who takes too strong an interest in Eager. Eager takes advantage of those affections and tricks Lisabeth into believing she has killed a man in order for Eager to blackmail her father (Edward Arnold), the district attorney standing between Eager and the opening of his dog track. Of course, Eager's plans unravel with tragic results when he actually falls for the girl.

Although *Johnny Eager* is no classic, it features good performances by Taylor, Lana Turner, and Edward Arnold, but especially by Van Heflin as Eager's best friend, Jeff Hackett. Heflin won an Oscar for Best Supporting Actor for his outstanding performance.

6. Quo Vadis - 1951

Robert Taylor and Deborah Kerr as lovers in *Quo Vadis*.

FORGOTTEN MOVIE STARS OF THE 30's, 40's, and 50's

Shortly after General Marcus Vinicius returns to Rome after three years of fighting in the field, he meets Lygia and falls in love with her. She is a Christian and as such doesn't want to have anything to do with a Roman general who specializes in killing people in battle. Though she grew up Roman, the adopted daughter of a retired general, Lygia is technically a hostage of Rome. Marcus gets Emperor Nero to give her to him for his glorious war record. Lygia resents this, but over time falls in love with Marcus anyway.

Meanwhile Nero's atrocities get more outrageous, turning even loyal Romans like Marcus against him. When Nero burns Rome and blames the Christians, Marcus goes off to save Lygia and her family. Nero captures them and many other Christians, and throws them to the lions. Do they all get eaten by lions? Watch the movie and find out.

This film, one of the first of the biblical-type spectacles, is, like many of these films, a bit starchy and preachy, but features good performances by Taylor as Marcus and Kerr as Lygia. Taylor is fairly convincing as he moves from hating to accepting Christians, and perhaps even becoming one himself. As in most of these good movies, there are good vibes between the two stars. The film also features a strong supporting cast, especially Leo Genn as Petrionius, the Senator with a heart, and Peter Ustinov as the loony emperor Nero. Another film like *Spartacus* where Ustinov is good playing a Roman. *Quo Vadis* was nominated for eight Oscars but did not win any.

> Biblical spectacles tend not to do too well at Oscar time. *Ben Hur* was an exception.

FORGOTTEN MOVIE STARS OF THE 30's, 40's, and 50's

7. The Law and Jake Wade - 1958

As the film opens, Jake Wade (Robert Taylor) sneaks into a jail and holds up the Marshal to spring Clint Hollister (Richard Widmark) who has been imprisoned for robbery and murder. As a result, Jake has ostensibly paid back an old debt owed his former partner from the days when the two rode together as outlaw members of Quantrill's Raiders; this included robbing banks and trains even after the Civil War ended for their own personal profit. Jake has since completely washed his hands of his former career and has used his abilities to good use by becoming a Marshal himself, but is satisfying his own personal code of honor by taking care of this one last thing before he marries his fiancée and settles down. Clint still holds a grudge for Jake's running out on him on their last bank robbery with $20,000 from that heist, from which Jake carries guilt for believing (incorrectly, as it turns out) that he had shot and killed a young boy during the robbery.

Clint gathers together a gang and kidnaps Jake and Peggy, coercing Jake into taking them to the place where he has hidden the money. During the trip the group fights it out between themselves and with the Comanche Indians before the inevitable duel between good and evil takes place.

The Law and Jake Wade is an excellent western that demonstrates an older, wizened, battle-weary Robert Taylor – now in his late 40's – pitted against the younger Widmark, playing one of his typical sadistic bad guys. Taylor's character certainly has his baggage from his outlaw days as a member of Quantrill's Raiders, but is making a real effort to turn his life around until he is forced to pay back an old debt. There is constant tension between the two leads throughout the film. The supporting cast includes Ray Middleton, Henry Silva, Patricia Owens, and DeForrest Kelley before Star Trek.

FORGOTTEN MOVIE STARS OF THE 30's, 40's, and 50's

Henry Silva has had a really impressive film career. Because of his exotic looks, he has played:

- ➢ A Native American in several Westerns
- ➢ A Mexican Bandido in *The Bravados*
- ➢ A Chinese Communist in *The Manchurian Candidate*
- ➢ A Rat Pack member in the original *Ocean's Eleven*
- ➢ Killer Kane, in the 1979 "Buck Rogers" TV show
- ➢ And of course, Henry Silva is… Italian.

Henry Silva in one of his many western roles.

Robert Taylor was a top-notch star of the 1930's through 1950's who in his heyday was probably the most famous star of all the forgotten stars in this book. During his peak, he was every bit the equal of Clark Gable, Cary Grant, Errol Flynn, or any other of the handsome leading men of his generation. While never a great actor, he was good in a variety of roles in many different types of motion pictures.

FORGOTTEN MOVIE STARS OF THE 30's, 40's, and 50's

Louis Hayward – 1909-1985

I always think of Louis Hayward as the poor man's Errol Flynn because of all the swashbuckler movies he starred in. Sure, he played in many other types of films, but gained his greatest notoriety from his costume drama roles, primarily in the 1930's and 1940's. He also was the first actor to star as The Saint in 1938's *The Saint in New York*. He was also "The Lone Wolf" on television in the 1950's. Although perhaps the least well known of any of the forgotten stars in this book, it is because of his adventures in these costume dramas that makes him one of my personal favorites of the Forgotten Stars. In addition, he starred in one of my favorite motion pictures.

FORGOTTEN MOVIE STARS OF THE 30's, 40's, and 50's

Louis Hayward was a suavely handsome, often tongue-in-cheek leading man who began his career with a provincial theater company in England. Hayward had most of his starring roles between the mid-1930's and 1950's but continued to act in movies and on television until the mid-1970's. His first important role – until he was quickly disposed of in the movie by Claude Rains – was as Frederick March/Anthony Adverse's father in *Anthony Adverse* (1935). But Hayward's most famous role was as the twin brothers Louis and Philippe - in the best (by far!) version of *The Man in the Iron Mask* in 1939.

> Anyone who thinks that the remake of *The Man in the Iron Mask* with Leonardo DiCaprio is a really good movie should watch the 1939 version to see how a really great swashbuckler movie is made.

He had the ability to play leading men in a variety of venues – swashbucklers, detectives, ne'er do wells that you still want to root for, military heroes, and even a horror film or two (*Son of Dr. Jekyll*). But clearly his best roles were in costume dramas. Even the mediocre ones were better than they otherwise would have been because of his presence. Interestingly enough, Hayward bears a strong resemblance to current actor Hugh Grant – at least, I think he does.

My favorite Louis Hayward films include the following:

- *The Man in the Iron Mask* – his best film, and a real classic, a must see
- *And Then There Were None*

FORGOTTEN MOVIE STARS OF THE 30's, 40's, and 50's

- *The Black Arrow*
- *Walk a Crooked Mile*
- *The Son of Monte Cristo*
- *Ladies in Retirement*
- *Anthony Adverse*

Biography

Born in Johannesburg, South Africa, Louis Hayward grew up in South Africa but was educated largely in England. While searching for a career, Hayward spent a short time managing a London nightclub and theater. There, he displayed some talent for and decided to try his luck in acting instead of managing a theater. Hayward was quickly tapped by playwright Noel Coward as his patron – some reports indicate that he and Coward were in fact a couple.

> I should point out that affairs, whether heterosexual or homosexual, were just kept much more secret in those days.

Matinee idol-handsome, Hayward developed acting skills as a co-star in the London staging of several Broadway plays, among them "Dracula" and "Another Language". He began his film career in the British *Self Made Lady* (1932) which was followed by five UK films through 1933.

Hayward came to New York and Broadway in 1935 to star in "Point Verlaine." It was his only Broadway venture, but it brought him a Hollywood contract. His first American film role was in *The Flame Within* (1935).

FORGOTTEN MOVIE STARS OF THE 30's, 40's, and 50's

After several supporting roles, in 1936 Hayward got his real break starring in the extended romantic prologue of Warner Bros. *Anthony Adverse* (1936). As the dashing officer Denis Moore, he was Anthony's father, rescuing his lover/soon-to-be-a-mother Maria at the very beginning of the film from an arranged marriage to the Marquis Don Luis, played by Claude Rains.

Shot with gauze focus in part to increase the dreamlike romantic interlude of the lovers, the prologue played to a bitter end with Hayward dispatched by an unlucky break in a sword duel with the outraged Don Luis, and Maria - now pregnant - forced to return to her husband. But Hayward had his defining moment.

Through the remainder of the 1930s Louis Hayward had ample opportunities to vary that class of swashbuckling character - starting with some early B tier efforts. Along with good looks he had an airy delivery of speech which worked as both hero and rogue or occasional suave villain.

The familiar British Simon Templar character was brought to the screen originally by Hayward in *The Saint in New York* (1938) to cap his B picture career, with Hayward the first actor to play the role. The stylish *The Man in the Iron Mask* (1939) gave him the opportunity to play the good and evil royal twins with impressive flair.

But the swashbuckling efforts did not pan out nearly as well for Hayward as they did for fellow British actor Errol Flynn. *The Son of Monte Cristo* (1940) was a *Prisoner of Zenda* look-alike but not nearly as good. Another bad break was his 1941 casting with a pivotal role in Orson Welles' *The Magnificent Ambersons* only to be edited away and left on the cutting room floor.

FORGOTTEN MOVIE STARS OF THE 30's, 40's, and 50's

Hayward became a United States citizen in 1941. During World War II, Hayward served as a photographer of many battles. While a Captain in the Army, he and his unit filmed the Battle of Tarawa. It was the first time in the history of amphibious warfare that photographers had landed to take a beachhead with the initial assault waves. The battle was one of the bloodiest in Marine history - three days of fighting cost the Marines nearly 3,000 casualties, with over 4,500 Japanese soldiers killed.

Hayward was awarded a Bronze Star for his courage under fire in this battle. However, the carnage Captain Hayward saw led to depression and a complete physical collapse.

Overcoming the psychological stress of his war experiences, Hayward returned to his movie career after World War II. Already with a few mysteries under his belt, he was cast as the leading man in the Agatha Christie thriller *And Then There Were None* (1945) which was a hit.

Thereafter the mix of romantic parts included yet another Monte Cristo (1946); the Robin Hood-like Robert Louis Stevenson adventure *The Black Arrow* (1948); and a succession of pirate parts - particularly - and unfortunately - two sequels playing Captain Blood (1950, 1952). There was also another twin sequel - this time a twist of the Jekyll/Hyde story but with the doctor's twin sons (1951).

There was also one more outing for an iron mask vehicle - this time with twin royal sisters and Hayward as a mature D'Artagnan in *The Lady in the Iron Mask* (1952). Amid all this blandness, Hayward had developed a good business sense to capitalize on his movie career. He was one of the first Hollywood stars to incorporate the one percentage-of-profits deal for both the theatrical and TV releases of his post-1949 films, ensuring him a comfortable lifelong income.

FORGOTTEN MOVIE STARS OF THE 30's, 40's, and 50's

> Hayward had the good fortune to play in "the best version of" a couple of movies that had many remakes, including *The Man in the Iron Mask* and *Ten Little Indians (And Then There Were None)*.

While staying with movies, Hayward ventured enthusiastically into TV, not only with some ten American Playhouse Theater productions and episodic TV through the 1960s but production investments of his own. In 1954, Hayward produced and starred in the 39-week TV series "The Lone Wolf" after buying exclusive rights to several of Louis Joseph Vance's original "Lone Wolf" stories. He also produced the British series "The Pursuers" (1966) and the American "The Survivors" (1969). He bowed out of acting in the mid 1970s.

Louis Hayward died in Palm Springs, California in 1985 at age 75 from lung cancer, blaming his illness on a five decade habit of smoking 3-4 packs of cigarettes daily. At his request, he did not have either a funeral or a memorial service.

> One final interesting fact about Louis Hayward. His real name is often listed as Seafield Grant, not Louis Hayward. However, he was actually born at a place called Seafield Grant in South Africa and his name was really Louis Charles Hayward. So there! Imagine – a guy who looks like Hugh Grant was born in a place called Seafield Grant.

FORGOTTEN MOVIE STARS OF THE 30's, 40's, and 50's

Recognition

Louis Hayward actually has two stars on the Hollywood Walk of Fame – one for movies and one for television. His star for movies is at 1500 Vine Street, and his star for television is at 1656 Vine Street.

> Of all the forgotten stars in this book, Louis Hayward is probably the least well known of this group today, including by people in my generation. However, he remains one of my favorites, largely because of his high percentage of swashbuckler movies, a genre which I really enjoy.

My Favorite Louis Hayward Films

1. The Man in the Iron Mask - 1939

Louis Hayward in the dual role of the twin sons of the King of France, Louis and Philippe. That is Joan Bennett by his side.

FORGOTTEN MOVIE STARS OF THE 30's, 40's, and 50's

Any discussion of Louis Hayward must start with the 1939 version of *The Man in the Iron Mask*, his signature film and the first and best version of the Alexander Dumas novel which is far superior to the more recent 1998 version with Leonardo DiCaprio. (I like DiCaprio, but this earliest version of the film is just much better.) Hayward plays twin sons of the King of France, Louis and Philippe – who at birth are secretly separated because there would be civil war if the French people realized that there were in essence two legitimate claimants to the throne of France.

So Louis is raised to be the next King while Philippe as a baby quickly and secretly goes to live in Gascony with the King's best friend, Dartagnan, and his pals, the three musketeers – Porthos, Athos, and Aramis – without his ever knowing of his real ancestry. So not only is this a tale of a man in an iron mask, but also a tale involving those wonderful musketeers.

As you might expect, Louis XIV becomes a pompous, arrogant, selfish, incompetent fool (sounds like a U.S. politician to me) who cares not one iota for the French people – only his mistress and raising taxes to support his lavish lifestyle (definitely a politician) - while Philippe is nobly but secretly raised as a musketeer to respect the people of France and fight for their good – "all for one and one for all" to be sure.

The brothers – unaware that they are twins – finally meet each other when the "five musketeers" are arrested for failure to pay taxes and come face to face with the king. Louis at first relishes having a twin and decides to pass Philippe off as himself and use him at events which he (Louis) thinks are beneath his dignity to attend – meeting the people of France and responding to their problems, and greeting Louis' fiancée, the beautiful Maria Theresa of Spain, played by the equally beautiful Joan Bennett.

FORGOTTEN MOVIE STARS OF THE 30's, 40's, and 50's

Eventually Louis begins to resent and fear Philippe and has him imprisoned in the Bastille. He plots to keep Philippe in an iron mask until he suffocates, away from the knowledge of the French people, who might actually prefer Philippe as King. But the Three Musketeers and their comrade D'Artagnan eventually locate Philippe's whereabouts and contrive to rescue him and place Louis in the Iron Mask instead. The film comes to a rousing conclusion with Louis' carriage toppling over a cliff and into the river and Philippe taking his place as the King of France, while all of France thinks it is still Louis. Got that?

This film is a true swashbuckler in the best sense of the word – costumes, swordplay, color, and plot - and Hayward is outstanding in the dual role of the dashing, heroic Philippe and the foppish Louis. He can be completely arrogant and unsympathetic in one moment and the next moment heroic and courageous. An outstanding cast includes Warren William as D'Artagnan, Joseph Schildkraut, and Alan Hale. However, Hayward drives the film as the noble and gallant Philippe and foppish and evil Louis. He is extremely convincing in both roles.

> Hayward had a real knack for playing foppish roles in films in order to pretend to be someone he was not. *Man in the Iron Mask* was one of those films. He was able to effect a high-pitched effeminate voice that made him appear less than masculine.

It is worthy of note that Hayward's double in this film was actor Peter Cushing, who would go on to an illustrious career in Hammer Films, generally playing Dr. Frankenstein, and also appearing in the original *Star Wars* film.

2. And Then There Were None - 1945

A group of guests trying to determine why their mysterious host invited them to a deserted island for the weekend. From left to right – Louis Hayward, C. Aubrey Smith, Barry Fitzgerald, Richard Haydn, Mischa Auer, and Walter Huston. Mischa Auer looks glum and he should – he is the first victim.

And Then There Were None was the first and best version of the Agatha Christie novel, Ten Little Indians, and starred Louis Hayward along with a cast of great, mostly English character actors. Hayward plays one of ten individuals who are invited to spend a weekend at a deserted island off the Coast of England by their host – the mysterious U. N. Owen, who turns out to be "unknown." It seems that Mr. or Ms. Owen has taken it upon himself to punish these ten people for their perceived misdeeds that were never officially dealt with in by the authorities in England. The guests are clearly stranded without any communications for three days (This is before the days of cell phones, folks!). When they start getting bumped off – one by one – the survivors come to realize that Mr. or Ms. "Unknown" is actually one of them.

FORGOTTEN MOVIE STARS OF THE 30's, 40's, and 50's

Hayward plays the dashing adventurer Charles Morley – or is he Philip Lombard? - in an effective performance as the mysterious hero of the cast who could also be the murderer. As the youngest and best-looking male in the cast, he stands out among his older co-starring character actors including Fitzgerald, Huston, Richard Hayden, C. Aubrey Smith, Dame Judith Anderson, and Roland Young. June Dupree plays the girl he comes to trust, but could that be fatal for one or both of them? This film's surprising tongue-in-cheek humor – there is a scene where five of the male stars are all spying on each other, and none of them realizes that they are also being spied on – and an outstanding cast sets it completely apart from other versions of this film. Of course, the key is that each character is killed eventually as described in the Ten Little Indians poem, which is recited after each murder as follows:

"Ten little Indians (Soldier boys is also often used) went out to dine;
One choked his little self and then there were nine.

Nine little Soldier boys sat up very late;
One overslept himself and then there were eight.

Eight little Soldier boys travelling in Devon;
One said he'd stay there and then there were seven.

Seven little Soldier boys chopping up sticks;
One chopped himself in halves and then there were six.

Six little Soldier boys playing with a hive;
A bumblebee stung one and then there were five.

Five little Soldier boys going in for law;
One got in Chancery and then there were four.

Four little Soldier boys going out to sea;
A red herring swallowed one and then there were three.

Three little Soldier boys walking in the zoo;
A big bear hugged one and then there were two.

Two Little Soldier boys sitting in the sun;
One got frizzled up and then there was one.

One little Soldier boy left all alone;
He went out and hanged himself and then there were none."

> Interestingly enough, Chancery is an English court. So the verse probably means that he got into trouble with the law, somehow.

Do they in fact all die, or does the real killer's identity become known in time? You will have to watch the film to find out. It is definitely worth watching, and Hayward holds his own with an outstanding cast.

> If you want to see a really mediocre version of this movie, try the 1965 rendition with Hugh O'Brian and – believe it or not – pop singing star Fabian, who can't act at all. Fortunately, he was dispatched early in the film. And the musical score is just plain awful – imagine a murder mystery with a funky musical score.

3. The Black Arrow – 1948

On the next page is a scene from *The Black Arrow*, another Hayward swashbuckler. As the "poor man's Errol Flynn," Hayward played in many swashbucklers, and this film represents perhaps the best of the rest of them after *The Man in the Iron Mask*. That's bad-guy George Macready in the center, no doubt plotting some mischief for our hero, Dick Shelton, played by Louis Hayward.

FORGOTTEN MOVIE STARS OF THE 30's, 40's, and 50's

The *Black Arrow*, based on the 1888 novel of the same name by Robert Louis Stevenson, takes place during the reign of King Henry VI of England and the War of the Roses. It tells the story of Richard (Dick) Shelton: how he becomes a knight, rescues his lady Joanna Sedley, and obtains justice for the murder of his father, Sir Harry Shelton.

Outlaws in Tunstall Forest organized by Ellis Duckworth, whose weapon and calling card is a black arrow, cause Dick to suspect that his guardian Sir Daniel Brackley (Macready) and his close associates are responsible for his father's murder. Dick's suspicions are enough to turn Sir Daniel against him, so he has no recourse but to escape from Sir Daniel and join the outlaws of the Black Arrow against him. This struggle sweeps him up into the greater conflict of the War of the Roses.

Hayward is at his typical daring best in this film. The cast includes Janet Blair and the always-villainous George Macready, who has his usual good performance as the villain and adversary of Dick Shelton.

FORGOTTEN MOVIE STARS OF THE 30's, 40's, and 50's

> If I ever do a book about supporting actors and actresses, George Macready will definitely be in it. He was in a ton of terrific films over a 30-year period, including *Paths of Glory, Gilda,* and a large number of high quality costume dramas. His unmistakably resonant voice was his calling card. I don't remember him ever playing anything but the villain in movies. I am sure in real life he was a very nice man.

4. Walk a Crooked Mile - 1948

Government agents Dennis O'Keefe and Louis Hayward in *Walk a Crooked Mile*.

FORGOTTEN MOVIE STARS OF THE 30's, 40's, and 50's

A spy ring has infiltrated Lakeview Laboratory of Nuclear Physics, a Southern California atomic research center. FBI agent Dan O'Hara and Scotland Yard detective Philip Grayson are on the case. This film presents a good pairing of Louis Hayward and American actor Dennis O'Keefe as a Scotland Yard detective (Hayward) and an FBI agent (O'Keefe) who work together to discover the spy ring. Raymond Burr played a Communist agent, well before his casting as TV's Perry Mason.

> Before he was cast as good guy lawyer Perry Mason in the late 1950's, Raymond Burr almost always played villains, usually the second banana guy who was the muscle, not brains, of the organization.

5. The Son of Monte Cristo - 1940

Here, the son of Monte Cristo – Louis Hayward – is convincing Zona – Joan Bennett – that he is on her side. A reteaming of the two stars from *The Man in the Iron Mask*.

FORGOTTEN MOVIE STARS OF THE 30's, 40's, and 50's

This film is an updated version of the Count of Monte Cristo story, with Hayward playing his son, Edmund Dantes, Jr. In 1865, General Gurko Lanen – what a name for a villain! - is dictator of "Lichtenburg" in the Balkans. Rightful ruler Zona, played by Joan Bennett in another of her performances as the royal damsel in distress, hopes to get aid from Napoleon III of France. The visiting Count of Monte Cristo falls in love with Zona and undertakes the task of aiding her, masquerading as a foppish banker and a masked freedom fighter (Hayward was adept at this). The movie is full of rapid-fire intrigue and swashbuckling scenes. While nowhere near as good of a film as *The Man in the Iron Mask,* it is still an adventure film that is worth watching.

> George Sanders, as the villainous Gurko Lanen, was another character actor who almost always played villains and was always good. His film roles included *Rebecca, All About Eve, Samson and Delilah*, and *The Picture of Dorian Gray*. He was also one of Zsa Zsa Gabor's many husbands in real life and reportedly her favorite one.

6. Ladies in Retirement - 1941

(Previous Page). Hayward and Ida Lupino in a publicity photo from *Ladies in Retirement*. At this time, they were husband and wife in real life.

The housekeeper to a retired actress living in the countryside of England tries at the same time to look after her own two emotionally disturbed sisters. As it develops, she learns that her two disturbed sisters are to be evicted from their apartment in London because of their behavior, and they have no place to go. The housekeeper convinces her employer to take in the two sisters "for a couple of days until arrangements can be made."

Weeks later, the sisters are still there and have no plans to go anywhere else. When one of the sisters brings dead branches and shells into the house, that becomes the final straw, and the retired actress gives them an ultimatum to move the next day. As it turns out, the actress leaves on a long vacation – we know better, of course – and the sisters remain in the house until the authorities start getting suspicious. As all this is taking place, one of their male cousins – a bank employee ne'er do well who has "borrowed" some funds from the bank – keeps popping in and out and causing further havoc.

This thriller features then-husband and wife Ida Lupino as the housekeeper and Louis Hayward as the ne'er do well cousin. As we can expect, the two of them work well together, as he demands to stay in the house as payment for his knowing what really happened to the retired actress. Hayward plays a charmingly devilish scoundrel in this film – while he is basically a small-time thief and overall nogoodnik, his charm makes him impossible to dislike.

A good supporting cast includes Elsa Lancaster as one of the strange sisters and Evelyn Keyes as the maid.

FORGOTTEN MOVIE STARS OF THE 30's, 40's, and 50's

This thriller was originally a stage play and you can see why – all the action takes place in the house, and there are only nine people in the entire cast.

> Ida Lupino was a very interesting actress. In the late 1940's, she became interested in directing, and went on to direct six films, becoming Hollywood's only female film director at that time and the first actress to produce, direct, and write her own product. Several of her films were on socially relevant projects such as rape (*Outrage*) and female independence. She is a role model today for female movie directors like Kathryn Bigelow and Penny Marshall.

7. Anthony Adverse - 1935

A very young Louis Hayward in *Anthony Adverse*. He is dispatched early, but makes a solid impression.

FORGOTTEN MOVIE STARS OF THE 30's, 40's, and 50's

The main reason I am including this film is that it is an early Louis Hayward picture and demonstrates the swashbuckling presence that he was to achieve in his later starring costume dramas.

> A costume drama or period drama is a period piece in which elaborate costumes, sets and properties are featured in order to capture the ambience of a particular era. It generally takes place in the 17th, 18th or 19th century.

In late 18th century Italy, a beautiful young woman finds herself married to a rich but cruel older man. However, she is in love with another, younger man. When the husband finds out, he kills the lover in a swordfight, and takes his wife on a long trip throughout Europe. Months later, she dies giving birth to a son.

Realizing that the son is not his son, the husband leaves the child at a convent, where he is raised until the age of 10; then he is apprenticed to a local merchant, who gives him the name "Anthony Adverse" because of the adversity in his life. Anthony falls in love with the cook's daughter, and the two of them pledge their undying love for each other.

But Anthony's adversity (catch that brilliant reference?) has only begun, as fate takes him to Cuba, Africa, and Paris. He represents his benefactor in business dealings with others, and for a time in Africa loses his way morally. But in returning to Italy, he rights himself and vows to find the woman he loves – the cook's daughter.

FORGOTTEN MOVIE STARS OF THE 30's, 40's, and 50's

Louis Hayward is only in this film for the first 20 minutes, playing the wife's lover, Denis Moore, who is dispatched by the husband, Claude Rains. But it does show Hayward's ability to play the handsome, swashbuckling hero. Frederick March and Olivia de Havilland, as Anthony Adverse and the woman he loves, are the real stars of the film.

A terrific supporting cast includes Rains, Anita Louise, Donald Woods, Edmund Gwenn (Santa in *Miracle on 34th Street*), and Gale Sondergaard.

This movie is an outstanding early talkies costume drama with an excellent cast headed by March. One of the criticisms of this film – probably valid – is that you can't really tell the whole story even in 140 minutes. The film seems to move forward without sufficient development at times, even for a film that long.

Because of his outstanding work in a number of swashbucklers and other movies, his work in television, and his smart career financial choices, I have included Louis Hayward in this book. If you are a fan of swashbucklers, as I am, other Louis Hayward costume drama vehicles, although not as good as the ones mentioned above, include:

- *The Return of Monte Cristo*
- *Fortunes of Captain Blood*
- *The Lady and the Bandit*
- *Lady in the Iron Mask* – you can detect a certain common theme here
- *Captain Pirate*

FORGOTTEN MOVIE STARS OF THE 30's, 40's, and 50's

Dana Andrews – 1909-1992

Dana Andrews has probably become my favorite star of this group of forgotten stars. He was really always good, no matter what the role, and always seemed to have the ability to come off as smarter than the guy he was playing should be. He never looked dumb or out of place in any picture he was in. I really appreciate the fact that he never over-acted and always underplayed his part; perhaps that was not appreciated as much as it should have been in his day.

FORGOTTEN MOVIE STARS OF THE 30's, 40's, and 50's

Dana Andrews was probably best at playing smart-guy detectives in a number of movies. However, he was also in westerns, civil war dramas, musicals like *State Fair*, and many other types of movies. His single best role was as one of the returning veterans in the 1946 classic, *The Best Years of Our Lives*. Though Frederick March won the Oscar for Best Actor for that movie, it was clearly Andrews who held the movie together.

> By the way, Bette Davis once called *The Best Years of Our Lives* the finest film ever made by Hollywood, according to TCM host Robert Osborne. Most critics put it in the top 50.

Andrews was teamed up with Gene Tierney, another of my favorites, in a total of five movies, including the classic *Laura* and *Where the Sidewalk Ends* – featured below in my specific selections on Dana Andrews.

Regarding his personal life, he was married to the same woman for over 50 years, invested well in real estate, and was a recovering alcoholic who became a spokesman for fighting the illness. His real name was Carver Dana Andrews, and he had early plans of becoming an opera singer. I remember seeing him and his wife, Mary Todd, appearing in a comedy at the Drury Lane Theater in Chicago in the 1970's.

My favorite Dana Andrews films are the following:

- *The Best Years of Our Lives*
- *Laura*
- *Where the Sidewalk Ends*
- *State Fair*

FORGOTTEN MOVIE STARS OF THE 30's, 40's, and 50's

- ➤ *The Ox Bow Incident*
- ➤ *A Walk in the Sun*
- ➤ *Daisy Kenyon*
- ➤ *Fallen Angel*

Biography

Dana Andrews was an American leading man star of the 1940's and 1950's and a native Texan. The son of a Baptist minister (and one of nine children including actor Steve Forrest), Andrews was born in Mississippi, but the family eventually settled in Huntsville, Texas. Dana Andrews studied business administration at Sam Houston State Teachers College in Texas, but took a bookkeeping job with Gulf Oil in 1929 just prior to graduating. Perhaps because of his early interest in dramatics, he quit a promising job as an accountant and instead decided to pursue a career as an actor (much to the disappointment of his Baptist minister father).

In 1931 he hitchhiked to California, hoping to get work as an actor. He held a variety of rather menial jobs during that period: driving a school bus, digging ditches, picking oranges, working as a stock boy, and pumping gas while trying without luck to break into the movies. He actually convinced his employer at a Van Nuys gas station to invest in him, asking to be repaid if and when Dana made it as an actor. Andrews studied opera and also entered the Pasadena Community Playhouse, the famed theatre company and drama school. He appeared in scores of plays there in the 1930s, becoming a favorite of the company. Playing opposite future star Robert Preston in a play about the British composers Gilbert and Sullivan, he was offered a contract by Samuel Goldwyn. It was two years before Goldwyn and 20th Century-Fox (to whom Goldwyn had sold half of Andrews' contract) put him in a film, but the roles, though secondary, were mostly in top-quality

FORGOTTEN MOVIE STARS OF THE 30's, 40's, and 50's

pictures such as *The Westerner* (1940) and *The Ox-Bow Incident* (1943). A starring role in the hit *Laura* (1944), followed by one in *The Best Years of Our Lives* (1946), made him a star. No later film quite lived up to the quality of these two – but that is easy to understand, since are two of the best films of that era. Andrews slipped into a steady stream of unremarkable films in which he gave sturdy performances, until age and other interests such as his real estate investments resulted in fewer appearances. In addition, his increased drinking leading to alcoholism, according to his own admission, caused him to lose the confidence of some producers.

> I remember watching a very moving episode of Ralph Edwards' "This Is Your Life" TV show in which Dana Andrews was the subject. He was candid in discussing his alcoholism and his recovery.

Andrews was popular enough with his fellow actors to be elected president of the Screen Actors Guild from 1963 to 1965. During his tenure, Andrews was one of the first to speak out against the degradation of the acting profession, particularly actresses doing nude scenes just to get a role. After becoming a recovering alcoholic, he was probably the first actor to do a public service announcement about alcoholism (in 1972 for the U.S. Department of Transportation), was a member of the National Council on Alcoholism, and did public speaking tours focused on this illness.

Andrews retired from films in the 1960s and made, he said, more money from real estate than he ever did in movies. Yet he and his second wife, actress Mary Todd, lived quietly in a modest home in Studio City, California. Andrews suffered from Alzheimer's disease in his later years and spent his final days in a nursing facility. He died of congestive heart failure and pneumonia in 1992 at age 83.

Recognition

Dana Andrews won a Golden Apple Award in 1946 as Most Cooperative Actor. He does not have a star on the Hollywood Walk of Fame, which is really an oversight and should be corrected. I have tried contacting the Hollywood Walk of Fame staff without any success.

My Favorite Dana Andrews Films

1. The Best Years of Our Lives - 1946

Dana Andrews and Teresa Wright together in *The Best Years of Our Lives*. They are falling in love and trying to decide what to do about it, since he is married, though very unhappily.

FORGOTTEN MOVIE STARS OF THE 30's, 40's, and 50's

Ranked 37th on the list of the best American films of all time by the American Film Institute, I personally would rank *The Best Years of Our Lives* at or near the top of the list. The film concerns three just-returning WWII veterans and the problems they encounter in returning to their previous pre-war lives in Boone City, USA (supposedly Cincinnati, Ohio according to some experts).

One – Frederick March – is a bank vice president who returns from the war with a social conscience. His idea of what an applicant for a bank loan brings to the table in terms of "collateral" has changed during those years, from financial to character assets.

The second – Harold Russell – faces the physical challenges of returning to civilian life without his hands and arms as well as whether his girlfriend views him with pity or love. Finally, Dana Andrews plays the most difficult role as he returns from a position as a captain to his old job as a soda jerk, with a wife who has been less than faithful to him and does not at all understand what these men went through during those years at war. As a result of his war experiences, he finds it extremely difficult to return to his old life as a drug store employee and spends the rest of the movie trying to "find himself," as we used to say in the 60's and 70's.

March and Russell got most of the credit – each won an Oscar for this movie – but Andrews clearly has the most difficult role as well as the highest amount of screen time of the three, and carries it off brilliantly. He finds himself falling in love with Frederick March's daughter, played by the ever-cute Teresa Wright, and not knowing what to do about it. He wants to salvage his marriage, which might not be possible, and can't find a decent job in spite of his impressive war record as an Army Air Force flyer.

FORGOTTEN MOVIE STARS OF THE 30's, 40's, and 50's

After 67 years, this film is as powerful today as it was in 1946. It swept most of the major Oscars – winning seven - and it is easy to see why. Returning veterans of Korea, Vietnam, Iraq, and Afghanistan face(d) many of the same challenges as the three leading characters in this film, and their stories have never been better told.

For his part, Andrews was never better, whether in dealing with his two new buddies that he shares a cab ride with at the beginning of the film as they return to their old town, in trying to please his difficult and sleazy wife (Virginia Mayo in a good performance), or in trying to understand a budding love with Teresa Wright.

The climax of the movie – with Andrews in the cockpit of one of the thousands of fighter planes about to be used as scrap for new housing as he relives those moments when he faced death in the skies, is the most powerful scene in the movie and one that still resonates with anyone seeing this film for the first or 21st time today.

> Harold Russell was a real WWII veteran who lost his hands during a training accident. He actually won two Oscars for this performance – a special one because the Academy did not believe he would win for Best Supporting Actor, and in a surprise, Best Supporting Actor. Russell is the only actor to ever win two Oscars for the same performance. For a non-actor, he did a remarkable job in this film. Russell died in 2002 at the age of 88.

FORGOTTEN MOVIE STARS OF THE 30's, 40's, and 50's

2. Laura - 1944

Dana Andrews, as the detective investigating the murder of Gene Tierney as Laura Hunt. Andrews is clearly falling in love with her, and after viewing that painting, what straight guy in his right mind would not be taken with her?

Laura is an outstanding detective story/film noir from 1944 starring Gene Tierney, Dana Andrews, Clifton Webb, Vincent Price, and Judith Anderson. Dana Andrews plays a rough New York City detective investigating the brutal murder of fashion designer Laura Hunt. Laura is engaged to ne'er do well Vincent Price and loved by radio talk show host Clifton Webb, whose character, Waldo Lydecker, remains another one of the great movie names of all time. After interviewing everyone connected with the case and continuously viewing the painting of Laura over her fireplace, Andrews too begins to fall in love with Laura. Imagine his surprise when she suddenly appears one night while the policeman is studying the painting. If Laura wasn't murdered, then who was, why was that person using Laura's apartment, and what role did Laura play in all this, if any? Who was the murderer, and who was he or she really trying to kill?

FORGOTTEN MOVIE STARS OF THE 30's, 40's, and 50's

Andrews and Tierney were outstanding in this film. Tierney was captivating, and Andrew was terrific as the supposedly dimwitted police detective who turns out to be a lot smarter than the rich New York City society people he is investigating. The supporting cast is outstanding, as you might imagine. And the title theme is played over and over at appropriate times throughout the film.

But it is the scenes between the two stars, where they both initially dislike each other primarily because of their differing social status but end up as lovers, that are the key to the film. Also, Andrews more than holds his own against the great acting talents of Webb, Price, and Anderson, all in supporting roles.

> This is one of five films that Andrews and Tierney appeared in together – *Tobacco Road, Belle Starr, The Iron Curtain,* and *Where the Sidewalk Ends* were the others. But this is the one that they will always be remembered for, and rightly so.

Directed by Otto Preminger, *Laura* remains a masterpiece of film noir – stylish, cynical crime dramas - and a great detective story to this day.

> They do play the "Laura" song quite a lot during the movie, practically any time Gene Tierney enters a scene. And this is one song that I can still play on the piano.

FORGOTTEN MOVIE STARS OF THE 30's, 40's, and 50's

Clifton Webb – as radio personality Waldo Lydecker - and Dana Andrews view the portrait of supposedly-murdered girl Laura Hunt (Gene Tierney).

3. Where the Sidewalk Ends - 1950

Gene Tierney comforting an injured Dana Andrews in *Where the Sidewalk Ends*.

FORGOTTEN MOVIE STARS OF THE 30's, 40's, and 50's

Another Dana Andrews/Gene Tierney cop movie directed by Otto Preminger, *Where the Sidewalk Ends* involves a big-city detective (probably New York), a tough cop who dislikes hoods so much that he gets demoted for being too aggressive with them. To make matters worse, he accidentally kills a murder suspect whom he feels is being set up by the mob and spends the rest of the movie trying to pin the murder on the hood who always seems to escape arrest because he is skilled at getting around the law. Tierney plays the widow of the murdered man (a small part for "Peter Gunn's" Craig Stevens), who was very abusive towards the Tierney character. Gary Merrill is the hoodlum and the cast also includes Karl Malden as the precinct commander and Tom Tully as Tierney's father.

This excellent example of film noir is an interesting part for Andrews. He is basically a good man but one who takes the law into his own hands when the system is not working. Ironically, on the one occasion where he is actually trying to calm down a suspect, he accidentally kills the man. The situation comes to a head when the father of the girl he loves (Tully) is falsely accused of murdering his daughter's abusive and now dead husband. How Andrews goes after the hood while dealing with the incorrect arrest of his girlfriend's father makes this movie a cut above the typical film noir. In addition, Andrews' performance as a guy you want to root for in spite of his flaws, really makes this movie.

4. State Fair – 1945

This 1945 Rodgers and Hammerstein musical about a farm family attending the Iowa State Fair stars Dana Andrews, Jeanne Crain, Dick Haymes, and Vivian Blaine and is definitely the best version of this musical, far superior to the 1962 Pat Boone/Ann Margaret version (which for some unexplained reason takes place in Texas instead of Iowa). The

FORGOTTEN MOVIE STARS OF THE 30's, 40's, and 50's

farming Frake family, with discontented sister Margy (Jeanne Crain) and brother Wayne (singing star Dick Haymes), travels to the Iowa state fair to watch Ma compete for the best mincemeat and pickles while Pa's prize pig Blue Boy competes for the best sow. Along the way, Margy falls in love with newspaper reporter Dana Andrews, while Wayne falls for nightclub singer Vivian Blaine. One of these romances works out and one does not. As a hint, can you picture a farm boy from rural Iowa marrying a nightclub singer?

Andrews is excellent as the fast-talking newspaper reporter Pat and there are good vibes between Andrews and Crain. Andrews shows that he can be effective in more lighthearted ventures.

> While Andrews studied opera and had a good singing voice, his character does not sing in this movie. This is in spite of the fact that in the stage play version, his character actually sings several songs.

State Fair is one of those rare musicals that was brought directly to the screen without first appearing on Broadway. While *State Fair* is not really one of Rodgers and Hammerstein's best musicals, this version is extremely well done and definitely worth seeing. The four stars are excellent as are Charles Winninger and Fay Bainter as Pa and Ma. "It Might as Well Be Spring" and "It's a Grand Night for Singing" are excellent songs, and the production moves along at a fast pace. Watch for an early Harry Morgan (Colonel Potter in M*A*S*H*) as a fast-talking carnival barker in a sideshow attraction.

FORGOTTEN MOVIE STARS OF THE 30's, 40's, and 50's

5. The Ox Bow Incident – 1943

This is a great western about the dangers of vigilantism and stars Henry Fonda, Dana Andrews, Anthony Quinn, and an even younger Harry Morgan, along with a supporting cast of outstanding character actors. A rancher is murdered, and the town's leading citizens decide to form a posse to find and hang the killer or killers.

They encounter Andrews and Quinn with the murdered man's cattle and assume that they killed the rancher and stole his cattle. Despite Andrews' protests that he bought the cattle and has a bill of sale to prove it, and that the rancher was fine when they left him, the posse will not be convinced otherwise. A few of the members, including Fonda and Morgan, believe that Andrews and Quinn are innocent, and want the men brought back to town for a trial, but they cannot convince the majority, who are bent on vengeance no matter the cost.

Andrews is very effective as the (as we find out) innocent victim of the mob, and Fonda is Fonda, the courageous hero trying to do the right thing. Andrews is so good that the viewer is clearly rooting for him to be saved and at least be given a chance to explain himself in a trial, but that is not to be the case. The film deals with themes such as vigilantism, courage under fire, and mob violence and is as poignant today as when it was first released. The letter that Andrews writes and asks Fonda to deliver and read to Andrews' widow at the very end of the movie is extremely moving and sums up the dangers of reacting too quickly as a mob.

> If you don't get a slight tear in your eye as Fonda first reads the letter to the men in the bar before setting out to find Andrews' widow, you are not very emotional.

FORGOTTEN MOVIE STARS OF THE 30's, 40's, and 50's

This 1943 classic western is one of Andrews' best early roles and set him up for bigger and better things to come. Jane Darwell is excellent as the lone female vigilante in the posse.

6. A Walk in the Sun – 1945

Richard Conte, Dana Andrews, and George Tyne (I believe) sizing up the situation in *A Walk in the Sun*.

A Walk in the Sun is one of the better, if not most well known, films about World War II. In the 1943 invasion of Italy, one American platoon lands, digs in, then makes its way inland to attempt to take a fortified farmhouse, as tension and casualties among the soldiers mount. This is an unusually realistic picture of war featuring long quiet stretches of talk among the soldiers. For example, as they walk, the men shoot the breeze and discuss their likes and dislikes, the nature of war and the food they wish they were eating. These quiet stretches are punctuated by sharp, random bursts of violent action related to taking the farmhouse, whose relevance to the overall mission is often unknown to the soldiers. So it goes with war.

FORGOTTEN MOVIE STARS OF THE 30's, 40's, and 50's

Andrews is quite effective as Sgt. Bill Tyne, who is forced to take over what is left of the 53-man platoon when senior officers either are killed or break down mentally. Rather than playing someone who has all the answers, Andrews portrays a common soldier who is seeking help in finding the right solutions and doing the right thing under a very stressful environment, albeit in a very courageous manner. A stellar cast includes John Ireland, Richard Conte, Lloyd Bridges, Norman Lloyd, Sterling Holloway, and – yes – Huntz Hall of the Bowery Boys. Andrews made several WWII movies, but this is the best one.

> In January 1945, Director Lewis Milestone showed the film to the U.S. Army for their approval. The Army was pleased with the film but requested two minor changes which were made.

7. Daisy Kenyon – 1947

Dana Andrews, Henry Fonda, and director Otto Preminger on the set of *Daisy Kenyon*. Preminger directed several of Andrews' best films.

FORGOTTEN MOVIE STARS OF THE 30's, 40's, and 50's

This film is interesting because it features three stars – Andrews, Joan Crawford, and Henry Fonda - in a soap-opera love triangle. While the title gives the impression that Joan Crawford as Daisy is the key figure in the movies, it is actually Dana Andrews who carries the story if one examines the film closely.

Joan Crawford technically stars as the distressed heroine, a Manhattan commercial artist. Daisy is torn between two men: a handsome, married, successful attorney (Dana Andrews) and an unmarried blue-collar guy, Henry Fonda. Deciding to do the "right thing," Daisy marries Fonda, but still carries a torch for the dashing Andrews. When the lawyer divorces his wife, he calls upon Daisy and tries to win her back. In the highly-publicized divorce trial (Andrews is kind of the Perry Mason of his day), Andrews is caught between fighting for custody of his two daughters – since they prefer their loving father over their abusive mother – and protecting Daisy's reputation. He decides the noble thing is to stop the proceedings, give over custody of the children to his wife, and protect Daisy's reputation. As a result, he nearly wins Daisy over, but her husband isn't about to give up so easily. Both men argue over Daisy, who is so distraught by the experience that she nearly has a fatal automobile accident.

In the end, Crawford (Daisy) realizes that she truly loves Fonda, and tells Andrews that it is over between them. Andrews leaves, probably to reconcile with his wife for the sake of his devoted daughters.

While he is having an affair with Daisy, it is clear that he is a decent man who adores his daughters but is married to an unsympathetic and abusive wife. Andrews is able to pull off convincing us that while he has not acted in a noble manner, he is basically a decent fellow.

FORGOTTEN MOVIE STARS OF THE 30's, 40's, and 50's

> Andrews actually received second billing in this film, behind Crawford but ahead of the now-more famous Henry Fonda. Andrews clearly had the more demanding role of the two.

8. Fallen Angel – 1945

Dana Andrews with coffee shop owner Percy Kilbride and waitress Linda Darnell, in a scene early on in *Fallen Angel*. Andrews becomes smitten with Darnell's character, much to her disadvantage.

Eric Stanton (Dana Andrews) is a fast-talking drifter and hustler who gets off the bus at a small town about 150 miles south of San Francisco because he only has a dollar left in his pocket. Stopping in the local diner, he immediately falls for a coffee shop waitress, Stella (Linda Darnell), who goes out with him but won't marry him unless he can afford to settle down. Acting as a front man for a fortune teller who happens to be in town, Stanton meets most of the local townspeople, including a wealthy spinster, played by Alice Faye. Stanton decides to marry the spinster, fleece her of much of her money, divorce her, and then marry Stella.

FORGOTTEN MOVIE STARS OF THE 30's, 40's, and 50's

He marries Faye's character in San Francisco, but his plans go awry when Stella is murdered the next evening. Of course, Stanton is a prime suspect in her murder when it was shown that he and Stella had an argument a few hours before her death. I won't give away the ending, but suffice it to say it has a definite twist.

Andrews is excellent in a good role – he is, of course, the "fallen angel" – probably a decent guy whose plans have always backfired throughout life. He definitely has some character faults, not the least of which is scheming to marry Alice Faye only for her money. But do those character faults include murder? Darnell is, as always, extremely alluring, and an excellent supporting cast includes Charles Bickford as the detective investigating the murder, John Carradine as the fortune teller who knows a good scheme when he sees one, Bruce Cabot as one of Darnell's boyfriends, Percy Kilbride (Pa Kettle from the Ma and Pa Kettle movies) as the owner of the coffee shop, and Anne Revere as Alice Faye's sister. Alice Faye gets top billing, but Dana Andrews is clearly the star of this movie, and he does an outstanding job in this role of a less than perfect character who has some good qualities but may also be a murderer. This movie definitely falls in the category of film noir.

Finally, the more research I did on Dana Andrews, the more I came to realize how good he was in the vast majority of films he was in. It is a shame that he does not have a star on the Hollywood Walk of Fame, a fact that should be rectified as soon as possible. I have tried contacting the folks at the Hollywood Walk of Fame about this obvious oversight, but was unsuccessful in getting anyone to call me back.

FORGOTTEN MOVIE STARS OF THE 30's, 40's, and 50's

Gene Tierney – 1920-1991

Any modern moviegoers who think that Angelina Jolie or any of today's stars is the most beautiful actress ever, might want to take a look at a few Gene Tierney films first. In my mind, she was one of the most beautiful movie stars ever, and a decent although not spectacular actress. When I met Turner Classic Movies host Robert Osborne at a program he was hosting in the Chicago area recently, I asked him who his favorite classic male and female stars were. Without pausing, he said that Cary Grant was his favorite male star, because he could play any role – comedy, drama, thrillers – and do it superbly. As for his favorite female star, he said, surprisingly, Gene Tierney. Not that she was in the realm of Kathryn Hepburn or Bette Davis as an actress, but because she lit up the screen in every part she played. I was surprised, but I have to say, I would agree wholeheartedly.

My favorite Gene Tierney films include the following:

- ➤ *Laura*
- ➤ *Leave Her To Heaven*
- ➤ *The Ghost and Mrs. Muir*
- ➤ *The Razor's Edge*
- ➤ *Son of Fury*

Biography

Gene Tierney was born Gene Eliza Tierney in Brooklyn, New York, on November 19, 1920, to well-to-do parents. Her father was a very successful insurance broker and her mother was a former teacher. Her childhood was lavish indeed. She also lived, at times, with her equally successful grandparents in Connecticut and New York. Gene was educated in the finest schools on the East Coast and at a finishing school in Switzerland. After two years in Europe, Gene tired of the European social circles and returned to the U.S. where she completed her education.

Gene was bored with society life and decided to pursue a career in acting. Her father felt that if she were to become an actress, it should be in the legitimate theatre. So Tierney studied acting at a small Greenwich Village acting studio in New York with Broadway director and actor Benno Schneider. She was also the protégé of producer-director George Abbott, the writer-director of "Damn Yankees!"

Her wealthy father set up a corporation whose sole purpose was to promote her theatrical pursuits. Gene's first role consisted of carrying a bucket of water across the stage, prompting one critic to announce that "Miss Tierney is, without a doubt, the most beautiful water carrier I have ever seen!"

FORGOTTEN MOVIE STARS OF THE 30's, 40's, and 50's

By 1938 she was performing on Broadway in "What a Life!" and understudying for "The Primrose Path" (1938) at the same time. Her subsequent roles in "Mrs. O'Brian Entertains" (1939) and "Ring Two" (1939) were meatier and received praise from the tough New York critics. Critic Richard Watts wrote "I see no reason why Miss Tierney should not have a long and interesting theatrical career; that is if the cinema does not kidnap her away."

After being spotted by the legendary Darryl F. Zanuck during a stage performance of the hit show "The Male Animal" (1940), Gene was signed to a contract with 20th Century-Fox. Her first role, in *The Return of Frank James* (1940), with Henry Fonda, would be the send-off vehicle for her career. Later that year she appeared as Barbara Hall in *Hudson's Bay*. The next year was a very busy one for Gene, as she appeared in *The Shanghai Gesture* (1941), *Sundown* (1941), *Tobacco Road* (1941) and *Belle Starr* (1941).

> For no apparent reason, she was often cast as an Asian woman at this point in her career. Perhaps the high cheekbones? Directors were certainly still trying to find her niche at this time.

Gene tried her hand at screwball comedy in *Rings on Her Fingers* (1942), which was a great success. Her performances in each of these films were well received by both critics and the public.

In 1944 she played what is probably her best-known performance in Otto Preminger's *Laura* (1944). Tierney played a (supposed) murder victim named Laura Hunt, with Dana Andrews, Clifton Webb, and Vincent Price in support.

FORGOTTEN MOVIE STARS OF THE 30's, 40's, and 50's

In 1945 she was nominated for a Best Actress Oscar for her portrayal of Ellen Brent in *Leave Her to Heaven* (1945). Though she did not win, merely being nominated solidified her position in Hollywood circles as a top-flight actress. She followed up with another great performance as Isabel Bradley in the hit *The Razor's Edge* (1946). In 1947 Gene played Lucy Muir in the acclaimed *The Ghost and Mrs. Muir*. By this time Gene had achieved stardom, and the 1950s saw no letup as she appeared in a number of good films, among them *Night and the City* (1950), *The Mating Season* (1951), *Close to My Heart* (1951), *Plymouth Adventure* (1952), *Personal Affair* (1953) and *The Left Hand of God* (1955). The last one was to be her last performance for seven years.

The pressures of a failed marriage to fashion designer Oleg Cassini also included giving birth to a daughter – Daria - who was born in 1943 with severe birth defects and required lifelong institutionalization. That experience, and several unhappy love affairs resulted in Gene having a nervous breakdown and being hospitalized for depression. As a result, her career suffered. (The couple's second child was also a daughter, named Christina.) When she returned to the screen in *Advise & Consent* (1962), her acting was as good as ever but, at 41, there was no longer a big demand for her services as a glamorous leading lady. Her last feature film was *The Pleasure Seekers* (1964), and her final appearance in the film industry was in a TV miniseries, "Scruples" (1980).

> In a nightmarish twist of fate, Tierney learned that a female Marine had ignored quarantine orders to meet her idol during Tierney's WWII hostessing duties at the Hollywood Canteen, where movie stars helped the war effort by entertaining the troops.

FORGOTTEN MOVIE STARS OF THE 30's, 40's, and 50's

> That was how the star contracted German measles late in her pregnancy - an innocent kiss from an admiring fan who wanted an autograph. It is very likely that this caused the severe birth defects in her daughter Daria.

Many people mistakenly believe that Gene spent the remainder of her life beginning in the late 1950's in various mental hospitals; however, that is completely mistaken. Gene married Texas oilman Howard Lee, a former husband of Hedy Lamarr, in 1960 and afterward made occasional movie and television appearances but otherwise was happy to be involved in various Houston-area charitable causes and social events for the next 30 years. She apparently experienced no additional dramatic mental health issues during the last 30 years of her life.

Gene died of emphysema in Houston, Texas, on November 6, 1991, just two weeks shy of her 71st birthday. As an ironic note, Gene only took up smoking because studio officials at Fox felt that smoking would give her a lower, sultrier voice.

Tierney had her share of affairs during her Hollywood reign, including a notorious one with a young John F. Kennedy. Kennedy broke it up because of his political ambitions. Tierney voted for Richard Nixon in the 1960 presidential election but sent a congratulatory note to Kennedy on his victory.

Recognition

Gene Tierney was nominated for an Academy Award for Best Actress in a leading role for the 1945 film *Leave Her to Heaven*. Tierney lost out to Joan Crawford for *Mildred Pierce*, Crawford's signature role. She has a star on the Hollywood Walk of Fame at 6125 Hollywood Boulevard.

FORGOTTEN MOVIE STARS OF THE 30's, 40's, and 50's

My Favorite Gene Tierney Films

1. Laura - 1944

Detective Dana Andrews admires the portrait of the reportedly-murdered Laura Hunt (Gene Tierney).

The famous portrait of Laura Hunt (Gene Tierney) being viewed by detective Dana Andrews tells you all you need to know about Gene Tierney's most famous role as Laura in the movie of the same name. Detective Andrews is called in to solve the murder of fashion designer Laura Hunt, who was unceremoniously dispatched as she answered the door to her apartment by her unknown murderer. Andrews begins to fall in love with her by hearing more about her as he interviews her friends, played by Clifton Webb, Vincent Price, and Dame Judith Anderson. After that, he spends an entire night in her apartment thinking about the case and viewing the famous portrait shown above. Imagine his surpise when Laura suddenly appears and wonders what a brash New York City detective is doing in her apartment late at night.

FORGOTTEN MOVIE STARS OF THE 30's, 40's, and 50's

Gene Tierney is at the same time strong yet vulnerable and absolutely gorgeous. You can certainly see why the male characters are all in love with her. Laura comes to trust the detective, probably because he is so different from her society friends, and the two of them set out to find the real killer of Laura's friend and look alike who was using her apartment while Laura was away for a weekend.

This film is a combination of a romance, film noir, and suspense. Tierney is breathtaking in every way, Andrews is excellent as her co-star, and the supporting cast is top notch, especially Webb in the role of radio talk show host Waldo Lydecker. Plus the haunting melody of the title song is heard throughout the film and gives the movie an added sense of mystery and intrigue.

Gene was on the set six days a week before the sun came up. She stayed until 8 or 9 p.m. each night. She made 28 costume changes and almost every close-up was preceded by an hour to two of testing the lights on Tierney's face while she was forced to sit there.[1]

If you only see one Gene Tierney film and want to make it the one where she looks her best, make sure you see *Laura*. She is absolutely breathtaking and also very vulnerable yet strong in the role of Laura Hunt. Definitely her signature role.

> The portrait of Laura is, in fact, a photograph painted over with oil paint. It was also seen in the Danny Kaye movie, *On the Riviera* and also in another Webb film, *Woman's World*.

---

[1] From the Gene Tierney website, **www.cmgww/stars/tierney**

FORGOTTEN MOVIE STARS OF THE 30's, 40's, and 50's

2. Leave Her to Heaven - 1945

Writer Cornel Wilde and his wife, Gene Tierney, in happier moments in *Leave Her to Heaven*. Little did he realize that she was beautiful but also psychotic. This was an outstanding performance by Gene Tierney in this film, one that made Hollywood realize that she could actually act.

A writer, played by Cornel Wilde, meets a young socialite (Gene Tierney) on board a train. The two fall in love and are married soon after, mainly because he is swept up by her charms. However, he soon begins to realize how highly possessive she is of everything that she wants. The fact that he resembles her deceased father is also a new and rather spooky situation. Still, he does not realize the extent of her possessiveness until two tragedies occur in their lives.

FORGOTTEN MOVIE STARS OF THE 30's, 40's, and 50's

This film resulted in Gene Tierney's one Academy Award nomination, for Best Actress in a Leading Role, and she certainly deserved it. She was at the same time controlling, frail and vulnerable, possessive, caring, and mentally unstable, all in the same package. She has the audience rooting for her to achieve happiness one moment, then realizing, with a subtle change of expression on her face, what a monster she can be in the next moment. Plus, as beautiful as she is in *Laura*, she is perhaps even more beautiful in Technicolor. *Leave Her to Heaven* co-starred Jean Crain as her sister – they do look quite alike – and also featured Vincent Price, Darryl Hickman, Chill Wills, and Ray Collins (Lt. Tragg from the Perry Mason television series).

> You will see that the name Ray Collins appears quite a lot in this book for his fine work in supporting roles.

3. The Ghost and Mrs. Muir - 1947

In early 1900's England, a young widow, Lucy Muir (Gene Tierney), moves to the seaside village of Whitecliff and into Gull Cottage with her daughter Anna (Natalie Wood) and her maid Martha (Edna Best), in spite of the fierce disapproval of her mother- in-law and sister-in-law. Despite discovering that the house is haunted, she rents it anyway. On the first night she is visited by the ghostly apparition of the former owner, a roguish sea captain named Daniel Gregg (Rex Harrison), who reluctantly promises to make himself known only to her. When Lucy's source of investment income dries up, the sea captain dictates to her his memoirs, entitled *Blood and Swash*. His racy recollections make the book a bestseller, allowing Lucy to stay in the house. During the course of writing the book, they fall in love, but as both realize it is a hopeless situation, Daniel

FORGOTTEN MOVIE STARS OF THE 30's, 40's, and 50's

tells her she should find a real (as in actually living!) man. (Having intimate relations with a ghost was probably out of the question, I assume.)

When Lucy visits the publisher in London she becomes attracted to suave Miles Fairley (our friend George Sanders again), a writer of children's stories who is known by his pen name of "Uncle Neddy". They begin a courtship which looks like it will lead to marriage until Lucy finds out that Fairley is already married. Lucy leaves heartbroken and returns to spend the rest of her life as a single woman in Gull Cottage with Martha to look after her.

The key to this film is a believable relationship between the captain and the widow, and it works in this film because of the two leads, Tierney and Harrison. Playing second fiddle to a ghost would work negatively for many actresses, but Gene Tierney pulls it off just fine.

> That is all well and good, but I have a tough time picturing Gene Tierney as a spinster! A widow or divorcee, perhaps, but definitely not a spinster.

> "The Ghost and Mrs. Muir" was also a popular television show from 1968 to 1970 and starred Hope Lange and Edward Mulhare as the two leads. It lasted for three seasons, and Hope Lange won a Golden Globe.

4. The Razor's Edge - 1946

Clifton Webb and Gene Tierney in *The Razor's Edge*. You can tell just by the hair that it is Gene Tierney.

This first and best film version of the W. Somerset Maugham novel about a young man trying to discover the meaning of life – even before the 1960's - featured an all-star cast including Tyrone Power, Gene Tierney, John Payne, Herbert Marshall, Clifton Webb, and Ann Baxter. Webb was nominated for an Oscar for Best Supporting Actor for this film, and Baxter won an Oscar as Best Supporting Actress. The basic plot of the melodrama centers around Power, a disenchanted World War I veteran who leaves his home in Chicago to travel around the world to find the meaning of life. He and his fiancée, Tierney, agree to rekindle their love after he has "found himself" and determined what he wants to do with the rest of his life. Ten years later he resurfaces, affecting the lives of everyone around him. Most of the movie takes place in Paris, with Power and Tierney playing the leads and the others playing key supporting roles as relatives or friends.

FORGOTTEN MOVIE STARS OF THE 30's, 40's, and 50's

Tierney is excellent in the role of the self-centered Isabel. At various times in the movie she can be kind, considerate, and loving, and at other times self-centered, devious, and scheming. After Power and Baxter, a recovering alcoholic, announce their engagement, it is Tierney who decides to test her former lover's fiancée to determine if she has truly recovered, with tragic results. Power and Tierney are handsome and beautiful and make a wonderful onscreen pair. Tierney more than holds her own playing against such acting heavyweights as Marshall, Webb, and Baxter. And as always, she is incredibly beautiful.

> Tyrone Power and Gene Tierney both looked great in this film and were perhaps the best-looking couple in cinema history.

The Razor's Edge was the first 20th Century Film to be given a big New York premier after World War II. It brought in more than $5 million in profits, making it 20th Century Fox's top-earning film up to that time. [2]

> Clifton Webb played a prominent role in *Laura* as well as this film, and Power and Tierney appeared together in three films – *The Razor's Edge, Son of Fury,* and *That Wonderful Urge*. They were very good friends off the set, but nothing more. They did share a common bond – uncommonly beautiful people who had to struggle to be taken seriously as actors.

---

[2] From *Leading Couples,* text by Frank Miller with an Introduction by Robert Osborne, Chronicle Books, 2008, Page 155.

FORGOTTEN MOVIE STARS OF THE 30's, 40's, and 50's

5. Son of Fury - 1942

Gene Tierney and Tyrone Power in *Son of Fury*.

Sir Arthur Blake – George Sanders - has inherited a title and lands from his brother. He also has his orphaned nephew Benjamin (Tyrone Power) working for him as a bonded servant. While he believes the lad was born out of wedlock and so cannot claim the inheritance, he is taking no chances, keeping him under close watch. Benjamin eventually rebels against his uncle and sets sail to avoid arrest as well as to try and make his fortune. Ben stows away on a ship bound for the South Seas, where he is forced to join the ship's crew. After a while, he joins shipmate Caleb Green (John Carradine) in jumping ship at a Polynesian island. There he wins the trust of the native islanders, finds fortune (pearls), and takes a new love, a native girl he calls "Eve" (Gene Tierney). When a Dutch ship happens by, allowing them to fulfill their ambitions, Ben decides to return to England to clear his name and claim himself as the rightful heir to the estate.

FORGOTTEN MOVIE STARS OF THE 30's, 40's, and 50's

This film is a typically good Tyrone Power swashbuckler, with Tierney his newfound love after he lands in Polynesia. Again, this film shows her propensity, early in her career, to being cast as an Asian woman. She was 22 at the time.

> To satisfy the Hollywood censors, writers had to add a tribal ritual scene to this movie to suggest that Power and Tierney were actually married before moving in together.

While it can be said that many Hollywood actresses of beauty and talent are here today and gone tomorrow, Gene Tierney will be long remembered for being one of the screen's greatest beauties, and as an actress who, when given good parts, gave performances equal to the best.

In Gene Tierney's case, I think that one final picture is appropriate. This is from the May 1945 issue of *Army Weekly*, a monthly magazine begun in 1942 to boost the morale of troops. This pic would have DEFINITELY boosted my morale!

Teresa Wright – 1918-2005

Teresa Wright was unbelievably cute – spunky would probably be a good term for her - and also a darn good actress. Moreover, she is the only actor or actress ever to be nominated for an Oscar in her first three films. Wright was a female lead or co-star in a number of great films, including *The Best Years of Our Lives, Mrs. Miniver*, and *Pride of the Yankees*. In *Pride of the Yankees*, she was Lou Gehrig's wife Eleanor and was the lead in Hitchcock's *Shadow of a Doubt*, one of Hitchcock's best movies and his own personal favorite. She and Dana Andrews were a likeable couple in *The Best Years of Our Lives*. Later on, in 1956, she appeared in The *Search for Bridey Murphy* with Louis Hayward (No. 2 star above) before turning to television and live theatre for most of her later acting work. She had the rare quality of being attractive and appealing without necessarily being glamorous as, for example, Gene Tierney was. Wright was definitely the kind of girl you would bring home to introduce to mom and dad.

FORGOTTEN MOVIE STARS OF THE 30's, 40's, and 50's

My favorite Teresa Wright films are the following:

- ➢ *The Best Years of Our Lives*
- ➢ *The Pride of the Yankees*
- ➢ *Shadow of a Doubt*
- ➢ *Mrs. Miniver*

Biography

Teresa Wright was born Muriel Teresa Wright in the Harlem district of New York City on October 27, 1918. Her parents divorced when she was quite young, and she lived with various relatives in New York and New Jersey after the divorce. She attended the exclusive Rosehaven School in Tenafly, New Jersey. Wright became excited about the possibility of an acting career when she saw the legendary Helen Hayes perform in a production of "Victoria Regina." After performing in school plays and graduating from Columbia High School in Maplewood, New Jersey, she made the decision to pursue acting professionally.

After her high school graduation, Teresa began an apprenticeship at the Wharf Theatre in Provincetown, Massachusetts during the summers of 1937 and 1938 in such plays as "The Vinegar Tree" and "Susan and God." She moved to New York and changed her name to Teresa after she discovered there was already a Muriel Wright in Actors Equity. She was an understudy to Dorothy McGuire and Martha Scott on Broadway at that time.

> In my opinion, Teresa Wright sounds better anyway. I just can't envision the name Muriel Wright on a movie theater marquee.

FORGOTTEN MOVIE STARS OF THE 30's, 40's, and 50's

Her first New York play was Thornton Wilder's "Our Town" in which she played a small part but also understudied the lead ingénue role of Emily. She eventually replaced Martha Scott in the lead after Scott was brought to Hollywood to make movies and specifically recreate the Emily role on film. It was during her year-long run in "Life with Father" that Teresa was seen by Goldwyn talent scouts, was tested, and ultimately won the coveted role of Alexandra in the film *The Little Foxes* (1941), her first film.

Even at this early stage of her career, she showed herself to be a serious actress. Wright accepted an MGM starlet contract on the condition that she not be forced to endure cheesecake publicity or photos for any type of promotion and could return to do live theater at least once a year. Oscar-nominated for her work alongside fellow cast members Bette Davis (as calculating mother Regina) and Patricia Collinge (recreating her scene-stealing Broadway role as the flighty, dipsomaniac Aunt Birdie), Teresa's star continued to rise even higher with her next several films.

Playing the good-hearted roles of the daughter-in-law to Greer Garson in the war-era tearjerker *Mrs. Miniver* (1942) and baseball icon Lou Gehrig's faithful wife in *The Pride of the Yankees* (1942) opposite Gary Cooper, Wright won both "Best Supporting Actress" and "Best Actress" nods respectively in the same year, ultimately taking home the supporting trophy for *Mrs. Miniver*. Of Garson, she said, "Very bright. Fantastically beautiful. There are actors who work in movies. And then there are movie stars. She was a movie star."

Teresa's fourth huge picture in a row was Alfred Hitchcock's psychological thriller *Shadow of a Doubt* (1943); she even received top billing over established co-star Joseph Cotten who played a murdering Uncle Charlie to her suspecting niece.

FORGOTTEN MOVIE STARS OF THE 30's, 40's, and 50's

Wed to screenwriter Niven Busch in 1942, Wright had a slip with her fifth picture *Casanova Brown* (1944) but bounced right back as part of the ensemble cast in the "Best Picture" of 1946, *The Best Years of Our Lives*, portraying the daughter of Fredric March and Myrna Loy who falls in love with damaged soldier-turned-civilian Dana Andrews.

With that last film, however, her MGM contract ended. Unbelievably, she made only one movie for the studio (*Mrs. Miniver*) during all that time. The rest were all parts in which she was loaned out to other studios. In those days, you were in essence "owned" by the studio that held your contract. They controlled your career, you did not.

As a freelancing agent, the quality of her films began to dramatically decline. Pictures such as *Enchantment* (1948), *Something to Live For* (1952), *California Conquest* (1952), *Count the Hours* (1953), *Track of the Cat* (1954) and *Escapade in Japan* (1957) pretty much came and went.

For her screenwriter husband she appeared in the above-average western thriller *Pursued* (1947) and crime drama *The Capture* (1950). Her most inspired films of that post-war era were *The Men* (1950) opposite film newcomer Marlon Brando and the low-budgeted but intriguing *The Search for Bridey Murphy* (1956) with Louis Hayward, which chronicled the fascinating story of an American housewife who claimed she lived a previous life. (Louis Hayward is one of my other forgotten stars.)

> *The Men* featured Marlon Brando's film debut, as he played a paralyzed war veteran attempting to adjust to civilian life.

FORGOTTEN MOVIE STARS OF THE 30's, 40's, and 50's

The "Golden Age" of TV was her salvation during these lean film years as she appeared in and performed excellent work in a number of dramatic showcases. She recreated for TV the perennial holiday classic "The 20th Century-Fox Hour: The Miracle on 34th Street" (1955) in which she played the Maureen O'Hara role opposite Macdonald Carey and Thomas Mitchell.

Divorced from Busch, the father of her two children, in 1952, Teresa made a concentrated effort to return to the stage and found consistency in such plays as "Salt of the Earth" (1952), "Bell, Book and Candle" (1953), "The Country Girl" (1953), "The Heiress" (1954), "The Rainmaker" (1955) and "The Dark at the Top of the Stairs" (1957) opposite Pat Hingle, in which she made a successful Broadway return. Marrying renowned playwright Robert Anderson in 1959, stage and TV continued to be her primary focuses, notably appearing under the theater lights in her husband's drama "I Never Sang for My Father" in 1968. The couple lived on a farm in upstate New York until their divorce in 1978.

By this time a mature actress now in her 50s, challenging stage work came in the form of "The Effect of Gamma Rays on Man-in-the Moon Marigolds," "Long Day's Journey Into Night," "Mornings at Seven," and "Ah, Wilderness!" Teresa also graced the stage alongside George C. Scott's Willy Loman (as wife Linda) in an acclaimed presentation of "Death of a Salesman" in 1975, and appeared opposite Scott again in her very last play, "On Borrowed Time" (1991). After almost a decade away from films, she came back to play the touching role of an elderly landlady opposite Matt Damon in her last picture, John Grisham's *The Rainmaker* (1997).

Teresa passed away from a heart attack in 2005 at the age of 87.

FORGOTTEN MOVIE STARS OF THE 30's, 40's, and 50's

Recognition

Teresa Wright won an Oscar as Best Actress in a Supporting Role for her performance in *Mrs. Miniver* in 1943, her third film. She was nominated for Best Actress in a Supporting Role for her performance in *The Little Foxes* in 1942, her first film, and was also nominated for Best Actress in a Leading Role for her performance as Eleanor Gehrig in *The Pride of the Yankees* in 1942, her second film.

> Transitioning from movies to television- was quite a common occurrence even in those days. Teresa Wright was also nominated for two Emmy awards. In 1956 she was nominated as Best Single Performance in a Lead or Supporting Role for her terrific performance as Annie Sullivan in *The Miracle Worker* on "Playhouse 90." In 1989, she was nominated as Outstanding Guest Actress in a Drama Series for "Dolphin Cove."

Because of her performance as Eleanor Gehrig, her name was read in 2006 among the list of New York Yankees who had died the previous year..

Teresa Wright has a star on the Hollywood Walk of Fame at 1658 Vine Street for motion pictures and at 6405 Hollywood Boulevard for television.

My Favorite Teresa Wright Films

1. **The Best Years of Our Lives – 1946**

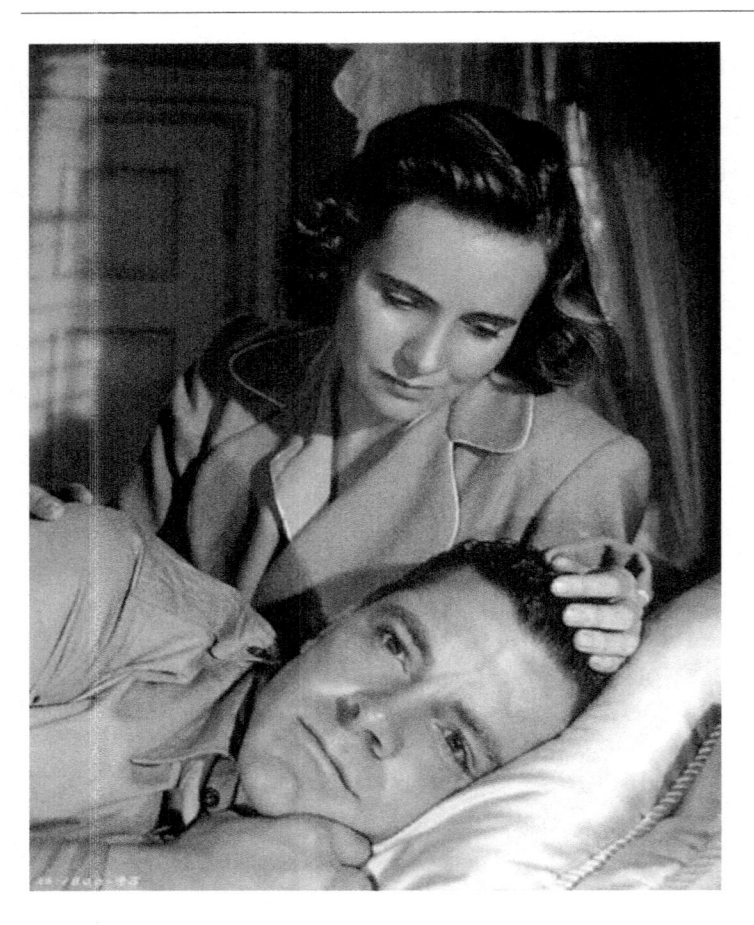

FORGOTTEN MOVIE STARS OF THE 30's, 40's, and 50's

Teresa Wright falls in love with an unhappily married man, played by Dana Andrews, in this scene from *The Best Years of Our Lives*.

I have already discussed this film under the section devoted to Dana Andrews. As I indicated, the film concerns three just-returning WWII veterans – Frederick March, Dana Andrews, and Harold Russell - and the problems they encounter in returning to their previous pre-war lives in Boone City, USA. The movie also focuses on the women in their lives.

FORGOTTEN MOVIE STARS OF THE 30's, 40's, and 50's

In this case, Wright plays the daughter of bank vice president Frederick March; she meets and falls in love with his new friend, played by Dana Andrews. Wright is conflicted by her love for Andrews and her sincere desire that his marriage to Virginia Mayo succeed. Unfortunately (or perhaps fortunately) it becomes increasingly clear that Mayo and Andrews are a mismatch bound for destruction, and he turns to Wright for friendship and consolation. That their friendship turns into love is no surprise – they are a perfect match - but it is just very difficult to bring these two people together. For one thing, her father, though a friend of Andrews, does not want his daughter involved with a married man.

As in so many good movies, there is a great deal of chemistry between Andrews and Wright. She seems at one time a mere schoolgirl and in the next scene demonstrates a level of maturity far beyond her years in trying to keep Mayo and Andrews together but realizing that whatever those two had going for them before the War, is completely gone now. The viewer comes to realize that no matter how difficult that road ahead will be for Andrews and Wright, they are much better off if they face it together rather than separately. They confront the ultimate challenge when Andrews' character Fred Derry decides to take the next airplane out of Boone City in any direction after his luck and marriage have run out.

No less an expert than film critic James Agee had this to say about Teresa Wright's performance in his review of *The Best Years of Our Lives* for *The Nation* (December 28, 1946): "I cannot ... resist speaking briefly ... of Teresa Wright. Like Frances Dee, she has always been one of the very few women in movies who really had a face. This new performance of hers seems to me one of the wisest and most beautiful pieces of work I have seen in years. If the picture had none of the hundreds of other things it has to recommend it, I could watch it a dozen times over for that personality and its mastery alone."[3]

The film won seven Academy Awards, including those for best picture, director, actor, supporting actor, editing, screenplay, and original score. Bette Davis called this three-hour movie "The greatest movie made in Hollywood," according to TCM host Robert Osborne. I would not argue with that assessment.

2.   The Pride of the Yankees – 1942

Teresa Wright as Eleanor Gehrig and Gary Cooper as Lou Gehrig in *The Pride of the Yankees*.

---

[3] Taken from a web site on Teresa Wright - http://www.reelclassics.com/Actresses/Teresa/teresa2.htm.

FORGOTTEN MOVIE STARS OF THE 30's, 40's, and 50's

I admit that I am a huge baseball fan, and *The Pride of the Yankees*, depicting the life story of baseball great Lou Gehrig, is probably my all-time favorite baseball movie. Therefore, it was pretty much a guarantee that I would include it in my list of favorite Teresa Wright films.

The Pride of the Yankees is the story of Lou Gehrig from his college days (Columbia Lou) through his famous goodbye speech at Yankee Stadium, where, in spite of his impending death from ALS, he manages to say that "Today, I consider myself the luckiest man on the face of the earth." Wright is his loving wife Eleanor, and Gary Cooper and Teresa Wright have great affection for each other in all their scenes – where she first meets him and calls him "Tanglefoot" through the best days of their marriage, through the confrontations with Gehrig's mother, through to the end, where she shares in his suffering as he confronts the disease named after him.

> Gehrig was reportedly what we would call a momma's boy with a domineering mother, and Eleanor was forced to deal with that and let Lou know that she, his wife, was now the main woman in his life. (According to Jonathan Eig's book, *Luckiest Man: The Life and Death of Lou Gehrig*, Simon and Shuster, 2005), which I have read.

Wright makes a perfect companion for the real-life hero, still recognized as the greatest first baseman of all time and one half of the greatest 3-4 lineup of all time, Babe Ruth and Lou Gehrig. When we see her in tears as he gives his famous farewell speech, it also moves us to tears. Wright is at various times sympathetic, loving, and tough as she fights for and with her husband.

There are a lot of great baseball movies around, but this one is my own personal favorite – partially because of the character of the hero, and partially because of the interaction between Cooper and Wright.

3.   Shadow of a Doubt – 1943

Joseph Cotten and Teresa Wright in a scene from *Shadow of a Doubt*. By this time in the film, she has begun to suspect that her beloved Uncle Charlie may actually be the Merry Widow serial murderer who is the subject of a nationwide manhunt by the authorities.

FORGOTTEN MOVIE STARS OF THE 30's, 40's, and 50's

While the police are on the lookout for the notorious Merry Widow killer, who gets his nickname by murdering lonely and rich widows for their money, the Newton family's Uncle Charlie comes to live with them. Teresa Wright plays the oldest child, Charlie, who at first adores her uncle but starts to wonder if he might in fact be the notorious Merry Widow killer. The cynical, film-noirish 1943 motion picture was shot on location in the small, story-book town of Santa Rosa, California - a representative place of sacred, wholesome, middle-American values where dark corruption is hidden within a family, and specifically within one family member.

Wright is excellent in the role of Charlie. At first she is swept up by her captivating uncle, played by Joseph Cotten, but a series of events leads her to suspect he is not as sweet and loving as he appears. So she starts to investigate the possibility of his being the killer, with suspenseful results.

Alfred Hitchcock directed this thriller and indicated that it was the favorite of all his American films. With outstanding performances by Wright and Cotten, and a superb supporting cast including Macdonald Carey, Hume Cronin, and Henry Travers, it is easy to see why. The delicate balance between good and evil and between what seems to be and what actually is, has perhaps never been better demonstrated than in this powerful movie. And the haunting Merry Widow Waltz is played throughout the film very effectively. The climax is typical Hitchcock – surprising but understandable.

> You may not recognize the name of supporting player Henry Travers, but he was Jimmy Stewart's guardian angel Clarence, trying to obtain his wings, in *It's a Wonderful Life*.

FORGOTTEN MOVIE STARS OF THE 30's, 40's, and 50's

I don't think I have ever seen a more appealing heroine in a film or a more dubious leading man than Cotten. Their performances are exceptional, although surprisingly neither was nominated for an Academy Award. Its only nomination came for best writing based on an original story, and even that did not win. What a shame this film did not receive more recognition in its time, although lovers of thrillers and of Hitchcock have typically recognized it as one of their favorites. Include me in that category.

4. Mrs. Miniver – 1942

Greer Garson as Mrs. Miniver and Teresa Wright in a scene from *Mrs. Miniver*.

Mrs. Miniver is the story of an English middle class family as they deal with the first years of World War II and its effect on the English people, including the bombing of England by the Axis forces. Clem Miniver is a successful architect and his beautiful wife Kay is the anchor that keeps the family together. With two young children to raise, Kay keeps busy in the quaint

FORGOTTEN MOVIE STARS OF THE 30's, 40's, and 50's

English village they call home. She is well-liked by everyone, and the local station master has even named his new rose after her. When their son Vincent comes home from Oxford for the summer he is immediately attracted to Carol Beldon (Teresa Wright), granddaughter of Lady Beldon, the richest woman around. Their idyllic life is shattered in September 1939 when England is forced to declare war on Germany. Soon Vincent is in the Royal Air Force, and everyone has to put up with the hardship of war, including blackouts and air raids. Mrs. Miniver has to deal with an escaped German flyer who makes his way to her home while husband Clem helps evacuate the trapped British Expeditionary Force from Dunkirk. Vincent and Carol are married but their time together is to be short. Throughout it all, everyone displays strength of character in the face of tragedy and destruction.

This film won six Academy awards in 1943, including Best Picture, Best Actress in a Leading Role (Greer Garson), and Best Actress in a Supporting Role (Wright). While Garson's performance is clearly the centerpiece of the movie, Wright adds depth as a young British wife who deals with the same issues as her new mother-in-law. Her performance was certainly deserving of the Oscar.

I have attempted to portray Teresa Wright as a spunky but thoughtful actress who starred in a number of outstanding films throughout her career. The four I have listed were truly excellent movies, and part of the reason they were so good was that Teresa Wright was in them.

FORGOTTEN MOVIE STARS OF THE 30's, 40's, and 50's

Victor Mature – 1913-1999

Before Arnold Schwarzenegger, before Sylvester Stallone, the biggest hunk in Hollywood in the 1940's and 1950's was Victor Mature – "That Beautiful Hunk of Man," a term coined by famed actress Gertrude Lawrence. At almost 6'3" and over 200 pounds, Mature can be easily dismissed as nothing more than a beefcake for his roles in movies like *One Million B.C.* and *Samson and Delilah*. However, when you see him in films like *My Darling Clementine*, *Kiss of Death*, and *The*

FORGOTTEN MOVIE STARS OF THE 30's, 40's, and 50's

Robe/Demetrius and the Gladiators, you realize that in the right part, Mature was a quite capable actor. He held his own with Henry Fonda as Doc Holliday in *My Darling Clementine*, as an ex-con trying to go straight opposite Richard Widmark's psycho killer in *Kiss of Death*, and in *The Robe*, where his performance as a Greek slave actually holds up better over time, in my opinion, than Richard Burton's.

Best known for his biblical and historical epics, Mature played a variety of roles and was perhaps at his best in film noir movies, including the above-mentioned *Kiss of Death*, *Cry of the City*, and *I Wake Up Screaming* (with Betty Grable). But, because of his swarthy good looks and olive complexion, he may have played a wider variety of ethnic roles, and played most of them very well, than almost any other leading man of his era. These roles included:

- ✓ Greek fishermen
- ✓ Hebrews
- ✓ Ex-cons
- ✓ Cavemen
- ✓ Egyptians
- ✓ Native Americans – several times
- ✓ Frontier scouts fighting Native Americans
- ✓ Cowboys
- ✓ Song and Dance men
- ✓ Hannibal
- ✓ Eastern Europeans
- ✓ Arabs/Indians
- ✓ Italians

> Victor Mature was actually half Italian and half Swiss.

FORGOTTEN MOVIE STARS OF THE 30's, 40's, and 50's

Mature held his own against the leading ladies of the era, including such notables as Susan Hayward, Gene Tierney, Jean Simmons, Rita Hayworth, Betty Grable, Hedy Lamarr (not Hedley Lamarr!), Janet Leigh, Lizabeth Scott, Jane Russell, Joan Bennett, Lucille Ball, Carole Landis, Linda Darnell, and many others.

My favorite Victor Mature films include the following:
- *My Darling Clementine*
- *Kiss of Death*
- *The Robe/Demetrius and the Gladiators*
- *Samson and Delilah*
- *Million Dollar Mermaid*

Biography

Victor Mature was born, surprisingly enough, Victor John Mature (to knife sharpener Marcellus George Mature, who was himself born Marcello Gelindo Maturi in Pinzolo, Trentino, Italy and a Swiss-American mother, Clara Ackley) in Louisville, Kentucky. According to Mature, he had an ancestral mix of French, Swiss, German, Italian and Greek. (No wonder he could play so many different nationalities!) Victor Mature worked as a teenager with his father as a salesman for butcher supplies.

What led Mature from Louisville to Hollywood? According to his sources, Mature had apparently said that he had aspirations to become an actor since he turned 17 years old. What led him to leave Louisville was supposedly a social rebuff by one of the high society belles when he asked her to dance. He told himself that he would never return "until the Mature name was so big that those society people would eat dirt." He packed up his car and set off to California to become famous with this advice of his father: "As long as people think you're

FORGOTTEN MOVIE STARS OF THE 30's, 40's, and 50's

dumber than you are, you'll make money." Victor arrived in California with 11 cents to his name. He registered with casting agencies and went to study at the famed actor training forum Pasadena Playhouse while taking various jobs to pay for tuition.

> Mature auditioned for *Gone with the Wind* (1939) for the role ultimately played by his fellow Playhouse student and lifelong good friend, George Reeves. After achieving some acclaim in his first few films, he served in the Coast Guard in World War II.

Mature made a couple of movies before the start of WWII, most notably *One Million B.C.* with Carole Landis, where he played a caveman. In July 1942 Mature attempted to enlist in the U.S. Navy but was rejected for color blindness. He enlisted in the U.S. Coast Guard after taking a different eye test the same day. Mature was assigned to the USCGC *Storis*, which was doing patrol work off Greenland. After 14 months aboard the *Storis*, Vic was promoted to the rank of Chief Boatswain's Mate. In 1944 he did a series of War Bond tours and acted in morale shows.

After the end of World War II, Mature became one of Hollywood's busiest and most popular actors though rarely was he given the critical respect he often deserved. His roles in John Ford's *My Darling Clementine* (1946) and in Henry Hathaway's *Kiss of Death* (1947) were among his finest work, though he moved more and more frequently into biblical and historical roles in films like *Samson and Delilah* (1949) and *The Egyptian* (1954). Never an energetic actor nor one of great artistic pretensions (he never took himself too seriously), he

FORGOTTEN MOVIE STARS OF THE 30's, 40's, and 50's

nevertheless continued as a Hollywood leading man both in formula films and in more prominent films like *The Robe* (1953). More interested in golf than acting, his appearances diminished through the 1960s, but he made a stunning comeback of sorts in a hilarious romp as a very Victor Mature-like actor in Neil Simon's *After the Fox* (1966). Golf eventually took over his activities and, after a cameo as Samson's father in a TV remake of his own "Samson and Delilah" in 1984, he retired for good. Rumors occasionally surfaced of another comeback, most notably in a never-realized remake of *Red River* (1948) with Sylvester Stallone, but nothing came of it. He died of cancer at his Rancho Santa Fe, California, home in 1999 at the age of 86.

Mature was an easygoing guy and never took his acting or himself all that seriously. He was also a very generous man. According to his web site, during and after World War II, Victor lived in his dressing room on the studio lot for ten months. When a reporter asked him, "Couldn't you find a place to live?" Vic replied, "I could have, but I thought it was rather crummy of me to rent myself a place when veterans with families were sitting on the curbs. The dressing room was okay. It had a bath. I ate all my meals out."

> What he had a passion for was golf. He once applied for membership to an elite golf club and was rejected because the club did not accept actors as members. His reported response: "I'm not an actor - and I've got 64 films to prove it!"

He was always well liked on the set by cast and crew because of his easygoing personality. Mature was married five times and had several affairs with leading ladies, including Esther

FORGOTTEN MOVIE STARS OF THE 30's, 40's, and 50's

Williams, Rita Hayworth, and Gene Tierney, but was happily married to his fifth wife for the last 25 years of his life.

He attributed his success in Biblical spectacles to his ability to "make with the holy look." That might be true, but Mature deserves more recognition than he has received. Another Mature quote: "Actually I am a golfer. That is my real occupation. I never was an actor. Ask anybody, particularly the critics." [4]

Recognition
Victor Mature has a star on the Hollywood Walk of Fame at 6780 Hollywood Boulevard.

My Favorite Victor Mature Films
1. My Darling Clementine – 1946

---

[4] Quote from the Victor Mature web site, www.victormature.net

FORGOTTEN MOVIE STARS OF THE 30's, 40's, and 50's

The picture on the previous page is (from left to right), Henry Fonda as Wyatt Earp, Victor Mature as Doc Holliday, and Linda Darnell as saloon hall singer and Holliday girlfriend Chihuahua. Clementine is Doc Holliday's girl from back East when he was a dentist.

Don't get me wrong. I am a big fan of the Wyatt Earp/Doc Holliday movie *Gunfight at the O.K. Corral*, with off-screen pals Burt Lancaster and Kirk Douglas chewing up the screen, but this rendition of the story is probably the best film version because of the unique pairing of Henry Fonda and Victor Mature. Mature really makes this movie special. He can be vicious and scary in one moment and your best and most caring friend in the next. Mature never acted better than in this 1946 version of the classic tale. His facial expressions alone demonstrate more character and emotion than you would expect in a typical Victor Mature film.

In case you're not familiar with the story, Wyatt Earp comes to Tombstone to help his brothers clean up the town and is joined by his pal Doc Holliday, an alcoholic one-time doctor. The brothers and Holliday go up against the Clantons, led by mean old pappy Ike (Walter Brennan) and several sons, including John Ireland and Grant Withers. Mature does a great rendition of Hamlet's "To Be or Not To Be" speech when the actor playing Hamlet and performing at the saloon cannot remember his lines, and Mature takes over.

> By the way, John Ireland plays in both renditions of the movie and in both cases is a member of the Clanton gang; in the Lancaster version, he plays Ringo, an old nemesis of Holliday.

You may wonder why the film is called *My Darling Clementine*. Clementine Carter is Doc Holliday's fiancée from the East, who comes West to find him after she has not heard from him in a long, long time. Her appearance demonstrates that there is more to the doctor than just an alcoholic tough guy. By the way, this version of the story has a slightly different and less positive ending than all other versions of the story that I have seen.

2. Kiss of Death - 1947

The picture shows Richard Widmark on the left and Victor Mature on the right. This was Widmark's first film, playing psycho gangster Tommy Udo. Widmark received his one and only Oscar nomination for this movie. Mature was actually 6'3" and Widmark 5'10".

FORGOTTEN MOVIE STARS OF THE 30's, 40's, and 50's

If *My Darling Clementine* is Victor Mature's best film, this 1947 crime drama/film noir is a close second. Mature is excellent as Nic Bianco, a gangster/bank robber who tries to go straight in order to take care of his two little daughters. After being sent to prison for bank robbery, a Federal agent (Brian Donleavy) tries to get Mature to squeal on his fellow robbers, but Vic won't because, as he says, "I'm no stoolie!" He maintains his stance until he finds out that his wife died and his two young daughters have become wards of the state. After that, Bianco turns state's evidence against his fellow criminals so that he can get his sentence shortened in order to go home and raise his daughters.

Something goes wrong, and the state is unable to get the promised conviction against one of Bianco's former criminal buddies, a complete psycho named Tommy Udo. Realizing that Udo will come after him for testifying against him, Bianco takes drastic but legal measures to assure his family's safety.

This is simply one of the best crime/gangster films ever made. While Widmark gets most of the publicity for this movie – including the famous scene where he pushes the wheelchair of an elderly woman down the stairs and kills her – it is Mature whose performance is the core of the film. Mature is very convincing as the gangster who wants to reform and the blue collar worker/father who wants a better life for his daughters. This movie is clearly a thrill from beginning to end and is a must see for people who believe Mature can only be convincing as a gladiator or biblical hero.

> If this film sounds familiar, you are probably thinking of the 1995 remake with David Caruso and Nicholas Cage. The Caruso/Cage film, however, can't hold a candle to the original.

FORGOTTEN MOVIE STARS OF THE 30's, 40's, and 50's

Here is that famous shot of Richard Widmark as Tommy Udo pushing wheelchair-bound Mildred Dunnock down the stairs to her death because she won't tell him the whereabouts of her son, in *Kiss of Death*. You can see why even a tough guy like Victor Mature was afraid of him in this movie!

> For a similar crime drama with a convincing Victor Mature, check out the 1941 film *I Wake Up Screaming*, where Mature co-stars with Betty Grable, Carole Landis, and Laird Cregar. Another example showing that Mature could actually be pretty good when not playing stilted biblical figures.

Richard Widmark was really a nice guy off the set but played some really mean heavies, and this was probably his best performance as a guy who was both bad and also a psycho.

3. The Robe/Demetrius and the Gladiators – 1953/1954

Victor Mature and Susan Hayward in a scene from Demetrius and the Gladiators. Her husband, the eventual emperor Claudius, stands behind her.

This is one of the first of those sequel series, where the original film was so popular that the studio decided to continue the story in a second film, in this case one starring Mature as the Greek slave Demetrius. In the initial film, *The Robe,* a true Hollywood blockbuster, Marcellus (Richard Burton) is a tribune during the time of Christ who hopes to return from Israel to Rome to wed the lovely Diana (Jean Simmons). In the meantime, Marcellus is in charge of the group that is assigned to crucify Jesus. Drunk, he wins Jesus' homespun robe after the crucifixion. However, he is tormented by nightmares and delusions after the event. Hoping to find a way to live with what he has done, and still not believing in Jesus, he returns to

Palestine to try and learn what he can of the man he killed. Marcellus' Greek slave, Demetrius, newly converted to Christianity, helps him discover Christ and become a Christian, along with Diana.

Over the decades, critics and movie fans have come to realize that Mature is actually superior to the great Richard Burton in this film. While Mature's performance comes across as genuine and heartfelt, Burton's appears somewhat stilted. There is no question in my mind that Burton overacts in this film. The final scene, where Marcellus and Diana accept death from the crazy Roman Emperor Caligula (a terrific performance by Jay Robinson as the demented Roman emperor) rather than renounce Christianity, is probably the highlight of the film. Before dying, Marcellus gives the robe to Demetrius for safe keeping.

Demetrius and the Gladiators picks up at the point where *The Robe* ends, following the martyrdom of Diana and Marcellus. Christ's robe is conveyed by Demetrius to the disciple Peter for safe-keeping, but emperor Caligula wants it back to benefit from its supposed magical powers. Demetrius seeks to prevent this, and while doing so catches the eye of Messalina, wife to Caligula's uncle Claudius (eventually the Roman emperor Claudius). Messalina tempts Demetrius, he winds up fighting in the arena as a gladiator, and wavers in his faith when he sees his girlfriend, played by Debra Paget, sexually assaulted by other gladiators and supposedly dying in the process. As we find out later, the key word here is supposedly.

After that incident, Demetrius renounces his Christian faith and is seduced by the lovely Susan Hayward as Messalina. She has plans for Demetrius beyond that of a gladiator (where Demetrius is a huge success). But of course Demetrius regains his faith with the help of Peter.

FORGOTTEN MOVIE STARS OF THE 30's, 40's, and 50's

Mature is perfect in the role of Greek slave/gladiator Demetrius, and he does a commendable job in the sequel. Mature holds his own against such strong performers as Michael Rennie and Susan Haywood, along with Jay Robinson, again outstanding as one of the worst emperors in Roman history. Who else but Mature could have been so convincing as a gladiator at the time this movie was made?

4. Samson and Delilah - 1949

In this photo, Delilah (Hedy Lamarr) leads a fallen and blinded Samson (Mature) up to the pillars in the arena for Samson's last act of vengeance against the Philistines, including George Sanders. (The Philistines are about to find out that regrowing his locks has also meant that Samson has regained his strength!)

FORGOTTEN MOVIE STARS OF THE 30's, 40's, and 50's

Another biblical spectacle, this time based on the story of Samson and Delilah, stars Mature as the Hebrew strongman and Hedy Lamarr (not Hedley Lamarr) as Delilah.

> Hedley Lamarr is the name of Harvey Korman's character in *Blazing Saddles*. In the film, people are constantly calling him "Hedy Lamarr," and he has to continually correct them. (Typical Brooks mix of past and present.)

Although his people, the Israelites, are enslaved by the Philistines, Samson, strongest man of the tribe of Dan, falls in love with the Philistine Semadar, a 24-year old Angela Lansbury, whom he wins by virtue of a contest of strength. But Semadar betrays him, and Samson engages in a fight with her real love, Ahtur, and his soldiers, at a wedding feast. Semadar is killed, and her sister Delilah, who had loved Samson in silence, now vows vengeance against the Hebrew strongman. She plans to seduce Samson into revealing the secret of his strength – of course, his hair, as we all know who are familiar with the story, and then to betray him to the Philistine leaders, the key leader being George Sanders.

As the story goes, Samson loses his long locks, is no longer powerful, and becomes a slave to the Philistines, who further punish him by blinding him. But after seeing her lover Samson so humiliated, Delilah repents and helps Samson get his revenge against the Philistines and their leaders.

Mature is the perfect choice to play the Hebrew strongman. When he fights a lion, you convince yourself that Mature himself might have had a chance! As with most Cecil B. DeMille spectacles, the scenery, story, and special effects are sensational for 1949, while the dialogue is so pious it is

FORGOTTEN MOVIE STARS OF THE 30's, 40's, and 50's

sometimes laughable. But as with most DeMille pics, this film was a huge box office success, mainly due to the presence of Mature and Lamarr.

> Speaking of Hedy Lamarr, never for once think that she was just a dumb actress with a foreign accent. In 1942, at the height of her Hollywood career, she invented and patented a frequency-switching system for torpedo guidance that was two decades ahead of its time! The U.S. Navy rejected it at the time (what does this female movie star know?) but implemented it two decades later.

5. Million Dollar Mermaid – 1952

Victor Mature as promoter Jimmy Sullivan in *Million Dollar Mermaid*.

FORGOTTEN MOVIE STARS OF THE 30's, 40's, and 50's

Mature is good as fast–talking promoter Jimmy Sullivan, and Esther Williams plays the real-life turn of the 20th century Australian *Million Dollar Mermaid*, swimmer and aquatic star Annette Kellerman. Kellerman pioneered aquatic performance shows, the one-piece bathing suit (as opposed to bloomers and corsets), and of course, the Australian crawl swimming stroke. Kellerman had polio as a child and used swimming to cure herself of the illness. On a cruise from Australia to London to accompany her father as he takes a job with the London Conservatory of Music, she meets fast-talking promoter Sullivan. After a stunt in which she swims 26 miles from London to Greenwich, Sullivan convinces Kellerman and her father to take their chances with him in America. They arrive, and after several trials, Kellerman becomes an aquatic star at New York's Hippodrome. Of course, in the meantime, she and Sullivan have a falling out but are reunited at the end of the film.

Mature is very good as the fast-talking promoter, and he and Williams are believable as a couple. In real life, Kellerman did in fact pioneer the modern one-piece swimming suit and was the first real aquatic star, in a field whose main personality was eventually – Esther Williams! Unlike many marriages of this type that go astray, Sullivan and Kellerman were married for over 55 years until his death in the early 1970's. Kellerman lived until the age of 88, which I guess proves that swimming is good for your health.

So remember! Whenever you are reminded of Sylvester Stallone, Vin Diesel, The Rock, Arnold Schwarzenegger, or any of the modern day beefcakes in movies, think of the guy they are modeled after – Victor Mature. The only difference is – he could actually act a bit when it was required.

FORGOTTEN MOVIE STARS OF THE 30's, 40's, and 50's

Paulette Goddard – 1910-1990

Paulette Goddard was an attractive and talented female star of the 1930's and 1940's who would have been an even bigger star if one thing in her life had been changed. She was all set to be cast as Scarlett O'Hara in *Gone with Her Wind* when David O. Selznick found and selected Vivian Leigh for the role instead. The rest is history. Leigh will forever be remembered by movie audiences because of her role as Scarlett, while Goddard is now a "forgotten star."

In truth, Goddard had several outstanding starring roles of her own, including a similar part in Cecil B. DeMille's 1942 sea adventure, *Reap the Wild Wind*. She was also Charlie Chaplin's companion and may have actually been married to Chaplin, although whether an actual marriage ever took place is uncertain. Still, Goddard was a lovely movie star, a quality actress, and as such definitely deserves mention as a forgotten star.

My favorite Paulette Goddard roles include the following:

- *Reap the Wild Wind*
- *So Proudly We Hail*
- *Northwest Mounted Police*
- *Modern Times*
- *The Great Dictator*
- *The Women*
- *Kitty*

Biography

Pauline Marion Goddard Levy was born in Whitestone Landing, New York, on June 3rd, 1910. She was a beautiful child who began to model for local department stores before she made her debut with Florenz Ziegfeld's Follies at the age of 13. For three years, she astounded audiences with her talent and gained fame with the show as "the girl on the crescent moon." At Washington Irving High School in New York City, one of her close friends was future star Claire Trevor. Goddard was married to a wealthy man by the time she was 16. (I guess in those days, that type of thing was more common).

FORGOTTEN MOVIE STARS OF THE 30's, 40's, and 50's

After her divorce, she and her mother went to Hollywood in 1931 at the ripe old age of 21, where she appeared in small roles in pictures for a number of studios. A stunning natural beauty, Paulette could mesmerize virtually any man she met, a fact she was probably well aware of. One of her bigger roles in that period was as a blond "Goldwyn Girl" in the Eddie Cantor film *The Kid from Spain* (1932). In 1932 she met Charles Chaplin, and they soon became an item around town. He cast her in *Modern Times* (1936), which was a big hit, but her movie career was not going anywhere because of her relationship with Chaplin, who was not well liked by the moguls in Hollywood. She and Chaplin were (supposedly) secretly married in 1936, but the marriage failed and they were separated by 1940. It was her role as Miriam Aarons in *The Women* (1939), however, that got her a contract with Paramount.

Paulette was one of the many actresses tested for the part of Scarlett O'Hara in *Gone with the Wind* (1939), but she lost the part to Vivien Leigh and instead appeared with Bob Hope in *The Cat and the Canary* (1939), a good film but hardly in the same league as *GWTW*. The 1940s were Paulette's busiest period. She worked with Chaplin in *The Great Dictator* (1940), Cecil B. DeMille in *Reap the Wild Wind* (1942) and then-husband Burgess Meredith (Rocky's trainer in the first two Rocky movies) in *The Diary of a Chambermaid* (1946). She was nominated for an Academy Award for Best Supporting Actress in *So Proudly We Hail!* (1943). But her star faded in the late 1940s, and she was dropped by Paramount in 1949.

After a couple of "B" movies, she left films and went to live in Europe as a wealthy expatriate; she married German novelist Erich Maria Remarque in the late 1950s. Coaxed back to the smaller screen once more, Goddard starred in the television movie "The Snoop Sisters: Pilot" (1972). She died in 1990 in Switzerland at the age of 79.

At least partly because of her marriages to rich men, Paulette Goddard was quite a wealthy woman when she died. In fact, she left more than $20 million to New York University on her death.

> In a sense, *Reap the Wild Wind* was her version of *Gone with the Wind*. It took place in the South before the Civil War, and Goddard's character was equally strong willed. Still it was NOT Scarlett O'Hara.

Recognition

Paulette Goddard was nominated for one Academy Award, in the category of Best Supporting Actress for the 1943 film *So Proudly We Hail*. She has a star on the Hollywood Walk of Fame at 1650 Vine Street.

My Favorite Paulette Goddard Films

1. **Reap the Wild Wind – 1942**

   Pictured on next page. Paulette Goddard in a publicity photo from *Reap the Wild Wind* with admirers John Wayne and Ray Milland. While Wayne and Milland got top billing for the movie, Goddard easily had the most screen time and was really the central character in the film. But Wayne and Milland were bigger stars at the time.

FORGOTTEN MOVIE STARS OF THE 30's, 40's, and 50's

Reap the Wild Wind was in many ways a consolation prize to Paulette Goddard for not getting the Scarlett O'Hara role in *Gone With the Wind*, made three years earlier. It is the typical Cecil B. DeMille spectacular featuring great special effects, an excellent plot and story, and even a fight to the finish between the two male stars – John Wayne and Ray Milland – and a giant squid in the film's climactic finishing scene. But in spite of a great cast featuring Wayne, Milland, Susan Hayward, Raymond Massey and Robert Preston, the star of the motion picture is clearly Paulette Goddard as salvage boat owner Loxie Claiborne.

The plot of *Reap the Wild Wind* is a good one: It takes place in Key West, Florida in the 1840's where sailing ships bringing their cargo between Havana and points north attempt to avoid driving their ships onto the notorious reefs of Key West. Meanwhile, salvage masters – some honest and some not – vie for salvage rights for the cargo of the broken ships, in some cases wrecks that are planned by the most notorious and villainous of the salvage masters, King Cutler, played by Raymond Massey. Loxi Claiborne (Goddard) is the honest owner of one of Cutler's rival companies.

FORGOTTEN MOVIE STARS OF THE 30's, 40's, and 50's

When she rescues Captain Jack Stuart (Wayne) from the remains of his ship (whose collision with the reefs may well have been planned by his first mate), the plot is set in motion. Soon Loxie goes to Charleston, South Carolina to help her new love make amends with his company and its chief lawyer and second in command, Steve Tolliver (Ray Milland) for letting his ship get wrecked. When Milland volunteers himself to investigate the mysterious sinking of Wayne's ship by sailing to Key West, the action is really set in motion.

Plot twists galore, a view of pre-Civil War South, fistfights, romantic rivalries, and the two male leads dueling each other and finding time to fight the giant squid make this one of the most exciting movies of the 1940's. As long as you understand that this film contains the usual hokey dialogue present in all of DeMille's movies, you won't be disappointed.

As owner of the Claiborne salvage company, Goddard is excellent in this film. She is on screen for virtually every scene in the movie. She plays a gorgeous lady who is also a tomboy and does extremely well in both roles. Plus, the husky quality of her voice (she even sings a bawdy song) gives her an extra sultry appearance in this movie. After viewing this film, you realize that she would have held her own as Scarlett in *GWTW*, had she been given the part.

> *Reap the Wild Wind* was released three months after the Japanese attack on Pearl Harbor on December 7, 1941 - and brought some much-needed escapism from the horrors of war to the United States at that time. Its budget of $4 million was high for that era.

2. So Proudly We Hail – 1943

Paulette Goddard as one of the nurses in *So Proudly We Hail*, for which she was nominated for an Oscar. Paulette is in the center of the photo, and that's Claudette Colbert wearing the hat, with Veronica Lake on the right.

This Oscar-nominated film, made during World War II, is unusual in that it focuses on the experiences of the nurses rather than the soldiers. A group of Army nurses who are headed for Honolulu is diverted to Bataan after the attack on Pearl Harbor. These women form a unique bond that sees them through the horrors of the war, the Japanese offensive, and other related hardships. Claudette Colbert, Paulette Goddard, and Veronica Lake head this all-star cast.

Paulette Goddard is the sexy, flirtatious nurse, engaged to two captains at the same time. But she turns out to be the most dedicated nurse in the entire group, refusing to sleep for days at a time while caring for the injured soldiers in her care. She is excellent in the part, and it is easy to see why she was nominated for an Oscar.

3. Northwest Mounted Police – 1940

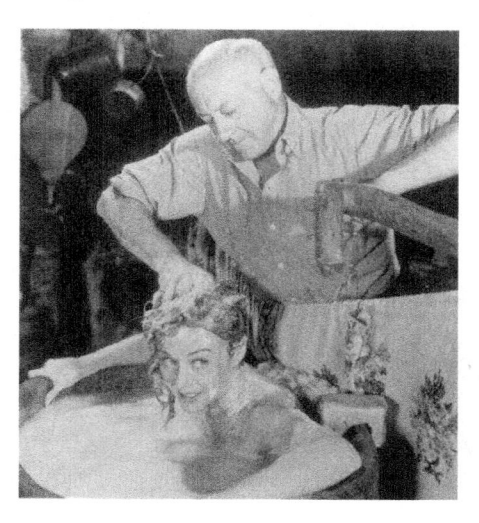

Paulette Goddard as the savage Louvette, in a publicity photo with director Cecil B. DeMille in *Northwest Mounted Police*. (I hope this was not payback for missing a line of dialogue!)

Northwest Mounted Police is a 1940 adventure featuring the typical Cecil B. DeMille themes – an outstanding cast, lots of good action, and dopey dialogue. In 1885, three mismatched frontiersmen (led by whiskey trader Corbeau), foment rebellion in western Canada; only the local Mounties stand in their way. Constable Ronnie Logan loves Corbeau's savage daughter Louvette (Goddard). His pal Jim Brett loves April, the district nurse, but finds a rival in visitor Dusty Rivers, a Texas Ranger who wants Corbeau for murder. Treachery, battles, and tense situations follow in rapid order, with some occasional lighthearted intervals. The outstanding cast includes Gary Cooper as ranger Dusty Rivers, Madeleine Carroll as April Logan, Paulette Goddard as Louvette, Preston Foster as Brett, and Robert Preston as Logan.

FORGOTTEN MOVIE STARS OF THE 30's, 40's, and 50's

Carroll plays the heroine and gets top billing, but Goddard is far more interesting as the conniving Louvette. Goddard chews up the screen in her scenes. Plus, DeMille's first Technicolor production makes her look especially alluring.

4. Modern Times - 1936 /The Great Dictator - 1940

Paulette Goddard, with then-husband (we think) Charlie Chaplin in a scene from *The Great Dictator*. Chaplin plays a barber named Adenoid Hynkel who happens to look exactly like a Hitler-type dictator.

Modern Times portrays Charlie Chaplin as a factory worker, employed on an assembly line – a modern-day factory, in other words. After being subjected to such indignities as being force-fed by a "modern" feeding machine and an accelerating assembly line where Chaplin screws nuts at an ever-increasing rate onto pieces of machinery, he suffers a mental breakdown that causes him to run amok and throw the factory into chaos. Chaplin is sent to a hospital. Following his recovery, the now unemployed Chaplin is arrested as an instigator in a Communist demonstration since he was waving a red flag that

FORGOTTEN MOVIE STARS OF THE 30's, 40's, and 50's

fell off a delivery truck (Actually, Chaplin was trying to return the flag to the driver.) In jail, he accidentally eats smuggled cocaine, mistaking it for salt. In his subsequent delirious state he walks into a jailbreak and knocks out the convicts. He is hailed a hero and is released.

Outside the jail, he discovers life is harsh, and attempts to get arrested after failing to get a decent job. He soon runs into an orphan girl played by his then-real life companion Paulette Goddard, who is fleeing the police after stealing a loaf of bread. A series of adventures follows. The most interesting one involves Goddard as a café/restaurant dancer. Goddard tries to get Chaplin a job as a singer. By that night, he becomes an efficient waiter though he finds it difficult to tell the difference between the "in" and "out" doors to the kitchen, or to successfully deliver a roast duck to the table. During the floor show, his pantomime act proves a hit. When police arrive to arrest Goddard for stealing the loaf of bread, they escape again. Finally, we see them walking down a road at dawn, towards an uncertain but hopeful future.

> Chaplin started making this picture as a talkie, since it was now the era of sound, but soon abandoned that angle and went back to his traditional silent film making instead.

Goddard is very good as the waif/dancer/girlfriend. This film provides an opportunity to see a young Paulette Goddard at age 26 in a silent film. Obviously, there is excellent chemistry between Chaplin and Goddard because of their off-screen relationship.

The two most famous scenes in this movie are when Chaplin gets stuck in the machine and turns into part of the product

FORGOTTEN MOVIE STARS OF THE 30's, 40's, and 50's

being assembled, and the very last scene, where Chaplin and Goddard are walking down the road toward an uncertain future. Clearly, this is Chaplin's vehicle, but Goddard is excellent as "the girl."

For another excellent Chaplin/Goddard vehicle, check out *The Great Dictator*, Chaplin's 1940 satire of Nazi Germany and Adolph Hitler. Tomanian Dictator Adenoid Hynkel – an Aryan who decides to persecute all Jews - has an exact double, a poor but kind Jewish barber living in the slums. One day the barber is mistaken for Hynkel, and all kinds of interesting plot details take place after that, all involving mistaken identify between the dictator and the barber. Goddard plays a simple washerwoman whom the barber falls in love with. Their romance is a key part of the story after that.

Chaplin's film followed only a few months after Hollywood's first parody of Hitler, the short subject *You Nazty Spy!* by the Three Stooges. I should note that Chaplin and - yes – The Three Stooges – were among the first to satirize Hitler, in both cases through comedy, well before the United States entered World War II. At the time of the release of *The Great Dictator*, 1940, the United States was still neutral toward Nazi Germany. That neutrality would change in about a year, but at this time it was not a popular idea to be making fun of Hitler.

> The Three Stooges – Moe, Larry, and Curly - were Jewish comics who obviously detested Hitler with a passion. They satirized him as a bumbling fool in at least two of their shorts. Moe played the Hitler character in both, of course.

FORGOTTEN MOVIE STARS OF THE 30's, 40's, and 50's

5. The Women - 1939

This scene from *The Women* features an obviously-angry Rosalind Russell taking out her anger on marriage breaker Goddard, who is having an affair with Russell's husband. That is Norma Shearer at the far left looking on with Joan Fontaine between Russell and Shearer. First-rate cast!

The Women is a classic and famous 1939 American comedy-drama film directed by George Cukor. The picture is based on Claire Boothe Luce's play of the same name. One of the great successes of its day, the film featured a truly outstanding cast of top Hollywood actresses including Norma Shearer, Joan Crawford, Rosalind Russell, Paulette Goddard, Joan Fontaine, Lucile Watson, Mary Boland, Marjorie Main, Virginia Grey,

Gone with the Wind's Butterfly McQueen, and even gossip columnist Hedda Hopper.

> Famed Hollywood gossip columnist Hedda Hopper also had a small part in another Goddard film – *Reap the Wild Wind*. Her son, William Hopper, played detective Paul Drake on the *Perry Mason* television series. Hopper was famous for wearing outrageous hats.

The film continued the play's all-female tradition - the entire cast of more than 130 speaking roles was female. Set in the glamorous Manhattan apartments of high society and in Reno where the women obtain their divorces, it presents a bitter commentary on the pampered lives and power struggles of various rich, bored wives and other women they come into contact with. Throughout the film, not a single male is seen — although the males are much talked about (generally not in a favorable light!), and the central theme is the women's relationships with them.

> The idea of an all-female cast was unheard of at the time. Hollywood moguls did not think the movie had a ghost of a chance. But due to the direction of George Cukor and a wonderful female cast featuring these outstanding ladies of the cinema, the film was a huge success!

Goddard plays a tough cookie chorus girl who breaks up at least one marriage but becomes friends with the women nevertheless. She is one of the assemblage of top-notch female talent that has never been surpassed before or since, and she holds her own with the likes of Shearer, Crawford, Russell, Fontaine, and other top female stars of that era.

6. Kitty – 1945

Kitty, played by Paulette Goddard, demonstrating the proper use of a fan in attracting a member of the opposite sex.

Kitty is a rags-to-riches film that combines the elements of Pygmalion with *Oliver Twist*. Kitty (Paulette Goddard) is a product of the London slums of 1783, complete with a cockney accent. She steals the shoes of painter Thomas Gainsborough but is caught and introduced to the famous painter. Seeing her incredible beauty masked behind a dirty face and ragged clothing, he agrees to release her if she will pose for him. She agrees, and the result is a painting called "An Anonymous Lady."

FORGOTTEN MOVIE STARS OF THE 30's, 40's, and 50's

Kitty draws the interest of one of Gainsborough's friends, Sir Hugh Marcy (Ray Milland), who agrees to teach her to lose the cockney accent and learn to speak and act like a lady (a la *Pygmalion* and *My Fair Lady*) in exchange for financial gain and a return to the foreign post he was expelled from. Kitty does far better than expected and climbs to tremendous wealth through marriage but continues to hold a torch for Milland. Will Sir Hugh realize that he loves Kitty before it is too late?

This film is a nice combination of comedy, drama, and English manners. It is not a memorable film by any measure, but Goddard's performance as the cockney wench turned into a duchess is very effective.

> *Kitty* also features another successful pairing of Paulette Goddard and Ray Milland. *Reap the Wild Wind* was of course, their other joint venture.

Paulette Goddard was a rare combination of beauty, brains, and talent in a successful career spanning almost 40 years. If she had just gotten the part of Scarlett O'Hara, she would certainly not be in this book of Forgotten Stars.

Glenn Ford – 1916-2006

Glenn Ford is the Forgotten Star whose death gave me the idea for this book, as I mentioned in the introduction. Glenn Ford starred in over 200 films and television productions in a long career by anyone's standards between 1939 and 1991, and a good chunk of them were certainly westerns. This includes perhaps his most famous film, the original version of *3:10 to Yuma*, remade in 2007 with Russell Crowe in the Glenn Ford role. But he was a very versatile actor who also appeared in crime dramas like *The Blackboard Jungle* and *The Big Heat*, comedies such as *The Courtship of Eddie's Father, Pocketful of Miracles,* and *Don't Go Near the Water*, thrillers like *Experiment in Terror*, and dramas like *Gilda*.

FORGOTTEN MOVIE STARS OF THE 30's, 40's, and 50's

> And, Ford was Pa Kent in the first *Superman* film with Christopher Reeve.

Ford's long career allowed him to perform for years beyond some of his contemporaries, with much of his best work taking place in the 1950's and 1960's. An example of Glenn Ford's star power was that he received top billing over Henry Fonda in a 1965 western called *The Rounders*. Ford was a good-looking guy, an easy guy to work with, a good actor able to demonstrate a variety of emotions, and a major star. But for some reason, his fame has not held up as well as other western stars like John Wayne, James Stewart, and Gary Cooper. That is a mistake.

My favorite Glenn Ford films include:

- *3:10 To Yuma*
- *The Blackboard Jungle*
- *Gilda*
- *Experiment in Terror*
- *The Man from Colorado*

Biography

Gwyllyn Samuel Newton Ford (Glenn Ford) was the son of a Canadian railroad executive who moved the family to Santa Monica, California, when Glenn was eight years old. His acting career began in a fairly normal fashion - with plays in high school, followed by acting in a company called West Coast, a travelling theatre company. In 1939 after being noticed by talent scout Tom Moore, Ford took a screen test for Columbia Pictures, which won him a contract. However, he debuted, not

FORGOTTEN MOVIE STARS OF THE 30's, 40's, and 50's

with Columbia, but at 20th-Century-Fox's *Heaven with a Barbed Wire Fence* that same year.

The head of Columbia pictures, Harry Cohn, had long resisted developing his own stable of contract stars, preferring instead to work with other studios like Warner Brothers, who would loan out their unruly stars – often those with outrageous salary demands or work assignment refusals - occasionally to Columbia. In the late 30's, however, Cohn finally relented, first signing Rosalind Russell and then Ford and fellow newcomer William Holden. Cohn figured that those two male stars could be used fairly interchangeably in case one became troublesome.

> Although they did often compete for the same parts, Ford and Holden actually were good friends in real life.

Ford's rise to stardom was interrupted by military service with the Marines during World War II. During his service, he helped build safe houses in France for those hiding from the Nazis. Ford continued his military career in the Naval Reserve well into the Vietnam War, becoming one of the few actors – James Stewart was another - to achieve officer rank. In 1943, he married legendary tap dancer Eleanor Powell with whom he had one son, Peter Ford. Like many actors returning to Hollywood after the war, he found it initially difficult to regain his momentum. However, he was able to resume his movie career with the help of Bette Davis, who gave him his first post-war break in the 1946 movie *A Stolen Life*. But it was not until his acclaimed performance in the 1946 classic film noir, *Gilda*, with Rita Hayworth, that he became a major star and one of the most popular actors of that era. His career during the 1940s and 1950s was extensive and varied, with Ford

FORGOTTEN MOVIE STARS OF THE 30's, 40's, and 50's

playing film noir in *The Big Heat* (1953), dramas like *The Blackboard Jungle* (1955), and comedies like *The Gazebo* (1959), *The Courtship of Eddie's Father* (1963), and *The Teahouse of the August Moon* (1956). He continued to make many notable films during his prestigious 50-year movie career, but he is best known for his fine westerns such as *3:10 to Yuma* (1957), *The Rounders* (1965), *Jubal* (1956), and *The Sheepman* (1958). In those roles, Ford was generally cast as a calm and collected everyday-hero, showing courage under pressure as, for example, a teacher fighting high school gang members in *Blackboard Jungle* (1955).

In the 1970s, Ford made his television debut in the controversial "The Brotherhood of the Bell" (1970) as a priest with a past, and appeared in two fondly-remembered television series: "Cade's County" (1971) and "The Family Holvak" (1975). During the 1980s and 1990s, Ford limited his appearances to documentaries and occasional films. Glenn Ford is remembered fondly for his more than 100 excellent films and his charismatic silver screen presence. He died in 2006 at the age of 90.

Recognition

As far as military recognition, Glenn Ford really did distinguish himself in military service. Committed to service in the armed forces, Ford also served two tours of duty in Vietnam with the Third Marine Amphibious Force in 1966-1968. He once went on a jungle mission at age 50 with a Special Forces Team during the Vietnam War. Ford was the only actor to have served with both the Green Berets and the French Foreign Legion. His military record is well recognized in both the United States and France as a highly decorated veteran and officer, achieving the rank of Colonel.

He was also recognized as the fastest draw of the western stars.

FORGOTTEN MOVIE STARS OF THE 30's, 40's, and 50's

Glenn Ford was a Golden Globe winner for Best Motion Picture Actor – Musical/Comedy for his performance in *Pocketful of Miracles* (1962). He was nominated for two other Golden Globes for best actor in a musical or comedy performance for *Teahouse of the August Moon* (1957) and *Don't Go Near the Water* (1958).

He was also nominated for several Laurel awards during his career and won the Laurel award for Top Male Comedy Performance for *Don't Go Near the Water* in 1958.

> The Laurel Award is given to those who, through their efforts, advance the art of film. It has nothing to do with Stan Laurel or Laurel and Hardy, although I am sure they would have been very deserving of the award.

Ford won Golden Globe Awards for most cooperative actor in 1948 and 1957. (Funny, I don't remember seeing an award for most cooperative actor on this year's Golden Globes. Perhaps no one is all that cooperative any more!) He won the Golden Boot award in 1987. The Golden Boot Award honors those who have contributed specifically to western films and is quite a prestigious award for fans of western films.

Finally, Glenn Ford has a star on the Hollywood Walk of Fame at 6933 Hollywood Boulevard.

My Favorite Glenn Ford Films

1. 3:10 To Yuma - 1957

FORGOTTEN MOVIE STARS OF THE 30's, 40's, and 50's

Outlaw Ben Wade (Glenn Ford) on the left and rancher Dan Evans (Van Heflin) appear on a poster for *3:10 To Yuma*. 3:10 is the time the train leaves to take the outlaw to the Yuma Federal prison, and rancher Evans is determined to see Wade gets on it.

This Glenn Ford/Van Heflin 1957 version is probably the better version of *3:10 to Yuma,* although in this case the updated version with Russell Crowe and Christian Bale is also very good. The unusual aspect of this movie is that Glenn Ford, who almost always played the hero, is the outlaw while Van Heflin, who often played the villain, is the hero.

FORGOTTEN MOVIE STARS OF THE 30's, 40's, and 50's

Outlaw/gang leader Ben Wade (Ford) is caught by the authorities, who are looking for local paid help (a sizeable reward, in other words) to get the outlaw transported to the railroad station – a trip of several days – so that they can put Wade on the 3:10 train to the Federal prison in Yuma, Arizona. Dan Evans (Heflin), desperate for money to save his ranch and earn the respect of his son, accepts the job in spite of the protestations of his wife about how dangerous this trip is. You see, Wade's gang is in hot pursuit and intends to rescue their leader before he boards the train. Of course, all of the others guarding Wade are either killed or back down along the way; only Evans is left at the end to assure that Wade in fact boards that train in spite of the efforts of his gang to rescue him.

Ford and Heflin are excellent in this film and work together very well. Their performances are clearly the highlights of this film. In the updated version, Crowe delivers a very effective performance as Ben Wade, but you know that there is no question that he is an outlaw and a cold-blooded killer to boot; but in the original, Ford is successful in convincing us that he is really a pretty good guy when in fact he is really an outlaw and a killer. The theme of the film is basically a typical one involving Western morality – when you give your word to do something, you don't back down just because the going gets a little tough or in this case, really tough - a very similar theme to that of *High Noon*, by the way. No matter whether your adversary is mean or tries to sweet talk you into changing your mind, you are not going to because you have given your word.

As I indicated, this is one of Ford's best films. He is very effective in an unusual role for him. In addition, the title song, sung by Frankie Laine, is excellent. This adaptation also has a slightly altered (and happier) ending than the Crowe/Bale update. This black and white version also seems a bit grittier than the later color version.

FORGOTTEN MOVIE STARS OF THE 30's, 40's, and 50's

> Speaking of Frankie Laine, he sang the title songs for the television series "Rawhide" and also the Mel Brooks hit, *Blazing Saddles*. "Rawhide" was also the song sung by the Blues Brothers in the movie of the same name. It appears in the film when the Blues Brothers and their rock band have shown up at a country and western bar, and the crowd is angrily demanding a country and western song.

2. The Blackboard Jungle - 1955

Glenn Ford as a high school teacher trying to get through to gang members in his class in an inner-city high school in New York City. The prime delinquent in this picture is Vic Morrow, pictured above. As in many of his movies, Ford displayed his calm under pressure style in this memorable movie.

This 1955 drama directed by Richard Brooks starred Glenn Ford and co-starred Anne Francis, Sidney Poitier, Louis Calhern, and Vic Morrow among others. Ford plays a new English teacher at a violent, unruly inner-city New York City school who is determined to do his job, despite resistance from both students engaging in anti-social behavior and faculty members who have given up on teaching these kids.

FORGOTTEN MOVIE STARS OF THE 30's, 40's, and 50's

The film features strong performances by all members of the cast, but particularly by Ford as the teacher who refuses to give up on these kids and take the easy way out by moving to a suburban school. Instead, Ford makes various attempts to engage the students in education and involvement in school affairs. With some students, especially Poitier, it works, while he is subjected to violence from others, especially Morrow, until the two have it out in a classroom showdown.

> What many people consider the first rock and roll song – "Rock Around the Clock" by Bill Haley and the Comets – was featured in this memorable film.

3. Gilda - 1946

Glenn Ford as a gambler who falls for the sultry Rita Hayworth. Can you blame him?

FORGOTTEN MOVIE STARS OF THE 30's, 40's, and 50's

The sinister boss of an Argentinean casino (George Macready) hires down-on-his-luck American gambler Johnny Farrell (Glenn Ford) to manage his casino. One day, the boss – Mundson - returns from a trip with a beautiful new wife, who is none other than Gilda (Rita Hayworth). Unaware that she was once Farrell's lover, Mundson assigns Farrell to keep an eye on her. Farrell keeps track of her, his loathing for her intensifying as she cavorts with men at all hours. A series of plots involve Johnny being approached by Nazis, faking his own death, and confronting a cartel headed by Mundson carrying on illegal activities. This drama is all set against the continuing saga of the love/hate relationship between Ford as the gambler and Hayworth as the boss's wife. A few surprises here and there, and you have a very effective film. Ford's character doubles as the narrator of the story.

Ford and Hayworth are very good as the lovers who fall between love and extreme dislike frequently during the course of this movie. Ford is believable as a sly gambler who is usually one step ahead of everyone else except when dealing with the love of his life, Hayworth. The most famous scene from the movie, the one that is always remembered, is Hayworth singing "Put the Blame on Mame, Boys" while she does a modified striptease (gloves only, however). It proves that you can make an extremely erotic scene while keeping your clothes on. George Macready is good, as always, in a villainous role as the casino boss/husband of Hayworth who has more than a few tricks and illegal activities up his sleeve.

> While one of the highlights of the film was Rita Hayworth's performance of "Put the Blame on Mame, Boys!," the vocals were actually sung by Anita Ellis, not Rita.

Rita Hayworth as Gilda

4. Experiment in Terror – 1962

A psychotic killer, Garland "Red" Lynch, uses a campaign of terror to force San Francisco bank teller Kelly Sherwood to steal $100,000 from the bank for him. Despite his threat to kill her or her teenaged sister if she goes to the police, Sherwood contacts the San Francisco office of the FBI anyway, where agent John Ripley (Glenn Ford) takes charge of the case. Ripley interviews a woman who implies that she's involved in some way in a serious crime, but before she can give Ripley the details, Lynch murders her. Sherwood continues to be terrorized with phone calls from Lynch, and an asthmatic condition makes the unseen Lynch's voice all the more sinister.

While the FBI knows who the stalker is, it does not have enough evidence against him to make an arrest. Lynch finally gives Sherwood a time and date to steal the money, and just to make sure that she does what he wants, he kidnaps her sister Toby and holds her captive. The climax is a chase through Candlestick Park after a night-time baseball game between the San Francisco Giants and Los Angeles Dodgers. Ripley and his men ultimately surround Lynch on the infield of the stadium and take him down.

Ford is a good choice as the FBI agent, determined to get the killer, and Lee Remick is effective as the tormented bank teller Kelly. I also liked Ross Martin as the psycho killer, Lynch. Perhaps the best thing about the movie is the creepy background music, which adds an additional sense of terror to the film. If the plot sounds a bit like that of *Dirty Harry*, including the San Francisco location, it IS similar!

> The creepy theme song of this movie is often used as the theme song for TV shows that feature the showing of horror or monster movies. It was written by Henry Mancini.

5. The Man from Colorado - 1948

Two friends – Glenn Ford and William Holden - return home after their discharge from the army following the Civil War. However, one of them (Ford), while seeming normal in his adjustment at first, has suffered deep-rooted psychological damage due to his experiences during the war. As his behavior becomes more erratic--and violent--his friend (Holden) tries to find a way to help him. When Ford is appointed a Federal judge, the damage from his experiences in the war show up in his decisions to place technicalities above justice and hang falsely accused men or those who have committed what are basically minor crimes.

FORGOTTEN MOVIE STARS OF THE 30's, 40's, and 50's

Holden is fine as the buddy who takes the straight and narrow path, but Ford is far more effective as the basically good man who suffers irreparable psychological damage during the war, resulting in decisions that alienate his friends and family. His resulting actions, including his lust for power, result in a very convincing performance by Glenn Ford.

> This movie represents the second western in which Ford and Holden were paired, the other being the 1941 film, *Texas*.

Ironically, the two very good Glenn Ford westerns I have illustrated here both portray Glenn Ford as the villain. However, Ford played the hero in the vast majority of his films, including his westerns. For a more representative look at Glenn Ford westerns, check out these excellent films:

- ✓ *The Man from the Alamo* - Glenn Ford as the lone survivor of the Alamo is forced to demonstrate his courage to justify why he too was not killed at the Alamo like everyone else
- ✓ *The Americano* – a South American western
- ✓ *The Violent Men* – Ford goes up against husband and wife Edward G. Robinson and Barbara Stanwyck
- ✓ *Jubal* – Ford is falsely accused of murder and must prove his innocence in an adult western featuring Ernest Borgnine, Rod Steiger, and Charles Bronson
- ✓ *Cowboy* – Chicago hotel clerk Jack Lemmon lives his dream and joins real cowboy Glenn Ford and others on a cattle drive
- ✓ *The Sheepman* – Sheep rancher Ford goes up against cattle ranchers and a young Shirley MacLaine

FORGOTTEN MOVIE STARS OF THE 30's, 40's, and 50's

Some pretty good non-western Glenn Ford films include the following:

- *The Big Heat*
- *The Courtship of Eddie's Father*
- *Teahouse of the August Moon*
- *Pocketful of Miracles*
- *A Stolen Life* with Bette Davis as twin sisters

In short, no one who considers himself or herself to be a fan of classic movies from this era should ever be saying, "Who the hell is Glenn Ford?"

FORGOTTEN MOVIE STARS OF THE 30's, 40's, and 50's

Barbara Stanwyck – 1907-1990

If people under 45 remember Barbara Stanwyck at all today, it is probably from watching reruns of *The Big Valley* on MeTV, where she appeared as the matriarch of the Barclay family, Victoria Barkley. But Barbara Stanwyck was an outstanding actress, maybe the best of her era after Bette Davis and Katherine Hepburn. She was not a classic beauty, but rather mixed her toughness with solid acting skills, genuine sex appeal, and an ability to play a wide variety of roles, including both good girls and bad girls. Amazingly, although she was nominated for four Academy Awards, she never won one. That was a real oversight, in my opinion!

FORGOTTEN MOVIE STARS OF THE 30's, 40's, and 50's

In a career that spanned almost 60 years, Barbara Stanwyck played villains, heroines, high society women, cowgirls, newspaper reporters, call girls, and just about everything in between. She also played in *Baby Face*, one of the Forbidden Hollywood pictures of the early 1930's before the censors moved in to make movies less frank, shall we say.

Not really a beauty in the classic Hollywood sense, she made up for it by being a really good actress. Stanwyck had a definite alluring appeal that was most easily seen in her best film, *Double Indemnity*. A very versatile actress, she deserves to be remembered as one of the best actresses of the golden age of Hollywood.

Barbara Stanwyck made a number of outstanding films. Among my own personal favorites are the following:

- *Double Indemnity (her best movie)*
- *Christmas in Connecticut*
- *Meet John Doe*
- *Ball of Fire*
- *The Lady Eve*
- *Sorry Wrong Number*
- *The Great Man's Lady*

Biography

Barbara Stanwyck was born Ruby Stevens on July 16, 1907, in Brooklyn, New York. She was the fifth and last child of Byron and Catherine McGee Stevens; the couple were working-class natives of Chelsea, Massachusetts and were of English and Irish extraction, respectively. When Stanwyck was four, her mother was killed when a drunken stranger pushed her off a moving streetcar. Two weeks after the funeral, her father joined a work crew digging the Panama canal and was never seen again.

FORGOTTEN MOVIE STARS OF THE 30's, 40's, and 50's

Barbara and her brother Byron were raised in foster homes and then by their sister Mildred, who was five years older than Barbara.

While in foster homes, Ruby attended various public schools in Brooklyn, where she received uniformly poor grades and routinely picked fights with the other students. One can see from this early experience how she became so mentally tough as an actress – after what she went through in her childhood, making motion pictures was probably a snap to her!

In her teens, Barbara went to work at the local telephone company for $14 a week, but she had the dream of somehow entering show business. When not working at the phone company, she sought work as a dancer. Eventually her persistence paid off. At 17, Barbara was hired as a chorus girl for the sum of $40 a week, much better than the wages she was getting from the phone company.

In 1928 Barbara decided to move to Hollywood, where she began one of the most lucrative careers in movie history. She was an extremely versatile actress who could adapt to any role. Barbara was equally at home in all genres, from melodramas, such as *Forbidden* (1932) and *Stella Dallas* (1937), to thrillers, such as *Double Indemnity* (1944), her best film, also starring Fred MacMurray (as you have never seen him before if your point of reference is "My Three Sons"). She also excelled in comedies such as *Remember the Night* (1940), *The Lady Eve* (1941), and *Christmas in Connecticut* (1945).

Another genre she excelled in was westerns, including *Union Pacific* (1939) being one of her first, and "The Big Valley" (1965) (her most memorable television role). In 1983, she played in the ABC hit mini-series "The Thorn Birds" which did much to keep her in the eye of the public.

FORGOTTEN MOVIE STARS OF THE 30's, 40's, and 50's

Barbara was considered a gem to work with for her serious but easygoing attitude on the set. Unlike many stars of her era, she was not a prima donna at all. Stanwyck worked hard at being an actress, and she never allowed her star quality to go to her head. Barbara died on January 20, 1990 at age 82, leaving 93 movies and a host of TV appearances as her legacy.

> Barbara Stanwyck played in more different kinds of movies than almost any other leading lady. Hollywood finally had the good sense to award her an honorary Oscar in 1982 for "superlative creativity and unique contribution to the art of screen acting." Why they never gave her an actual competitive award is beyond me.

Barbara Stanwyck was married to one of our other forgotten stars, Robert Taylor, from 1939 through 1952. He had several affairs, including one with Ava Gardner, which ultimately led to their divorce. Stanwyck's retirement years were active, with charity work done completely out of the limelight.

Her decline in health started following a robbery and beating at her Beverly Hills home in 1981, in which a cigarette case from her second husband Robert Taylor was stolen; affecting her greatly. The following year, while filming "The Thorn Birds," the inhalation of special-effects smoke on the set caused her to contract bronchitis. The illness was compounded by her cigarette habit; she had been a smoker since age nine until four years before her death. Barbara Stanwyck died in 1990.

FORGOTTEN MOVIE STARS OF THE 30's, 40's, and 50's

> In 1944, when she earned $400,000, the government listed Stanwyck as the nation's highest-paid woman. I guess she was the Oprah of her day, salary-wise.

Recognition

Unlike many of the stars on this list, Barbara Stanwyck actually received quite a bit of recognition during her career. There are certainly three factors involved here:

1) She was in the limelight for a long time in both movies and television
2) She was a really, really good actress
3) She continued acting into a time when there was more acknowledgment given to actors and actresses than merely the Oscars or Golden Globes

Her awards included the following:

> ➤ She was a four-time Oscar nominee for Best Actress – that she never won seems very shortsighted as we look back on her career. She was nominated for *Stella Dallas* in 1937, *Ball of Fire* in 1941, *Double Indemnity* in 1944, and *Sorry:Wrong Number* in 1948.

> For *Double Indemnity*, she lost out at the Oscars to Ingrid Bergman in *Gaslight*, which is certainly understandable. But I personally enjoyed Barbara's performance more – I thought it was a more difficult part.

- ➢ She was awarded the American Film Institute's Lifetime Achievement Award in 1987 for her 60 years in films.
- ➢ She won Emmys for her work in "The Barbara Stanwyck Show" (1960), "The Big Valley" (1965), and "The Thorn Birds" (1983).
- ➢ She won two Golden Globe awards, including the Cecil B. DeMille award which is given for "outstanding contributions to the world of entertainment," and was nominated for three other Golden Globes for "The Big Valley."
- ➢ Barbara won the Screen Actors Guild Life Achievement Award in 1967.

She has a star on the Hollywood Walk of Fame at 1751 Vine Street.

My favorite Barbara Stanwyck Films

1. **Double Indemnity – 1944**

FORGOTTEN MOVIE STARS OF THE 30's, 40's, and 50's

Barbara Stanwyck and Fred MacMurray in two scenes from *Double Indemnity* – no doubt hatching their plot to murder her husband for his considerable amount of life insurance (previous page), then dealing with some loose ends later on (below).

Double Indemnity makes the top ten list of many fans of classic movies, and it certainly makes sense. This 1944 classic starred Barbara, Fred MacMurray, and Edward G. Robinson. Insurance salesman MacMurray is making his daily sales calls and renewals, stopping at the house of Stanwyck and her husband to try to get the husband to buy a nice-sized life insurance policy, going through the standard shtick that every insurance salesman goes through to make a sale. However, on a return visit to obtain the husband's signature, Stanwyck and he concoct a plot to murder her husband but make it look like an accident so she can collect double on the policy – double indemnity – and split the pot between the two of them.

FORGOTTEN MOVIE STARS OF THE 30's, 40's, and 50's

All goes according to plan, except when the guy in Fred's company responsible for reviewing insurance claims for possible fraud – Edward G. Robinson in an outstanding performance – gets Stanwyck's claim and starts suspecting something is rotten in Denmark about this one. After all, he can smell a phony claim (the little man inside him can, he says), and this is one of them. Stanwyck and MacMurray spend the rest of the film trying to outwit Robinson – while at the same time double-crossing each other to try to avoid being found out as the guilty party.

Everything about this movie is absolutely terrific. The main plot and subplots are all very exciting, and Billy Wilder's direction keeps you on the edge of your seat the entire movie. MacMurray is very good (Is this the same guy we saw all those years as the widowed dad in "My Three Sons?"). Robinson is doggedly convincing as the insurance investigator who suspects fraud, and Stanwyck is probably the best of all – alluring, cunning, and trying to convince everyone of her innocence while being three steps ahead of everyone else.

There is also a good subplot about Stanwyck's stepdaughter. The movie leads to an inevitable conclusion and the entire film is told in a flashback format by MacMurray as the duped insurance salesman Walter Neff, trying to make a killing (literally and figuratively) but eventually realizing that he is no match for Stanwyck.

Double Indemnity is a must-see film that should be at the top of everyone's list of classic movies! The film was nominated for seven Academy Awards, including Best Picture, Best Director, Best Actress (Stanwyck), and Best Screenplay, but undeservedly did not win a single award. It lost out to *Going My Way*, a decent enough film but frankly nowhere near as good as this one.

FORGOTTEN MOVIE STARS OF THE 30's, 40's, and 50's

2. Christmas in Connecticut – 1945

Barbara Stanwyck and sailor Dennis Morgan in a scene from *Christmas in Connecticut*.

I had never seen *Christmas in Connecticut* until about a year ago. A friend told me what a good holiday film it was, and he was certainly right.

> *Christmas in Connecticut* is a charming film, a romantic comedy that can entertain everyone from age 2 to 92, with a good screenplay and cast, and especially another outstanding performance by Stanwyck.

FORGOTTEN MOVIE STARS OF THE 30's, 40's, and 50's

A food writer (and perfect housewife and mom) for a major publication based in New York - think Martha Stewart - is told by her boss to invite a returning war hero and himself to her home for a traditional family Christmas. It would be very heartwarming and inspirational and also great publicity for the publication, he explains. Unfortunately, what her boss does not realize is that she is not married, has no kids, and can't boil water – she gets all her recipes from her friend who owns a New York City restaurant. Her goal is to try to pull this off without the boss, the sailor, or anyone else figuring out that she is a phony.

Everyone arrives at the Connecticut home, including the boss and a baby borrowed from a neighbor, and Stanwyck spends the rest of the movie trying to look like the real McCoy. As you might expect, she learns a lot about herself in the process and falls in love with the sailor, played by singer/actor Dennis Morgan.

Again, the performance of Stanwyck, plus the overall plot, make this film very appealing. Her maturation process throughout this film shows a lot of range in acting ability. She shows she is equally good in comedy and dramatic roles. In addition, *Christmas in Connecticut* features an all-star supporting cast that includes Sidney Greenstreet as the boss, Reginald Gardiner, Una O'Connor, and the delightful S.Z. Sakall as the restaurant owner and friend.

> S.Z. Sakall was a delightful character actor – nicknamed Cuddles – who was in many a Hollywood film in the 1930's and 1940's, including *Casablanca.* You can see from the photo on the next page why he was nicknamed "Cuddles."

FORGOTTEN MOVIE STARS OF THE 30's, 40's, and 50's

His credits included the following films, which included lots of musicals:

- *Casablanca*
- *Yankee Doodle Dandy*
- *Ball of Fire*
- *The Daughter of Rosie O'Grady*
- *In the Good Old Summertime*
- *Wonder Man*
- *Christmas in Connecticut*
- *Tea for Two*

And, he was really good in all of them!

FORGOTTEN MOVIE STARS OF THE 30's, 40's, and 50's

3. Meet John Doe – 1941

Barbara Stanwyck and Gary Cooper in a scene near the end of *Meet John Doe* – a really classic inspirational film. Cooper is trying to decide whether to go through with his promise to kill himself because he is such a failure in life.

In this depression-era film directed by Frank Capra, Barbara Stanwyck plays a hard-charging, aggressive reporter for a big-city newspaper who becomes angry after being laid off from her job as a columnist from *The New Bulletin*. So Ann Mitchell (Stanwyck) prints a fake letter from a so-called unemployed "John Doe," threatening suicide in protest of society's ills. When the published letter causes a sensation, the newspaper is forced to rehire her. Now, however, she has to find a John Doe and pretend that he is the individual who wrote the letter.

FORGOTTEN MOVIE STARS OF THE 30's, 40's, and 50's

After reviewing a number of derelicts who have shown up at the paper claiming to have penned the original suicide letter, Ann and sidekick Henry Connell (James Gleason) decide to hire Long John Willoughby (Gary Cooper) to play John Doe. Cooper is a down-on-his-luck former baseball player and current unemployed hobo who is in need of money to repair his injured arm. Walter Brennan plays his sidekick.

The Doe philosophy of helping others and putting the needs of others ahead of one's own self spreads across the country, developing into a national political movement with John Doe clubs springing up everywhere, and with financial support from the newspaper's publisher, D.B. Norton (Edward Arnold). The publisher secretly plans to channel the support for Doe into support for his own political ambitions (which have nothing to do with helping others, by the way.)

When Willoughby, who has come to believe in the Doe philosophy himself, realizes that he is being used, he tries to expose the plot, but is stymied in his attempts to talk to a nationwide radio audience at a political rally, and then is exposed as a fake by Norton (who claims to have been deceived, like everyone else, by the staff of the newspaper).

Now spurned by his former followers and viewing himself as a complete failure, Willoughby announces his intent to commit suicide by jumping from the roof of City Hall on Christmas Eve, as was stated in the original John Doe letter. Only the intervention of Stanwyck (who has become a sympathetic figure and falls in love with Cooper) and followers of the John Doe clubs persuade him to renege on his threat to kill himself.

At this point in the movie, a reference to Jesus Christ is made, that a historical "John Doe" has already died for the sake of humanity. The film ends with Henry Connell turning to Norton and saying, "There you are, Norton! The people! Try and lick that!"

FORGOTTEN MOVIE STARS OF THE 30's, 40's, and 50's

This is a typical Frank Capra inspirational film about average Americans trying to exist in a difficult world, and is perhaps my own favorite Capra movie. Gary Cooper and Barbara Stanwyck head an all-star grouping, with Cooper perfect as the everyman John Doe and Stanwyck terrific as always as the tough as nails reporter who shows herself to have a heart of gold when it really matters. A stellar cast includes Edward Arnold, James Gleason, Spring Byington, Gene Lockhart, and especially Walter Brennan as Cooper's hobo friend and conscience.

> Brennan coins one of the greatest speeches in movie history when he refers to Cooper's becoming successful and becoming a "helot."

"All right. You're walking along, not a nickel in your jeans, your free as the wind, nobody bothers ya. Hundreds of people pass you by in every line of business: shoes, hats, automobiles, radios, everything, and they're all nice lovable people and they lets you alone, is that right? Then you get a hold of some dough and what happens, all those nice sweet lovable people become helots, a lotta heels. They begin to creep up on ya, trying to sell ya something: they get long claws and they get a stranglehold on ya, and you squirm and you duck and you holler and you try to push them away but you haven't got the chance. They gots ya. First thing ya know you own things, a car for instance, now your whole life is messed up with a lot more stuff: you get license fees and number plates and gas and oil and taxes and insurance and identification cards and letters and bills and flat tires and dents and traffic tickets and motorcycle cops and tickets and courtrooms and lawyers and fines and... a million and one other things. What happens? You're not the free and happy guy you used to be. You need to have money to pay for all those things, so you go after what the other fellas got. There you are, you're a helot yourself."

FORGOTTEN MOVIE STARS OF THE 30's, 40's, and 50's

And that very true statement about our ridiculous desire for "stuff" beyond what we really need is just one of the many reasons I like this movie so much, and Stanwyck is one of the keys to its success.

4. Ball of Fire – 1941

Barbara Stanwyck and Gary Cooper in a scene from *Ball of Fire*. I think she is trying to convince Cooper not to be such a stick in the mud. It seems to be working!

A group of professors have lived together, isolated for years in an urban residence in Manhattan, compiling an encyclopedia of all human knowledge. The youngest, Professor Bertram Potts (Gary Cooper as an eccentric bookworm), is a scholar of languages who is researching modern American slang. They are accustomed to working in relative seclusion at a leisurely pace with a prim housekeeper keeping tabs on them, but they are suddenly pressured by their financial backer to complete their work as soon as possible.

FORGOTTEN MOVIE STARS OF THE 30's, 40's, and 50's

Venturing out to do some independent research, Bertram becomes interested in the slang vocabulary of saucy night club singer "Sugarpuss" O'Shea (Stanwyck). She is willing to assist him in his research if he can find her a place to hide from the police, who want to question her about her boyfriend, mob boss Joe Lilac (Dana Andrews in a rare role as a villain). Sugarpuss takes refuge in the house where the professors live and work, despite the objections of Bertram (Cooper).

The professors soon become enamoured with her informality and casual manner, not to mention her use of slang terms they have never heard before, and she unexpectedly begins to become quite fond of them. She teaches them to conga and demonstrates to Bertram the meaning of the phrase "yum yum" (kisses). She becomes attracted to Bertram, who reciprocates with a vengeance by proposing marriage to her. She accepts, but before they can do anything, O'Shea is whisked away by Lilac's henchmen. Lilac also wants to marry her, but only so she cannot testify against him. He is a thug who has no real love for her at all.

After a series of adventures inside and outside the mansion, the professors eventually outwit Lilac and his henchmen and rescue Sugarpuss, with Bertram knocking out the mob boss just as the police arrive. Sugarpuss decides she is not good enough for Bertram, but his forceful application of "yum yum" convinces her to change her mind.

Like all great romantic comedies, the two leads have to genuinely like each other, and that spark is certainly apparent here. Stanwyck is really good as the alluring nightclub singer who turns out to really care for others, and Cooper, though seemingly an odd choice as the nerdy bookworm professor, is quite convincing in the part. And the supporting cast is top notch all the way – including Dana Andrews, Oskar Homolka, S.Z. Sakall, Henry Travers, Richard Haydn, and Dan Duryea.

FORGOTTEN MOVIE STARS OF THE 30's, 40's, and 50's

> It's difficult to picture Gary Cooper as a nerdy professor, but he pulls it off quite well. As for the rest of the professors, they can easily pass as nerds!

This is a must-see movie for all fans of romantic comedies, as well as individuals who want to learn about slang terms of the early 1940's. It is interesting to note that slang terms can be specific to a give era – after all, who today refers to kisses as "yum yum?"

5. The Lady Eve – 1941

Barbara Stanwyck and Henry Fonda in a scene from *The Lady Eve*. The seductress Stanwyck has her eyes on the wealthy but nerdy Henry Fonda.

FORGOTTEN MOVIE STARS OF THE 30's, 40's, and 50's

A conniving father and daughter meet up with the heir to a brewery fortune—a wealthy but naïve snake enthusiast— on a cruise ship and attempt to bamboozle him at the card table. Their plan is quickly abandoned when the daughter falls in love with their prey.

But when the heir gets wise to her gold-digging ways, she must plot to re-conquer his heart. This is one of Director Preston Sturges's most clever and beloved romantic comedies; *The Lady Eve* balances broad slapstick and sophisticated sexiness with perfect grace.

What is delightful about Stanwyck's performance is that she can effectively play a villain and a heroine in the same movie. In the beginning, she is simply a crook, and yet the Henry Fonda character trusts her unquestionably. She is an alluring seductress, and yet a pushover for old-fashioned romance. She's a gold digger, and yet she wants nothing from him.

And Fonda plays a naive innocent who knows only that her perfume smells mighty good to someone who has been "up the Amazon" for a year. He plays his typical good-guy, Midwestern straight-laced hero – Fonda was born and raised in Grand Junction, Nebraska - as he does in many other films, from *The Grapes of Wrath* to *Mister Roberts*. A good supporting cast includes Charles Coburn, Eugene Pallette, and William Demarest.

> So now we have two films in a row where Gary Cooper and then Henry Fonda play nerds. Pretty good acting on their part!

FORGOTTEN MOVIE STARS OF THE 30's, 40's, and 50's

6. Sorry Wrong Number – 1948

In the late 1940's, Barbara Stanwyck was in her early 40's and began playing more mature roles, and this film is a good example. A film noir suspenseful thriller, Stanwyck plays Leona Stevenson, a spoiled, bedridden daughter of a millionaire. The telephone is her sole connection with the outside world. One day, while listening to what seems to be a crossed phone connection, she eavesdrops on two men planning a woman's murder. Leona calls the phone company and police, only to be ignored. Adding to Leona's dilemma is the fact that her husband Henry (Burt Lancaster) is missing.

After a number of phone calls, the terrorized Leona begins to piece together the mystery. Her uneducated husband, who works for her wealthy father, turns out to be not all he seems. Finally, to her horror, Leona realizes *she* is the intended victim. Could her husband actually be the one planning to murder her?

Barbara Stanwyck was again nominated for an Oscar for her performance in this movie, and again she did not win.

> Burt Lancaster, who played her husband, is easily one of my all-time favorite movie stars. I did not include him in this book because I do not believe he is in the "forgotten" category. However, if you are unfamiliar with his work, you owe it to yourself to watch some of his movies. Perhaps more than any other actor I have ever seen, when Lancaster is on screen, he commands your entire attention.

FORGOTTEN MOVIE STARS OF THE 30's, 40's, and 50's

Some of the best Burt Lancaster films include *Elmer Gantry* (his Academy Award winning performance), *Sweet Smell of Success, Seven Days in May, The Birdman of Alcatraz, From Here to Eternity,* swashbucklers like *The Crimson Pirate* and *His Majesty O'Keefe,* film noir classics like *The Killers* and *I Walk Alone,* and a group of westerns that include *Gunfight at the OK Corral, The Professionals,* and *Vera Cruz.* Wow, what a resume! And those are just some of his highlights. He and Kirk Douglas were buddies and played in seven movies together, with Lancaster generally in the lead. One of his last roles was as Doc Graham in *Field of Dreams.*

Burt Lancaster in his very first film — *The Killers.* That's Ava Gardner on the right.

FORGOTTEN MOVIE STARS OF THE 30's, 40's, and 50's

7. The Great Man's Lady – 1942

In Hoyt City, a modern metropolitan city in the West, a statue of city founder Ethan Hoyt (Joel McCrea) is being dedicated, and 100 year old Hannah Sempler Hoyt (who lives in the last residence among skyscrapers) is at last persuaded to tell her story to a "girl biographer." Flashback: to 1848, teenage Hannah (Stanwyck) – a Philadelphia rich girl - meets and flirts with pioneer Ethan Hoyt, who is visiting her father to secure funds for an adventure to develop the West. On a sudden impulse, they elope. We follow their struggle to found a city in the wilderness, hampered by the Gold Rush, silver mines, the railroads, star-crossed love, floods, and heartbreak. In flashback, she tells her story to the biographer, from age 16 to age 100. All the trials and tribulations, including whether or not she was really married to Ethan Hoyt.

How Barbara Stanwyck did not even get an Oscar nomination for this picture is beyond me. She is terrific as she ages from 16 to 100 and is completely believable at each age. She demonstrates courage, toughness, and sweetness at alternating points in the film. The point of the film is that this so-called Great Man would never have gotten anywhere without the pluck and savvy of Hannah Sempler, his first wife. Stanwyck and McCrea worked on six films together, and they apparently got along very well professionally.

> By the way, according to TCM's Robert Osborne, she gave McCrea the best two items of advice that he ever received in his career. They were to:
>
> a) show up on time, and
>
> b) know your lines when you show up.

FORGOTTEN MOVIE STARS OF THE 30's, 40's, and 50's

Brian Donlevy is also in this movie, as her protector Steely Edwards, the guy who really loves her but never quite connects with her.

As I have said previously, whereas in these days where every city in America seems to have a film festival and give awards, the recognition that Barbara Stanwyck received in her day is quite an achievement. She may not have been a stunner like some of the other female stars on my list, but Barbara Stanwyck was really memorable for an outstanding body of work in both movies and television.

FORGOTTEN MOVIE STARS OF THE 30's, 40's, and 50's

Ray Milland – 1905-1986

Ray Milland was one of the most durable, versatile, and long-lasting Hollywood stars of the Golden Age of Hollywood in the 1930's, 1940's, and 1950's. Born in Wales in 1905, he was neither as big of a leading man as some of the real Hollywood heavyweights, nor as good an actor as someone like a Spencer Tracy or Frederick March. Yet he hung around in films for almost 60 years, made a couple of great films – *The Lost Weekend*, for which he won an Oscar for Best Actor, and *Beau Geste* – and three of my personal favorites: *Reap the Wild Wind, It Happens Every Spring*, and Alfred Hitchcock's *Dial M for Murder*. He also starred as a detective in a popular television show, "Markham," in 1959-1960.

FORGOTTEN MOVIE STARS OF THE 30's, 40's, and 50's

Ray Milland also made a series of low budget, mostly tacky horror and science fiction movies in the 1960's. However, because of his great performance in The *Lost Weekend* and considerable success over a very long career, he is one of my favorites and deserves to be showcased in this book.

My favorite Ray Milland films include:

- *The Lost Weekend*
- *Reap the Wild Wind*
- *Beau Geste*
- *Dial M for Murder*
- *The Big Clock*
- *It Happens Every Spring*

Biography

Ray Milland, born Reginald Alfred John Truscott-Jones (sounds very British) in the Welsh town of Neath, Glamorgan in 1905, spent his youth participating in sports rather than planning on a career in acting. Unlike many stars, he did not come from a broken or extremely poor family. He became an expert horseman early on, working at his uncle's horse-breeding estate while studying at the King's College in Cardiff.

At 21, he was selected to go to London as a member of the elite Household Cavalry (the ones guarding the Royal Family). There, he underwent a rigorous 19 months of training, becoming adept at fencing, boxing, horsemanship, and shooting. He won trophies with his unit's rifle team.

However, after four years, he suddenly lost his means of financial support and had to turn elsewhere to make a living. Broke, he tried his hand at acting in small parts on the London stage.

FORGOTTEN MOVIE STARS OF THE 30's, 40's, and 50's

> There are several stories as to how he derived his stage name (instead of going by Reggie Jones, I assume). Most likely he took the name from 'mill-lands', an area near his home town. When he first appeared on screen in British films, he was billed first as Spike Milland, then Raymond Milland. (Not sure where Spike came from. Perhaps he had a treasured dog named Spike.)

While having lunch with English actress Estelle Brody in 1929, a producer joined them and persuaded the handsome Welshman to appear in a motion picture bit part. After that, larger parts followed, including the male lead in *The Lady from the Sea* (1929). The following year, he was signed by MGM and went to Hollywood, but was given little work, except for the role of Charles Laughton's ill-fated nephew in *Payment Deferred* (1932). After a year, Ray was out of his contract and returned to England.

His big break did not come until two years later – 1934 - when he joined Paramount, where he was to remain for the better part of his Hollywood career. During the first few years, he served an apprenticeship playing second leads in low-budget films, usually as the debonair man-about-town in light romantic comedies. By 1936, he had graduated to starring roles, first as the injured British hunter rescued on a tropical island by Dorothy Lamour in *The Jungle Princess*.

After that, he was the title hero of *Bulldog Drummond Escapes* and, finally, won the girl (rather than being "the other man") in Mitchell Leisen's screwball comedy *Easy Living* (both 1937).

FORGOTTEN MOVIE STARS OF THE 30's, 40's, and 50's

> I watched *Bulldog Drummond Escapes* recently and can definitely vouch for it as a low-budget film. Very cheaply made, a low number of sets, most of it filmed at night, and only about 60 minutes in length.

From those experiences came his big break in being cast as one of the three valiant Geste brothers in the Gary Cooper classic *Beau Geste* (1939).

In 1940, Ray was sent back to England to star in the screen adaptation of Terence Rattigan's *French Without Tears*, for which he received his best critical reviews to date. He was top-billed (above John Wayne) running a ship salvage operation in Cecil B. DeMille's lavish Technicolor adventure drama *Reap the Wild Wind* (1942), besting Wayne in a fight and later wrestling (along with Wayne) a giant squid.

> Somehow, I just can't picture Ray Milland beating the 6'4" 200+ pound John Wayne in a fight in real life! But that's Hollywood for you.

Also that year, he was directed by Billy Wilder in a charming comedy, *The Major and the Minor* (co-starring Ginger Rogers), for which he garnered good notices from all the major critics. Ray then played a ghost hunter in *The Uninvited*, and the suave hero caught in a web of espionage in Fritz Lang's thriller *Ministry of Fear* (both 1944).

FORGOTTEN MOVIE STARS OF THE 30's, 40's, and 50's

Then came his really big break. On the strength of his previous roles, Billy Wilder chose to cast Ray against type in the ground-breaking drama *The Lost Weekend* (1945) as alcoholic writer Don Birnam. Milland gave the defining performance of his career, his intensity catching critics - used to him as a lightweight leading man - by surprise. Ray Milland won the Oscar for Best Actor, as well as other major awards for the film.

Rarely given such good material again, he nonetheless featured memorably in many more good or better films, often exploiting the newly discovered 'darker side' of his personality as, for example, the reporter framed for murder by Charles Laughton's heinous publishing magnate in *The Big Clock* (1948). In 1954, Ray played calculating ex-tennis champ Tony Wendice, who blackmails a former Cambridge chump into murdering his wife, in Hitchcock's *Dial M for Murder*.

> I should say "attempting" to murder his wife, Grace Kelly, who avoids being murdered with the help of a well-placed scissors.

Turning to direction, Ray Milland turned out several off-beat, low-budget films with himself as the lead, notably *The Safecracker* (1958) and *Panic in the Year Zero* (1962). At the same time, he cheerfully made the transition to character parts, often in horror and sci-fi outings. In accordance with his own dictum of appearing in anything that had "any originality," he worked on two notable pictures with Roger Corman: first, as a man obsessed with catalepsy in *The Premature Burial* (1961); secondly, as obsessed self-destructive surgeon Dr. Xavier in *X-the Man with X-Ray Eyes* (1963), a film which despite its low budget won the 1963 Golden Asteroid in the Trieste Festival for Science Fiction.

FORGOTTEN MOVIE STARS OF THE 30's, 40's, and 50's

As the years went on, he turned his attention to television, lending dignity through his presence to many run-of-the-mill television films, such as "Cave-I" (1979) and melodramas like "Love Story" (1970). He also enjoyed a brief run on Broadway, starring as Simon Crawford in "Hostile Witness" (1966), at the Music Box Theatre. He starred as international detective Roy Markham in the television series "Markham" in 1959 and 1960 and guest starred in TV shows like "Night Gallery" and "Battlestar Galactica."

> Although he was bald for most of his career, Ray Milland wore a hairpiece until the 1960's.

In his private life, Ray was an enthusiastic yachtsman who loved fishing and collecting information by reading the Encyclopedia Britannica. In spite of his on-screen personality as somewhat of a rogue, Milland was married to the same woman for 54 years until his death in 1986.

In later years, he became very popular with interviewers because of his candid spontaneity and humor. In the same self-deprecating vein he wrote an anecdotal biography, *Wide-Eyed in Babylon,* in 1976. Milland died of cancer at the age of 81.

Recognition

Ray Milland won the Oscar for Best Actor in 1946 for *The Lost Weekend.* He was also awarded Best Actor at the Cannes Film Festival and a Golden Globe in the same year for the same picture. He received the best actor honor for this film by the New York Film Critics Circle and the National Board of Review. Pretty much a clean sweep, and deservedly so.

Milland also was nominated for an Emmy as Best Supporting Actor in a Drama Series for "Rich Man, Poor Man" in 1976. He was nominated for a Golden Globe as Best Actor in a film for *The Thief* in 1952. Milland has two stars on the Hollywood Walk of Fame – at 1625 Vine Street for his motion picture work, and at 1620 Vine Street for his television work.

My Favorite Ray Milland Films

1. The Lost Weekend – 1945

Ray Milland as alcoholic Don Burnham, and Doris Dowling in a scene from *The Lost Weekend*. Milland's fortunes are obviously on the downside in this scene. Milland won an Oscar for Best Actor in 1946 for this film. He was outstanding in this movie, his best role, and he swept all the major awards.

FORGOTTEN MOVIE STARS OF THE 30's, 40's, and 50's

This trend-setting 1945 film was one of the first of a series of films to deal with social problems and may have been the first major film to deal specifically with alcoholism as an illness and not a moral weakness. "I'm not a drinker--I'm a drunk." These words, and the serious message behind them, shocked audiences flocking to *The Lost Weekend*. The speaker was Don Birnam (Ray Milland), a handsome, talented, articulate writer who is also an alcoholic. The movie pulled no punches in its depiction of Birnam's massive four-day weekend bender, a tailspin that finds him reeling from his favorite bar to other bars and eventually to Bellevue Hospital to dry out.

Shooting the film in New York helped add to the street-level atmosphere, especially a sequence in which writer Birnam tries to hock his typewriter for booze money. He desperately staggers past shuttered storefronts, but the pawnshops are closed. The sequence in the hospital, where he is withdrawing from the booze, is especially shocking. It is only when Birnham realizes that he is no longer a social drinker but an alcoholic, that he begins to turn his life around. He seeks help and decides to write about his life as an alcoholic.

The film won Oscars for Best Picture, Best Director (Billy Wilder), Best Screenplay and of course Best Actor for Ray Milland. *The Lost Weekend* was a landmark film because it brought a new kind of frankness and darkness rarely seen before the end of World War II, to Hollywood's treatment of a social problem.

> Interestingly enough, at first the film may have seemed too bold; Paramount Pictures nearly killed the release of the picture after it tested poorly with preview audiences.

FORGOTTEN MOVIE STARS OF THE 30's, 40's, and 50's

Once in release, *The Lost Weekend* became a substantial hit, and is easily Milland's best film. He gets to the core of the character in a shockingly convincing, no-holds-barred performance that is clearly the signature performance of his career.

2. Reap the Wild Wind - 1942

John Wayne takes the witness stand with Ray Milland as the prosecuting attorney determined to find out who was responsible for wrecking The Southern Cross, in a scene from *Reap the Wild Wind*.

As I have previously indicated, *Reap the Wild Wind* is one of my all-time favorite films. The plot of *Reap the Wild Wind* is a good one: It takes place in Key West, Florida in the 1840's where sailing ships bring their cargo between Havana and points north while attempting to avoid wrecking their ships on the notorious reefs of Key West. Meanwhile, salvage masters – some honest and some not – vie for salvage rights for the cargo of the wrecked ships, in some cases wrecks that are planned by the most notorious and villainous of the salvage masters, King Cutler, played by Raymond Massey.

FORGOTTEN MOVIE STARS OF THE 30's, 40's, and 50's

Loxi Claiborne (Goddard) is the honest owner of one of Cutler's rival companies. When she rescues Captain John Stuart (Wayne) from the wreckage of his ship, whose wreck may well have been planned by his first mate, the plot is set in motion. Soon Loxie goes to Charleston, South Carolina to help her new love make amends with his company and chief lawyer/second in command, Steve Tolliver (Milland), for letting his ship get wrecked. When Tolliver volunteers to investigate the mysterious sinking of Wayne's ship by sailing to Key West himself, the action is really set in motion.

Milland and John Wayne are rivals for Paulette Goddard, with Milland the quick-thinking lawyer and Wayne the honest but not as sharp ship's captain. They work together and at odds to find the real reason these sailing ships are being wrecked. Milland more than holds his own against the two-fisted Wayne in this DeMille classic.

Plot twists galore, a view of pre-Civil War South, fistfights, romantic rivalries, and the two male leads dueling each other and finding time to fight the giant squid in the movie's famous climax, make this one of the most exciting movies of the 1940's. As long as you understand that this film contains the usual hokey dialogue present in all of DeMille's movies, you won't be disappointed in this film.

> The giant rubber squid used in the underwater battle was donated by the studio to the war effort in 1942. The Japanese had conquered Malaya and Indochina, source of most of the world's rubber. The last scene of the film, featuring the battle with the giant squid, took two months to film. But the film did receive the Oscar for Best Special Effects, and you can certainly see why if you watch the movie.

FORGOTTEN MOVIE STARS OF THE 30's, 40's, and 50's

3. Beau Geste - 1939

Ray Milland as John Geste and Robert Preston as his brother, Digby, in a scene near the end of *Beau Geste*. Gary Cooper played the oldest Geste brother, Beau. In this film, Milland and Preston were brothers; they were on decidedly less friendly terms in *Reap the Wild Wind*.

Beau Geste is a terrific adventure story with a great cast featuring Gary Cooper, Ray Milland, and Robert Preston as the three inseparable Geste brothers, a lovely Susan Hayward as the girl in their lives, and Brian Donlevy as the despicable Sergeant Markoff. This version is clearly the best of all the Beau Geste movies. Beau, John, and Digby Geste are three inseparable, orphaned, adventurous brothers who have been adopted into the wealthy household of Lady Brandon.

FORGOTTEN MOVIE STARS OF THE 30's, 40's, and 50's

When money in the uppercrust household grows tight, Lady Brandon is forced to sell her most treasured jewel - the spectacular "Blue Water" sapphire. The household gets it out for one final look, the lights go out, and it vanishes, apparently stolen by one of the brothers. That night, Beau, Digby, and John each "confess" in writing to the theft and one by one run away, John leaving behind Isobel (Hayward), whom he loves.

They all join the French Foreign Legion, and Beau and Digby (Cooper and Preston) are split from John (Milland) and put under the command of the ruthless and sadistic Sergeant Markoff. The three are joined together again as conditions begin to deteriorate badly when the rest of the Legionnaires plot a mutiny against Markoff, in the midst of an attack by Arab hordes on their fort in the middle of the Sahara Desert. After an unsuccessful mutiny against the brutal treatment of Markoff, the fort is attacked by the enemy and the men have to join forces to fight for their lives.

This is an inspiring, action-packed movie, never equaled, with an all-star cast. In particular, the performances of the Geste brothers – Cooper, Milland, and Preston – as well as Donlevy as the evil Sergeant Markoff – should be noted. The three stars work well together, and any movie with Gary Cooper as one of its heroes has got to be good. The story itself is outstanding, and holds us in suspense as we learn which brother actually stole the Blue Water sapphire and why. And does Ray Milland actually end up with the love of his life? You will have to see *Beau Geste* to find out.

> I will always remember the scene where the evil Sergeant Markoff stacks up the bodies of the dead soldiers at their posts during the attack in order to give the appearance that all the soldiers are actually still alive; of course, he goes one step too far.

And then comes the famous line that a Viking always dies with a dog at his feet, and the symbolism that the line carries at the beginning and end of the film for the brothers.

4. **Dial M for Murder - 1954**

Robert Cummings, Grace Kelly, and Ray Milland in a scene from *Dial M for Murder*. Ray is up to something bad, but Kelly and Cummings don't know it yet.

Dial M for Murder is a classic Alfred Hitchcock murder mystery/thriller starring Ray Milland, Grace Kelly, and Robert Cummings. Milland is Tony Wendice, a retired tennis player living in London with his wife (Kelly) whom he has neglected throughout their marriage. He finds out that his wife is having an affair with Cummings, an American writer, and decides that the best way of getting rid of the problem is by getting rid of her. He finds an old acquaintance from Cambridge – Swann - that he has the goods on, and threatens to blackmail him unless the "buddy" does a slight favor for him – kill his wife. (After all, Milland is an upper-crusty Englishman who does not want to do the dirty work himself.)

FORGOTTEN MOVIE STARS OF THE 30's, 40's, and 50's

Milland and his army friend concoct an elaborate plot to ensure that no one could possibly expect that Milland plotted the murder. He manages to call his wife at their apartment at an exact time, and while he is on the phone with his wife, the buddy, to whom Milland has given a key to their place, will step in and strangle Kelly. All goes according to plan, except that while in the process of being strangled, Kelly manages to find a pair of scissors and stabs the poor blackmailed buddy in the back, killing him instantly.

> The attempted murder scene is the one from this movie that is always shown when discussing *Dial M for Murder*.

In any case, because of some shrewd and quick work by Milland, the police believe that Swann was blackmailing Kelly and that she committed murder rather than self defense; she is arrested, tried, and convicted. Milland's plans have gone as well as could be expected until the chief investigator on the case starts suspecting that something is not quite as it seems and begins to reopen the case with the help of Cummings.

Grace Kelly is good, as always, in this film, but Milland is even better as the husband, seeming to be completely in love while plotting her demise and changing plans when his first plan is not successful. He comes across well as the high-society Englishman who is all charm and reasonableness, but we in the audience know better – He is motivated by jealousy and greed, for his wife is much wealthier than he is. About the only valid criticism of the movie is that it has the look of a stage play – just about the entire film is set in their apartment. But that is hardly the fault of the actors, who turn in solid performances in one of the better Hitchcock films.

FORGOTTEN MOVIE STARS OF THE 30's, 40's, and 50's

> Unlike most of Hitchcock's films, which feature an innocent man falsely accused of murder, this one involves an innocent woman falsely accused of murder. And it was originally made in 3D, to boot.

5. **The Big Clock – 1948**

Charles Laughton and Ray Milland in a scene from *The Big Clock*.

The Big Clock is a mystery/film noir starring Ray Milland as a man falsely accused who has to find the real killer (it's not a Hitchcock film) with an outstanding cast that also includes Charles Laughton, Maureen O'Sullivan, George Macready, Rita Johnson, Elsa Lanchester, and Harry Morgan (Colonel Potter from the "M*A*S*H" television show).

FORGOTTEN MOVIE STARS OF THE 30's, 40's, and 50's

The story, as in many good film noir movies, is told in flashback. George Stroud (Ray Milland), editor-in-chief of *Crimeways* magazine, is shown hiding from building security in the office building where he works behind the "big clock" — the largest and most sophisticated one ever built, which dominates the lobby of the giant publishing company in New York City. At that point, he proceeds to tell the viewer his story.

A workaholic, Stroud wants to spend more time with his wife (Maureen O'Sullivan) and plans a long-postponed vacation from his job. He sticks to those plans despite being fired for it by his tyrannical publishing boss, Earl Janoth (Charles Laughton). Instead of meeting his wife at the train station as planned, however, Stroud finds himself preoccupied with the attention being shown him by Janoth's glamorous mistress, Pauline York (Rita Johnson), who proposes a blackmail plan against Janoth. When Stroud misses their scheduled train, his wife angrily leaves without him, so he begins drinking and spends the evening out on the town with York, even if he has no real plans to participate in this blackmailing scheme.

Later that night, Janoth spots a man leaving York's apartment, but does not get a clear enough look at him to see that it is Stroud. Although Stroud's evening with York had ended platonically (in the movie if not in the book on which the movie is based), Janoth assumes otherwise, leading to a quarrel with York that ends when he murders her. Janoth determines to locate the man he had seen leaving the apartment and then frame that man for the crime. Ironically, Janoth re-hires Stroud to lead the effort to find the man who left her apartment. Of course, it is our hero, George Stroud.

Stroud then must balance the tasks of outwardly appearing to diligently lead Janoth's investigation and, at the same time, trying to prevent that investigation from uncovering the fact that it is he who is the very target of it, even if he is completely innocent of murder. At the same time, he must also secretly carry out his own investigation to gather the evidence necessary to prove who is the real murderer.

The film features standout performances by all, especially Milland as the innocent victim and Laughton as the real murderer. As I indicated, it has the feel of an Alfred Hitchcock movie even if it is not.

> The film is directed by John Farrow, husband of Maureen O'Sullivan and father of actress Mia Farrow.

6. It Happens Every Spring - 1949

Ray Milland as King Kelly

FORGOTTEN MOVIE STARS OF THE 30's, 40's, and 50's

Ray Milland as chemistry professor turned star baseball pitcher King Kelly of the St. Louis Cardinals, in *It Happens Every Spring*. This film proves there was a bit of cheating and skullduggery in baseball even before steroids and human growth hormone.

The "it" in the title refers to baseball. A college chemistry professor is working on a long-term scientific experiment when a baseball comes through the window, destroying all of his glassware. The resultant fluid causes the baseball to be repelled by wood. Suddenly, he realizes the possibilities and takes a leave of absence to test his solution. He tells no one at all, not even his fiancée, what he is up to. Kelly decides to test his solution by going to St. Louis to try out as a pitcher for the St. Louis Cardinals. Of course, with no experience, he is initially rejected until he insists on being given a tryout, where none of the St. Louis hitters can hit his pitches. (Of course not, since his fluid causes the baseball to repel wood. Which is why he looks terrible warming up in the bullpen but unhittable on the pitching mound.) He goes on to become a star pitcher for the Cardinals and leads his team to the World Series.

> They chose the Cardinals rather than my favorite team, the Chicago Cubs, probably because it was too preposterous of an idea to think of the Cubs in a World Series. Otherwise, they would have had to call this film a fantasy instead of a comedy.

This is simply a very nice comedy/baseball film that you sit down and enjoy without taking it too seriously. Sure, Milland at 44 is too old to be a baseball player, and yes, you can't tell me that no one ever found out where he was hiding his solution (in the brim of his cap), but it's a lot of fun. Milland is fine as the professor turned baseball player, and a good

FORGOTTEN MOVIE STARS OF THE 30's, 40's, and 50's

supporting class includes Jean Peters, Paul Douglas as his catcher and friend, and Ed Begley. A good film to watch, especially in the spring. Since we know that baseball happens every spring.

In the 1960's and 1970's, Ray Milland had a number of character actor parts, including playing Ryan O'Neal's father in the 1970 soaper, *Love Story*. Ray also starred in a number of science fiction movies. Some were pretty good – *Panic in the Year Zero, Premature Burial, Terror in the Wax Museum*, and *The Man with the X-Ray Eyes* come to mind - and some were just awful. The latter category includes *The Thing with Two Heads*; which is one of the worst movies ever made, with Milland a dying racist scientist who develops a plan to save his head and attach it to the body of another man – in this case, former pro football star Roosevelt Grier. The heads of Ray Milland and Rosie Grier spend the rest of the movie insulting each other and trying to figure out how to get rid of the other head without killing himself.

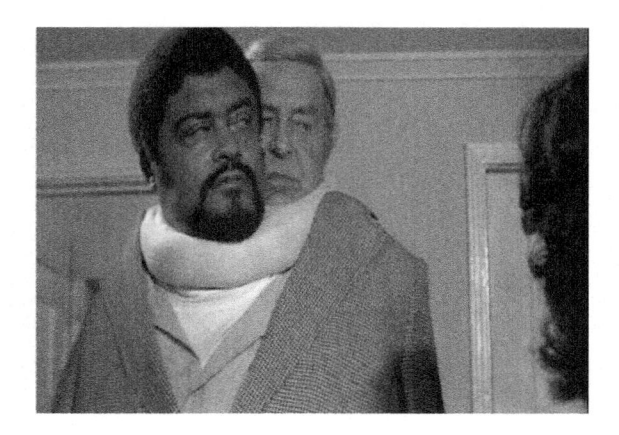

EEK!! That is all I can say about this film. This is one of those films where the actor just says, "I did it for the paycheck."

FORGOTTEN MOVIE STARS OF THE 30's, 40's, and 50's

> Just picture yourself walking down the street and running into a man with two heads – a bald Ray Milland and football player Rosie Grier.

Ray Milland also directed several films that he starred in – *Hostile Witness, Panic in the Year Zero, The Safecracker, Lisbon,* and *A Man Alone.* All were good films, none were spectacular but none were clunkers, either.

Let's remember Ray Milland for the large number of quality films he made, led by one of the best movies ever made about a social issue – *The Lost Weekend* – and forget about *The Thing with Two Heads.*

FORGOTTEN MOVIE STARS OF THE 30's, 40's, and 50's

Joseph Cotten – 1905-1994

Joseph Cotten was certainly an overlooked star. Nowhere near as handsome as a Robert Taylor or Tyrone Power, he was still a solid leading man for most of the 1940's through 1960's. He made a couple of really classic pictures with Orson Welles, and had a career which lasted well into the 1980's. This included a TV career in the 60's and 70's. Good acting skills and sincerity were his strengths, and if you like leading men who relied on talent and hard work rather than just good looks, you probably would like Cotten.

My favorite Joseph Cotten films include the following:

- *Shadow of a Doubt*
- *Citizen Kane*

FORGOTTEN MOVIE STARS OF THE 30's, 40's, and 50's

- *Duel in the Sun*
- *The Third Man*
- *Niagara*

Biography

Joseph Cheshire Cotten was born into an affluent Southern family, the eldest of three sons born to Sally Bartlett and Joseph Cotten, Sr. Cotten studied acting at the Hickman School of Expression in Washington, D.C. and worked as an advertising agent after that. By 1924 he tried to enter acting in New York but was unsuccessful and left for Miami. There he found a variety of jobs: lifeguard, potato salad salesman, a stint as entrepreneur – but more significantly, drama critic for the *Miami Herald*. That also led to his appearing in plays at the Miami Civic Theater. Through a connection at the newspaper, he managed to land an assistant stage manager job in New York. By 1930 he made his Broadway debut.

> Cotton actually was a Tip Top potato salad salesman for a short time.

To augment his income as an actor in the mid-30s, Cotten took on radio shows in addition to his theatre work. At one audition he met a young, budding actor/writer/director/producer named Orson Welles. Welles's drive led him to found The Mercury Theatre Players. Coming on board were later Hollywood stalwarts such as Everett Sloane, Agnes Moorehead, Ruth Warrick, and Ray Collins (Lt. Tragg on "Perry Mason"). In 1937, Cotten starred in Welles's Mercury productions of "Julius Caesar" and "Shoemaker's Holiday." But after a year, nothing had developed until Welles met with writer Herman J. Mankiewicz, resulting in the *Citizen Kane* (1941) idea in early 1940.

FORGOTTEN MOVIE STARS OF THE 30's, 40's, and 50's

Citizen Kane is the fictional story of a tyrannical newspaper publisher similar to William Randolph Hearst with Welles as Kane and Cotten, in his Hollywood debut, as his college friend turned confidant/theater critic, Jed Leland. Eventually the movie would become film history, but at the time it was not well received by the public. After all, Hearst owned the majority of the country's press outlets and as such forbade advertisements for the film. The film was nominated for nine Academy Awards in 1942 but was largely ignored by the Academy, only winning for Best Screenplay for Welles and Mankiewicz.

> Wonder why Citizen Kane was not a commercial success? No advertisements from the Hearst newspapers! I can't believe any other film had as tough a task.

The following year Cotten and Welles collaborated again in *The Magnificent Ambersons* (1942), acclaimed but again ignored at Oscar time, and the next year's Nazi thriller *Journey Into Fear* (1943). Cotten wrote the screenplay with some help from Welles. After that, Welles with his notorious overrunning of budgets was dropped by RKO.

Later in 1943 Cotten's friendship with young producer David O. Selznick resulted in a movie contract and the launching of his more mainstream and very successful movie career as a romantic leading man. Thereafter he appeared with some of the best of Hollywood's leading ladies - a favorite being Jennifer Jones, Selznick's wife, with the two of them being his best friends. Cotten got the opportunity to play a good range of roles through the 1940s - the darkest being the killer in Alfred Hitchcock thriller *Shadow of a Doubt* (1943) with Teresa Wright.

FORGOTTEN MOVIE STARS OF THE 30's, 40's, and 50's

Perhaps the most fun was *The Farmer's Daughter* (1947) with a vivacious Loretta Young. Cotten starred with Jennifer Jones in four films: the wartime domestic drama *Since You Went Away* (1944), the romantic drama *Love Letters* (1945), the western *Duel in the Sun* (1946), and later in the critically acclaimed *Portrait of Jennie* (1948).

Welles and Cotten did not work together again until *The Third Man* (1949), directed by Carol Reed. For Cotten, the role as the hapless boyhood friend and second-rate novel writer Holly Martins would be a defining moment in a part both comedic and bittersweet, its range making it one of his best performances. However, he was again overlooked for an Oscar.

Cotten was kept in relative demand into his mature acting years. In the 1950s, he reunited with Teresa Wright to do the memorable bank caper *The Steel Trap* (1952). He costarred with Jean Peters in *Blueprint For A Murder* (1953). But for the most part, the movie roles were becoming more B than A.

Turning to television, Cotten reunited with Alfred Hitchcock to star on three episodes of the acclaimed TV series "Alfred Hitchcock Presents" (1955-59). In the Episode "Breakdown", he portrayed a man who survived an auto accident but was believed to be dead. He stared in his own TV series "The Joseph Cotten Show - On Trial" (1956). He later played numerous major and minor parts and after 1967, had various appearances in TV and on the big screen. His last role was as a priest in the feature "The Survivor" (1981).

Cotten's hobbies in retirement included gardening and entertaining friends with his second wife, actress Patricia Medina (His first wife died after they were married for 30 years). He also had the time to write an engaging autobiography, *Vanity Will Get You Somewhere* (1987).

FORGOTTEN MOVIE STARS OF THE 30's, 40's, and 50's

Cotten's somewhat matter-of-fact and seemingly gruff acting voice served him well. Certainly his command of varied roles deserved more than the snub of never being nominated for an Academy Award. He was not the only actor to suffer being underrated, but that is largely forgotten in those memorable roles that speak out for him.

> If you listen closely you can detect a mild Southern drawl in his speech.

Recognition

Joseph Cotten was awarded Best Actor at the 1949 Venice Film Festival for *Portrait of Jennie*.

He has a star on the Hollywood Walk of Fame at 6382 Hollywood Boulevard.

My Favorite Joseph Cotten Films

1. Shadow of a Doubt - 1943

Cotten and Wright

FORGOTTEN MOVIE STARS OF THE 30's, 40's, and 50's

Previous page. Joseph Cotten, as beloved Uncle Charlie, and Teresa Wright, as his niece Charlie, in a scene from *Shadow of a Doubt*. **Young Charlie is starting to wonder if her uncle is truly the beloved figure everyone else believes him to be.**

While the police are on the lookout for the notorious Merry Widow killer, who gets his nickname by murdering lonely and rich widows for their money, the Newton family's Uncle Charlie – Joseph Cotten - comes to live with them. Teresa Wright plays the oldest child, Young Charlie, who at first adores her Uncle Charlie, but because of his quirky behavior, starts to wonder if he might in fact be the notorious Merry Widow killer. The cynical, film-noirish 1943 film was shot on location in the small, story-book town of Santa Rosa, California - a representative place of wholesome, middle-American values where dark corruption is hidden within a family, and specifically within one family member.

When Federal agents show up in Santa Rosa and start watching Uncle Charlie, Young Charlie becomes even more suspicious. And when they ask for her help, Charlie is conflicted between her loyalty to her family and her obligation to do what is right.

> Hitchcock said this was his own personal favorite of all his films. And that speaks volumes when you also consider his other great films like *Rear Window, North by Northwest, Strangers on a Train, Vertigo, Saboteur,* and *Psycho.*

I don't think I have ever seen a more dubious leading man than Joseph Cotten in this movie. He is convincing as both the upstanding uncle and also as a possible serial killer – you can believe he could be both people. It's a shame that this film did not receive more recognition in its time, although lovers of thrillers and of Hitchcock have typically recognized it as one of their favorites. Include me in that category. The delicate balance between good and evil and between what seems to be and what actually is, has perhaps never been better demonstrated than in this powerful movie. And the haunting Merry Widow Waltz is played throughout the film very effectively. The climax is typical Hitchcock – a surprise ending.

2. Citizen Kane - 1941

Orson Welles, Joseph Cotten, and others in a scene from *Citizen Kane*. Staff of the *Chronicle* discover that Kane (Welles) has bought their newspaper and is going to make some dramatic changes, and not necessarily pleasant ones for the staff.

FORGOTTEN MOVIE STARS OF THE 30's, 40's, and 50's

Generally ranked as one of the top five films of all time, *Citizen Kane* tells the story of newspaper publisher Charles Foster Kane, at least partly based on the life of newspaper magnate William Randolph Hearst. The opening scene sets the stage and tells it all: *Citizen Kane* opens with the camera panning across a spooky, seemingly deserted estate in Florida called Xanadu – the spectacular mansion of Charles Foster Kane.

The camera lingers on a "No Trespassing" sign and a large "K" wrought iron gate, then gradually makes its way to the house, where it appears to pass through a lit window. A person is lying on a slab-like bed. Snowflakes then suddenly fill the screen.

As the camera pulls back, a snow-covered cabin comes into view. The camera pulls back more quickly to show that what we have been looking at is actually just a scene inside a snow globe in the hand of an old man. The camera focuses on the old man's mouth, which whispers one word: "Rosebud." He then drops the globe, which rolls onto the floor and shatters.

Reflected in the curve of a piece of shattered glass, a door opens and a white-uniformed nurse runs into the room. She folds the old man's arms over his chest and covers his face with a sheet. And that's just the first five minutes of this movie, rated #1 of all time by the American Film Institute.

A reporter hired by the producer of a newsreel depicting the life story of Kane is not satisfied; the newsreel only tells the events of the man's life, but not his character. So the producer tells the reporter to find out about the essence of the man, including the meaning of the word "rosebud." The reporter interviews a series of people who were close to Kane, and these characters relate their memories of the man through flashbacks.

FORGOTTEN MOVIE STARS OF THE 30's, 40's, and 50's

Jerry Thompson (the reporter) speaks first with Kane's good friends and employees, including his former friend and associate with the newspaper, Jedediah Leland, played by Joseph Cotten. Each person, including Leland, gives his or her own version of an abandoned, lonely boy who grows up to be an isolated, needy man.

All reveal in some way that Kane is arrogant, thoughtless, morally bankrupt, desperate for attention, and incapable of giving love. Cotten's story in itself reveals the many sides of Charles Foster Kane. These faults eventually cause Kane to lose his paper, fortune, friends, and even his beloved second wife.

No one is able to reveal the meaning of the word "Rosebud" until the viewer discovers it in the last scene of the film. Spoiler note! If you read a few lines forward, you will find the answer to this mystery.

One of the most innovative American films of all time, the film features an outstanding narration and effective and unusual camera angles from Orson Welles. Featured in this movie are Welles' stalwarts including Cotten as his friend and associate, Jed Leland, in a very effective performance, along with Everett Sloane, Agnes Moorehead, and Ray Collins. And of course, Orson Welles as Charles Foster Kane from a young to an older man.

> As it turns out, "Rosebud" is the trade name of a cheap little sled a young Kane was playing with on the day he was taken away from his home and his mother. Apparently, Kane was never the same after that.

FORGOTTEN MOVIE STARS OF THE 30's, 40's, and 50's

3. Duel in the Sun – 1946

Cotten with actress and good friend Jennifer Jones in a scene from *Duel in the Sun*. This movie really belonged to Jennifer Jones and Gregory Peck as the star-crossed lovers, but Cotten was also effective as the refined son.

This blockbuster western features Jennifer Jones as the beautiful half-breed Pearl Chavez, who becomes the ward of her dead father's first love and finds herself torn between her sons, one good and the other bad - both of whom love her.

Joseph Cotten is effective as the good son but Gregory Peck – in an unusual role for him – is even better as the bad son. This is definitely not the typical Gregory Peck role. Lionel Barrymore and Lillian Gish are two Hollywood stalwarts who are also members of this outstanding cast.

FORGOTTEN MOVIE STARS OF THE 30's, 40's, and 50's

A very long (144 minutes) western set in Texas in the 1880's, it was not particularly well received by critics but is worth watching because of the performances of its stars, especially Peck as the brutish son; Lillian Gish in an Oscar-nominated performance; and of course, Jennifer Jones, in an unusual bit of casting from her normal straightforward and very pious roles. In today's Hollywood, someone like Salma Hayek would be perfect in this part. Cotten is effective as the refined son, who loves Jones but is unable to control her as she drifts between him and his brother.

4. The Third Man - 1949

Alida Valli and Joseph Cotten with a shadow of Orson Welles in the background as Harry Lime.

FORGOTTEN MOVIE STARS OF THE 30's, 40's, and 50's

Set in bombed-out, post-World War II Vienna, Holly Martins (Joseph Cotten), a writer of pulp westerns, arrives as a penniless guest of his childhood chum Harry Lime (Orson Welles), only to find Lime is dead – killed in a traffic accident. Martins develops the ultimate conspiracy theory after learning of a "third man" present at the time of Harry's death, running into interference from investigating British officer Major Calloway, and falling head-over-heels in love with Harry's grief-stricken lover, Anna, played by Alida Valli. Cotten is excellent as the narrator, trying to find the truth behind his pal's supposed death when some of the details behind the death show a great deal of inconsistency.

The Third Man is an excellent film featuring superior performances throughout, especially from Cotten as the friend investigating the crime, and of course Welles as Harry Lime. The film also features a wonderfully bizarre zither score by Anton Karas, perhaps the single item most remembered about this film. When I met TCM host Robert Ludlum a few years ago, I had an opportunity to ask him what was his all-time favorite movie. He said it was probably *The Third Man*.[5]

> If you have never heard of Alida Valli, you are probably not alone. Alida Valli had a short career as a Hollywood star, then returned to her native Italy in 1951 and appeared in scores of movies there for another 50 years. She was dubbed "The Next Garbo," but that never really panned out. Her other major U.S. film was *Miracle of the Bells* with Frank Sinatra and Fred MacMurray. She died in Rome in 2006 at the age of 84.

---

[5] Discussion with Robert Osborne at the Prairie Center for the Performing Arts in Schaumburg, Illinois, sometime in the summer of 2008 or 2009.

5. Niagara – 1953

Joseph Cotten is about to do in Marilyn Monroe in a scene from *Niagara*. Marilyn has gone a bit too far in trying to drive husband Cotten insane.

Unhappily married couple Rose and George Loomis (Marilyn Monroe and Joseph Cotten) are vacationing in a bungalow at Niagara Falls. George, a World War II veteran, is slowly unraveling and believes he is going insane because he has been plagued by extremely bad luck the past few years. As a result, their relationship is getting worse and worse. They meet the Cuttlers, spending a late honeymoon in the next bungalow. By accident, Polly Cuttler (Jean Peters) discovers that Rose has a lover, and we realize that Rose and her lover are attempting to drive George crazy in an effort to murder him that day. George finds out and attempts to turn the tables on his wife and her

FORGOTTEN MOVIE STARS OF THE 30's, 40's, and 50's

lover. He manages to drag Polly in during an exciting conclusion around the Falls itself.

This film features an excellent cast headed by Marilyn Monroe, Joseph Cotten, and Jean Peters, as well as good photography and chase scenes using Niagara Falls as a backdrop. As you can see from the photo, Monroe's plot to drive husband Cotten insane has worked only too well. Cotten turns in a solid performance as a man obsessed with his gorgeous, younger, and bored wife, an obsession that, coupled with his other problems, has made him extremely dangerous.

Joseph Cotten is certainly not my favorite male movie star on this list. However, the more I thought about it, the more I realized that he was quite a good actor who definitely deserves to be included in this book.

Other good Joseph Cotten films are the following:

- *The Magnificent Ambersons* – nominated for four Oscars, including Best Picture.
- *Since You Went Away*
- *The Farmer's Daughter* – featuring Loretta Young's Oscar-winning performance
- *The Abominable Dr. Phibes*
- *Hush..Hush Sweet Charlotte*

> Cotten was good in *The Abominable Dr. Phibes*, but Vincent Price was simply great as the doctor who seeks revenge on those he considers responsible for his late wife's death.

FORGOTTEN MOVIE STARS OF THE 30's, 40's, and 50's

John Garfield – 1913-1952

John Garfield was an outstanding actor and major star of the 1940's who passed away much too soon because of heart problems that plagued him all his life. Garfield was especially adept at playing brooding, rebellious, working-class character roles. His acting style was more in the method acting style of Montgomery Clift, James Dean, or even Marlon Brando than it was of other stars of his generation. In fact, you might be correct in saying that he was the forerunner of those three individuals. As a result, he is often referred to as the first rebel in the movies. Although he died early at the age of 39, he left a lasting impression through a number of quality films, including *The Postman Always Rings Twice, Gentlemen's Agreement, Body and Soul,* and *Pride of the Marines.*

FORGOTTEN MOVIE STARS OF THE 30's, 40's, and 50's

A paragraph on TheMave.com describes his impact on films perfectly: "Unlike reigning tough guys of the time, Garfield had a touching vulnerability just under his abrasive surface that proved to be remarkably appealing. Add to that little-boy-lost quality a thick shock of unruly hair and a killer smile and you had ...dynamite; a tribute to a man and actor who has not received the recognition he deserves"[6]

> I could not agree more with that statement. It was that vulnerability and the singsong quality to his voice that separated him from other leading men of the era.

My favorite John Garfield films are the following:

- Body and Soul
- The Postman Always Rings Twice
- The Sea Wolf
- Pride of the Marines
- Gentleman's Agreement

Biography

John Garfield was born Jacob Julius Garfinkle on the Lower East Side of New York City to David and Hannah Garfinkle. Jules was raised by his father after his mother's death in 1920, when he was 7. Being a difficult child, he was sent to a special school for problem children, where he was introduced to boxing and drama.

> There's an unusual combination: boxing and drama. But in his case, it worked!

---

[6] Taken from John Garfield's page on **www.themave.com**

FORGOTTEN MOVIE STARS OF THE 30's, 40's, and 50's

Garfield won a scholarship to Maria Ouspenskaya's drama school – yes the same Maria Ouspenskaya who played the old gypsy woman in *The Wolfman*. Achieving some success there, he joined the Civic Repertory Theatre in 1932, changing his name to Jules Garfield and making his Broadway debut in that company's play "Counselor-at-Law. "

Garfield then joined the Group Theatre Company, winning acclaim for his role in "Awake and Sing." Embittered over being passed over for the lead in *Golden Boy*, which was written for him but given to William Holden, he signed a contract with Warner Brothers, who changed his name to John Garfield. There, he won enormous praise for his role as the cynical Mickey Borden in *Four Daughters* (1938) and received an Oscar nomination for that performance. He appeared in similar cynical-type roles throughout his career despite his efforts to play varied parts, including the films I have listed as my personal favorites.

At the onset of World War II, Garfield immediately attempted to enlist in the armed forces, but was turned down because of his heart condition. Frustrated by his inability to enlist, he turned his energies to supporting the war effort.

He and actress Bette Davis were the driving forces behind the opening of the Hollywood Canteen, a club offering food and entertainment for American servicemen. This outstanding organization was universally heralded for its treatment of the armed forces. He later traveled to Yugoslavia to help entertain for the war effort.

> When his Warner Bros. contract expired in 1946, he opted to start his own independent production company instead. He was one of the first Hollywood actors to do so.

FORGOTTEN MOVIE STARS OF THE 30's, 40's, and 50's

> The Hollywood Canteen operated at 1451 Cahuenga Boulevard in Hollywood, California between October 3, 1942, and November 22, 1945 (Thanksgiving Day), as a club offering food, dancing and entertainment for servicemen, usually on their way overseas. A serviceman's ticket for admission was his/her uniform and everything at the canteen was free of charge.

Active in liberal political and social causes, he found himself unfairly embroiled in the Communist scare of the late 1940s. Though he testified before the House Un-American Activities Committee of Congress (HUAC) that he was never a Communist (and there was no evidence that he was a member of the Communist Party), his ability to get work declined. While separated from his wife – who was actually a member of the Communist Party - he succumbed to long-term heart problems, dying suddenly in the home of a woman friend at age 39. His funeral was mobbed by thousands of fans, in the largest funeral attendance for an actor since Rudolph Valentino.

> This shows you how many fans John Garfield had – that his funeral rivaled that of the legendary Rudolph Valentino. Valentino was the biggest star of the silent film era and died suddenly of a perforated ulcer and subsequent blood poisoning at the age of 31. He was just reaching the zenith of his popularity when he passed away.

FORGOTTEN MOVIE STARS OF THE 30's, 40's, and 50's

Recognition

John Garfield was nominated for two Oscars - for Best Actor in a Leading Role for *Body and* Soul in 1947 and for Best Actor in a Supporting Role for *Four Daughters* in 1938. He did not win on either occasion. He seems to be one of those individuals whose star has actually risen over the years, however.

John Garfield has a star on the Hollywood Walk of Fame at 7065 Hollywood Boulevard.

My favorite John Garfield films

1. Body and Soul - 1947

John Garfield as boxer Charley Davis in a scene from the boxing movie, *Body and Soul*.

FORGOTTEN MOVIE STARS OF THE 30's, 40's, and 50's

Body and Soul is probably John Garfield's signature role, and he was nominated for Best Actor for his role as Charley Davis in this film. The story centers on Davis taking up boxing to help his mother and himself out of poverty. Davis wins an amateur boxing match and is spotted by promoter/trainer Quinn (William Conrad). The plot follows Davis and his new trainer, who feels Davis could be a professional fighter. Charley's mother doesn't want him to fight; however, when Charley's father is killed in an accident, Charley agrees to fight because the family suddenly needs the money.

Charley's career blossoms as he wins fight after fight, but soon an unethical promoter begins to pursue him. His promoter/trainer Quinn falls in with the mob and tries to drag Davis down with him. As a result, Charley finds himself faced with increasingly difficult moral decisions.

Regarded as perhaps one of the best boxing movies ever, *Body and Soul* is truly one of John Garfield's best flicks. He is completely believable as a boxer, not just some Hollywood actor posing as a boxer. (There have been many boxing movies where the actor/boxer looked completely foolish in the ring.) And in the non-boxing scenes, he shows his ability to act in a sensitive manner. Lili Palmer, Anne Revere, and William Conrad (from TV's "Cannon" and "Nero Wolfe") head up a strong supporting cast.

> Garfield's early training in boxing definitely came in handy in this film. His acting skills also helped. Ironically, Garfield finally got to play the lead in the Broadway production of "Golden Boy" in 1951, a few months before his untimely death from a heart attack.

2. The Postman Always Rings Twice - 1946

Lovers Lana Turner and John Garfield in a scene from *The Postman Always Rings Twice*. They are undoubtedly plotting something here, probably how to get rid of her much older husband.

Based on James M. Cain's novel, this film stars John Garfield as drifter Frank Chambers, who finds himself in a tight spot. After taking a job as a handyman at a roadside restaurant owned by an older man, Nick Smith, played by Cecil Kellaway, he finds himself having an affair with the proprietor's young and sexy wife Cora Smith (Lana Turner in perhaps her signature role). She convinces Frank to kill her husband but make it look like an accident, so they can take his insurance money. But their best-laid plans don't always work out perfectly, as they find out.

FORGOTTEN MOVIE STARS OF THE 30's, 40's, and 50's

Again, this is a really good film that benefits from a strong performance by Garfield, and also by Lana Turner, and unbelievable sparks between the two stars. This is probably Garfield's most enduring performance.

> This film really put John Garfield on the Hollywood map as an actor. The vibes between the two stars are really what makes the film stand out.

3. The Sea Wolf - 1941

John Garfield confronts unmerciful sea captain Edward G. Robinson in a scene from *The Sea Wolf*.

Based on the novel by Jack London, *The Sea Wolf* concerns an odd group of three people who find themselves aboard the Ghost, a sealing schooner captained by the brutal taskmaster, Wolf Larson (Edward G. Robinson). George Leach (Garfield) is on the run from the police as is Ruth Webster (Ida Lupino), who has escaped from a women's penitentiary.

FORGOTTEN MOVIE STARS OF THE 30's, 40's, and 50's

Also aboard is a young writer, Humphrey van Weyden (Alexander Knox). He and Webster were fished out of the sea and Larson refuses to put them ashore. Larson is a cruel, unsympathetic bully who will have his sailors beaten for the smallest infraction. The three try to escape but without success. Even when Larson allows several of the people to leave, they realize that he has played tricks on them.

Another excellent performance by Garfield. Because his character is the toughest of the three individuals, he is also the least willing to accept Larsen's brutal leadership tactics. As a result, Larson and Leach continually clash.

4. Pride of the Marines - 1945

John Garfield and Eleanor Parker in a scene from the excellent WWII flick, *Pride of the Marines*.

FORGOTTEN MOVIE STARS OF THE 30's, 40's, and 50's

At the beginning of World War II, welder Al Schmid (Garfield) is set up on a blind date with Ruth Hartley (Eleanor Parker). The two hit it off and begin dating. Al learns of a friend's enlistment in the Marine Corps and decides to also join. Al and Ruth have a last date, with Al insisting that she forget about him as he is about to go into combat. However, when Ruth goes to meet his departure train, he gives her an engagement ring. Assigned to Guadalcanal, Al and his squad are tasked with preventing the Japanese from breaching their line. During a night attack, many of his fellow Marines are slain, but Al ends up single-handedly saving the day, killing scores of Japanese. However, he is wounded by a suicide bomber near the end of the battle.

At the hospital, Al learns that he is blind, a condition that persists even after surgery. Feeling sorry for himself, he dictates a letter to a nurse, informing Ruth that he is relieving her of any obligation to marry him. Neither his friends nor the medical staff can persuade Al to try rehabilitation in order to attempt a return to a "normal" life. Finally, he has to be kicked out of the hospital. He returns home, but does not want to see Ruth. She sees him and pledges her love, but he is still discouraged, as he does not feel that he is a real man anymore, and his pride will not allow her to take care of him. For his bravery, Lee is awarded the Navy Cross. But will he overcome his pride and move forward with his life?

> The names of the wars may change, but the problems faced by returning veterans – particularly disabled ones – remain constant. This film and others, like *The Best Years of Our Lives* – clearly highlight their stories.

FORGOTTEN MOVIE STARS OF THE 30's, 40's, and 50's

Because of Garfield's moving performance, this is perhaps my favorite John Garfield film. His difficulties in readjusting to civilian life are particularly moving. This includes a scene where he has difficulties with a Christmas tree. A tremendous performance that should have garnered Garfield an Oscar nomination, but did not.

> You may recognize Eleanor Parker in perhaps her most famous role 20 years later – as the baroness who almost marries Colonel Von Trapp in *The Sound of Music*.

5. Gentleman's Agreement - 1947

In this photo, John Garfield and Dorothy McGuire are in a restaurant discussing issues related to discrimination. The film concerns covert discrimination against Jewish people, and Garfield – who was Jewish - plays a Jew in the film.

FORGOTTEN MOVIE STARS OF THE 30's, 40's, and 50's

This is really a Gregory Peck film, not a John Garfield film, but Garfield plays a key supporting role. Philip Green (Peck) is a highly respected writer who is recruited by a national magazine to write a series of articles on anti-Semitism in America. He's not too keen on the series, mostly because he's not Jewish and therefore is not sure how to tackle the subject. He resolves that issue by pretending to be Jewish, and by doing so, personally experience the degree of racism and prejudice that existed in the United States after WWII. Green soon learns the liberal-minded firm he works for doesn't hire Jews – They don't have a formal policy on it but it is a "Gentleman's Agreement" not to hire Jews - and that his own secretary (played by Celeste Holm) even changed her name and kept the fact that she is Jewish a secret from everyone. Green then finds that he won't be invited to certain parties, that he cannot stay in so-called "restricted" hotels, and that his own son is called names in the street. His anger at the way he is treated also affects his relationship with fiancée Kathy Lacy (Dorothy McGuire), his publisher's niece and the person who suggested the series in the first place.

In this film John Garfield plays a supporting role as Dave Goldman, a Jewish friend of Gregory Peck's character. Goldman constantly lives in a world of anti-Semitic racism and confides in Peck's character the troubles he faces on a daily basis. This comes to a head in a moving restaurant scene shown on the previous page, where Garfield overhears a customer mocking Jews and loses his temper.

An outstanding supporting performance, Garfield shines in this role. The film is one of three outstanding social awareness films made right after World War II; the others are *The Best Years of Our Lives*, depicting the problems of veterans after the war in adjusting to civilian life, and *The Lost Weekend*, which dealt with alcoholism.

FORGOTTEN MOVIE STARS OF THE 30's, 40's, and 50's

> *Gentleman's Agreement* was nominated for eight Oscars and won three – Best Supporting Actress (Celeste Holm), Best Director (Elia Kazan), and Best Picture. By the way, Celeste Holm played Ted Danson's mother in *Three Men and a Baby*. Celeste Holm died in 2012 at the age of 95.

In summation, because of an early death at 39, John Garfield's body of work did not measure up with others in terms of sheer volume. However, he starred in a number of top-quality films, including the five mentioned here. If you were to ask me who were the top actors in this entire group of 25, I would probably pick Barbara Stanwyck, Susan Hayward, Ronald Colman, and John Garfield.

Not just a good looking star, John Garfield was also a terrific actor with great range in his performances. Individuals who like Marlon Brando, James Dean, and Montgomery Clift, in particular, should really take a close look at John Garfield and his films.

Susan Hayward – 1917-1975

Susan Hayward was one of those rare female stars who could be sweet, sexy, and deadly serious, and her career seemed to reflect that. Susan Hayward went to Hollywood as part of the nationwide casting call for someone to play Scarlett O'Hara in *Gone with the Wind*, a part that went of course to Vivien Leigh. Early on, Hayward was often cast as the sweet leading lady or even second banana in films like *Beau Geste* and *Reap the Wild Wind*. Later she was an alluring sex goddess, in films like *David and Bathsheba* and *Demetrius and the Gladiators*. As she matured, she got better parts and turned in several academy-award-winning-type performances, including *With a Song in My Heart, I'll Cry Tomorrow,* and *I Want to Live,* in which she won an Oscar for an outstanding performance as convicted murderer Barbara Graham.

FORGOTTEN MOVIE STARS OF THE 30's, 40's, and 50's

> With the natural Southern accent she displayed in several films, you would have assumed she was born and raised in the South; however, you would be wrong. Susan Hayward was born and raised in Flatbush, better known as Brooklyn, New York. I guess that proves she was a good actress!

If you wanted a perfect combination of brains, talent, and beauty, you would have to look no further than Susan Hayward. Her five Oscar nominations alone can attest to the talent that this key leading lady of the 30's, 40's and 50's possessed. And just think – she was the original choice to play the lead in *All About Eve*, a part that eventually went to Bette Davis because the studio felt Susan was too young for the part.

> Even though *Reap the Wild Wind* is one of my favorite movies, and Susan Hayward is in it, I have not listed it here. Susan Hayward is basically window dressing – *Reap the Wild Wind* is Paulette Goddard's film.

My favorite Susan Hayward films are the following:

- *Demetrius and the Gladiators*
- *With a Song in My Heart*
- *I'll Cry Tomorrow*
- *I Want to Live*
- *Beau Geste*

FORGOTTEN MOVIE STARS OF THE 30's, 40's, and 50's

Biography

Susan Hayward was born Edythe Marrener in Brooklyn, New York, on June 30, 1917. Her father was a transportation worker, and Susan lived a fairly middle-class life as a child. When she was seven, she was hit by a car and fractured a hip; it took about a year for her to recover fully. After graduation from high school, she planned on becoming a secretary, but her plans changed when she started doing some modeling work for photographers in the New York City area.

By 1937, she went to Hollywood when the nationwide search was on for someone to play the role of Scarlett O'Hara in Margaret Mitchell's *Gone with the Wind* (1939). Although she--along with several hundred other aspiring Scarletts--lost out to Vivien Leigh, Susan stayed and found bit parts of films.

While she was not necessarily happy with these roles, she also realized she had to "pay her dues." In 1939 she finally landed a part with substance, playing Isobel Rivers in the hit action film *Beau Geste* opposite a trio of male stars in Gary Cooper, Ray Milland, and Robert Preston.

In 1941 she played Millie Perkins in the offbeat thriller *Among the Living* (1941). This quirky little film showed Hollywood Susan's considerable dramatic qualities for the first time. She then played a Southern belle in Cecil B. DeMille's *Reap the Wild Wind* (1942), one of the director's bigger successes, and once again showed promise in a relatively small part.

Following that movie she starred with Paulette Goddard and Fred MacMurray in *The Forest Rangers* (1942), playing tough gal Tana Mason. Although such films as *Jack London* (1943), *And Now Tomorrow* (1944) and *Deadline at Dawn* (1946) continued to showcase her talent, she still hadn't gotten the meaty roles she deserved.

FORGOTTEN MOVIE STARS OF THE 30's, 40's, and 50's

> Interestingly, posters for *Reap the Wild Wind* now list John Wayne and Susan Hayward as the leads. This is because they are the most well known stars of the film today. However, if you list the stars in order of screen time, it would go Paulette Goddard, Ray Milland, John Wayne, Raymond Massey, Robert Preston, and finally, Susan Hayward.

In 1947, Susan's acting talent finally was able to be recognized, and she received the first of five Academy Award nominations, this one for her portrayal of Angelica Evans in *Smash-Up: The Story of a Woman* (1947). She played the part well but lost out to Loretta Young for *The Farmer's Daughter* (1947). In 1949 Susan was nominated again for *My Foolish Heart* (1949) but once more lost out when Olivia de Havilland won for *The Heiress* (1949). Now, however, with two Oscar nominations under her belt, Susan demanded and got better parts.

Good scripts finally started to come her way and she chose carefully because she wanted to appear only in good quality productions. Her caution paid off, as she garnered yet a third nomination in 1953 for *With a Song in My Heart* (1952). Later that year she starred as Rachel Donaldson Robards Jackson in *The President's Lady* (1953). She was superb as Andrew Jackson's embittered wife, who died before he took office as President of the United States. After her fourth Academy Award nomination for *I'll Cry Tomorrow* (1955), playing an alcoholic, Susan probably began to wonder if she would ever take home an Oscar, but was soon rewarded. In 1958 she gave the performance of her life as real-life California killer Barbara Graham in *I Want to Live!*; Graham was convicted of murder and sentenced to death in the gas chamber.

FORGOTTEN MOVIE STARS OF THE 30's, 40's, and 50's

Susan was absolutely riveting in her portrayal of the doomed woman. Many film buffs consider it to be one of the finest performances of all time[7], as she won the Oscar for Best Actress of 1958.

After that role she appeared in about one movie a year. In 1972 she made her last theatrical film, *The Revengers* (1972). That year she was diagnosed with multiple inoperable brain tumors and given a few months to live. Since her will to live was just as strong as her will to achieve success as an actress, she survived for two and a half years. The disease finally claimed her life on March 14, 1975, in Hollywood. She was only 57.

Away from movies, she was more of an outdoors woman than most leading ladies. Hayward loved sport fishing, and owned three ocean-going boats for that purpose. Movie directors enjoyed Susan's professionalism and her high standards. She was considered easy to work with, but she was not chummy after the cameras stopped.[8]

Recognition

Susan Hayward was nominated for – count them – five Academy Awards for Best Actress in a Leading Role. They are as follows:

- *Smash Up: The Story of a Woman* – 1947
- *My Foolish Heart* - 1949
- *With a Song in My Heart* – 1952
- *I'll Cry Tomorrow* – 1955

---

[7] International Movie Data Base (IMDB.com) biography of Susan Hayward

[8] IMDB biography of Susan Hayward

FORGOTTEN MOVIE STARS OF THE 30's, 40's, and 50's

> *I Want to Live* – 1958

She won for her performance as convicted murderer Barbara Graham in *I Want to Live*. Ms. Hayward also won Golden Globes for Best Actress in *I Want to Live* and *With a Song in My Heart,* the Cannes Film Festival award for Best Actress for *I Want to Live*, and the New York Film Critics Award for Best Actress for *I Want to Live*. She won the Photoplay award for Most Popular Female Star in 1952, and either won or was nominated for a variety of other awards throughout her career.

Susan Hayward has a star on the Hollywood Walk of Fame at 6251 Hollywood Boulevard.

My Favorite Susan Hayward Films

1. Demetrius and the Gladiators – 1954

Even with her husband Claudius behind her, Susan Hayward as the temptress Messalina appears to be in charge of the situation. She is confronting Victor Mature as Demetrius in this scene. Her husband Claudius became emperor of Rome after the assassination of the tyrant Caligula.

FORGOTTEN MOVIE STARS OF THE 30's, 40's, and 50's

As I previously mentioned in the section on Victor Mature, *Demetrius and the Gladiators* picks up at the point where *The Robe* ends, following the martyrdom of Diana and Marcellus. Christ's robe is conveyed by Demetrius to St. Peter for safekeeping, but the nutty emperor Caligula wants it back to benefit from its powers. Marcellus' former slave Demetrius seeks to prevent this, and while doing so catches the eye of Messalina, wife to Caligula's uncle Claudius (eventually the Roman emperor Claudius). Messalina tempts Demetrius, he winds up fighting in the arena as a gladiator, and wavers in his faith when he sees his girlfriend, played by Debra Paget, raped by other gladiators and supposedly dying in the process. As we find out later, the key word here is "supposedly."

After that incident, Demetrius renounces his Christian faith and is seduced by the lovely Susan Hayward as Messalina. She has plans for Demetrius beyond that of a gladiator (where Demetrius is a huge success) and he becomes her lover. Temporarily, he rejects his Christian values for a life of pleasure. But of course Demetrius regains his faith with the help of St. Peter, played by Michael Rennie in both films.

Susan Hayward is perfect as the sultry, amoral temptress Messalina, who leads Demetrius away from the noble Christian life after Demetrius believes that God has failed him. That Hayward would lead a man away from the noble life with her wiles and temptations is not difficult to imagine after watching her performance in this film. She serves in stark contrast to the pure and virginal (and rather uninteresting) Debra Paget and is very effective in the role.

> *The Robe* was such a huge hit that making a sequel was inevitable. This time Victor Mature and Susan Hayward were the stars.

FORGOTTEN MOVIE STARS OF THE 30's, 40's, and 50's

> In real life, after Claudius became emperor, Messalina continued to find other lovers, and plotted with one of them to kill her husband. Unfortunately for her, Claudius found out about the plot and had her executed. This seemed to be a common theme among wives of Roman emperors. Which again proves you had better be careful when dealing with Roman emperors.

2. With a Song in My Heart – 1952

A poster from *With a Song in My Heart*, with Susan Hayward as real-life singer Jane Froman. Among Froman's hits were With a Song in My Heart and I'll Walk Alone, two great songs.

FORGOTTEN MOVIE STARS OF THE 30's, 40's, and 50's

Jane Froman (Susan Hayward), an aspiring songstress, lands a job in radio with help from pianist Don Ross (David Wayne), whom she later marries. Jane's popularity soars, and she leaves on a European tour. But her plane crashes in Lisbon, and she is partially crippled. Her doctors tell her she will never walk again, but Froman vows to prove them wrong.

Unable to walk without crutches, Jane nevertheless goes on to entertain the Allied troops in World War II. The film also includes her real-life romance and marriage to the co-pilot who rescued her from the accident as well as her comeback from the terrible accident.

Susan Hayward is excellent as songstress Jane Froman. She definitely brings the necessary vitality and believability to the role. The film also features many of Froman's greatest hits, including "With a Song in My Heart" and "I'll Walk Alone. "

> The song, "I'll Walk Alone," was a popular song during WWII. Unlike other WWII songs, however, "I'll Walk Alone" is written from the point of view of the stay-at-home lover, promising to be true. The song was also recorded by Dinah Shore and later on by Ricky Nelson and Nancy Wilson, among many others.

3. I'll Cry Tomorrow – 1955

Next page. Susan Hayward as an alcoholic/recovering alcoholic in *I'll Cry Tomorrow*. On the right is Eddie Albert of Green Acres television fame but also a veteran of many movies, including Oklahoma!

FORGOTTEN MOVIE STARS OF THE 30's, 40's, and 50's

I'll Cry Tomorrow tells the real rags to riches to rags to redemption story of actress/singer Lillian Roth, a major star of silent films and early talkies whose battle with alcoholism is clearly and bravely depicted in this film. Deprived of a normal childhood by her ambitious mother, Lillian Roth became a star of Broadway and Hollywood before she was twenty. Shortly before her marriage to her childhood sweetheart, David Tredman, he dies and Lillian, emotionally distraught, takes her first drink of many down the road to becoming an alcoholic.

She enters into a short-lived marriage to an immature aviation cadet followed by a divorce and then marriage to sadistic abuser Tony Bardeman (played by Richard Conte). After a failed suicide attempt, she enters rehabilitation as a last resort; while there, Burt McGuire (Eddie Albert), himself a recovering alcoholic, comes to her aid and helps her find the road back to happiness after a lifetime of personal problems, including her bout with alcoholism.

FORGOTTEN MOVIE STARS OF THE 30's, 40's, and 50's

Susan Hayward is just sensational in this no-holds-barred, gutsy film on the life of Lillian Roth, including all the ups and all the downs, and there are plenty of both. She demonstrates great acting range and the ability to be much more than a romantic lead in this film, which is about as realistic as a movie could be in the mid-1950's. Susan could easily have won an Oscar for her performance in this film, but that was reserved for *I Want To Live*, an equally good performance.

> By the way, the songs that Ms. Roth are best known for are probably "When the Red Red Robin Comes Bob Bob Bobbing Along" and "Sing you Sinners." Both were big hits in their time. Every once in a while, you hear "Red Red Robin" in a commercial on the radio or television.

4. I Want To Live - 1957

Susan Hayward in her Oscar-winning performance as convicted murderer Barbara Graham in a scene from *I Want to Live*.

FORGOTTEN MOVIE STARS OF THE 30's, 40's, and 50's

Barbara Graham is the true story of a woman with clearly dubious moral standards, often a guest in seedy bars. More bluntly, she was a petty thief and also a prostitute at times. She had been sentenced and had served time for various petty crimes. Two men whom she knows are discussing stealing money from an older woman who they believe keeps a good deal of money in her home.

Graham becomes involved in this scheme; when the woman won't tell them where she stores her money, they murder her. When the men get caught they start to think that Barbara helped the police find and arrest them. For revenge, they tell the police that Barbara was the murderer. The film depicts Graham's imprisonment in San Quentin and execution in the gas chamber.

I Want to Live focuses on Graham's (Hayward's) attempt to show her side of the story, that she was innocent of the murder. (The truth is that the evidence showed that Graham was actually involved in the murder and may have been the actual murderer.)

In any case, Hayward's performance as the sleazy Graham fighting for her life against all odds is the kind of once-in-a lifetime performance that deserved an Oscar and resulted in Hayward winning her first and only Academy Award.

> For a more modern-day equivalent of this motion picture, just think of Charlize Theron as Aileen Wuornos in *Monster*. And what do you know, Ms. Theron also won an Oscar for her performance. And I am also a big fan of Charlize Theron. One of my favorite modern-day stars.

FORGOTTEN MOVIE STARS OF THE 30's, 40's, and 50's

5. Beau Geste - 1939

As mentioned in the discussion of Ray Milland, *Beau Geste* is a terrific adventure story with a great cast featuring Gary Cooper, Ray Milland, and Robert Preston as the three inseparable Geste brothers, a lovely Susan Hayward as the girl in their lives, and Brian Donlevy as the despicable Sergeant Markoff. Susan Hayward is the female romantic lead who grows up with the three Geste brothers but eventually falls in love with the youngest, John (Ray Milland). I include this film, not because it is a great performance by Hayward – she does not have a great deal of screen time – but because:

- *Beau Geste*, and especially this version, is one of the all-time great adventure films; and
- It was Susan Hayward's first leading role in a major film.

You only need to remember that Susan Hayward started out as being one of the many young women who was auditioned for the role of Scarlett O'Hara. Unlike Paulette Goddard, who was probably the front runner until David O. Selznick found Vivian Leigh, Susan Hayward bombed in her audition. However, that certainly did little to undermine her long-term career. She progressed all the way from playing romantic leads with little to do in films like *Beau Geste* and *Reap the Wild Wind,* to a series of Oscar-nominated performances in the 1950's, including *With a Song in My Heart, I'll Cry Tomorrow,* and *I Want to Live.* She was definitely a major star, a very gifted actress, and certainly deserves inclusion in this book.

William Powell – 1892-1984

A classic picture of William Powell. The best words to describe him are probably dapper and elegant. He seemed to be always wearing a suit and tie or tuxedo in his movies.

I have to admit that I am not really a big William Powell fan in comparison to most of the other stars in the book. However, he starred as Nick Charles in the *Thin Man* series in the 1930's and 1940's, a series so good that he deserves mention in this book just for that body of work alone. William Powell began in silent films and had several other successful films before his last movie, *Mr. Roberts,* in 1955, but it was clearly the *Thin Man* series and his performances as Flo Ziegfeld in *The Great Ziegfeld* as well as his work in *My Man Godfrey* that make him memorable.

FORGOTTEN MOVIE STARS OF THE 30's, 40's, and 50's

> Powell's voice and mannerisms also were used and mimicked by Don Adams as Maxwell Smart in the "Get Smart" TV series.

One other interesting film note about William Powell. He starred with Clark Gable and Myrna Loy in the 1934 hit gangster film, *Manhattan Melodrama*. But there is another reason that movie is still famous today. This was the flick that bank robber John Dillinger had just seen (and was exiting the theater from) when he was gunned down in front of Chicago's Biograph Theater on July 22, 1934 by FBI agents. Dillinger was number one on the FBI's most wanted list.

My favorite William Powell films are the following:

- *The Thin Man Series* – beginning in 1934
- *My Man Godfrey*
- *Manhattan Melodrama*
- *The Kennel Murder Case*

Biography

William Horatio Powell was born and raised in Pittsburgh, PA, in 1892, and in his early teens the family moved to Kansas City, MO. His father was an accountant and planned a career in law for him, but the younger Powell changed those plans after he worked on a high-school production of Richard Brinsley Sheridan's "The Rivals." A quiet and studious boy, he enjoyed the freedom that acting gave him, and came to seek out more plays and watch professional actors at work. Powell frequented the city's theaters and even took a job as an usher at an opera house to learn what he could from watching actors at work.

FORGOTTEN MOVIE STARS OF THE 30's, 40's, and 50's

Powell enrolled at the University of Kansas in an attempt to satisfy his father but was gone almost as soon as he arrived, in pursuit of an acting career. He had to support himself, as his father refused to contribute to his tuition, so he went to work for the telephone company in 1910. By the following year, he'd conceived of a plan to go to New York. He wrote to a wealthy aunt appealing for her assistance and a loan of $1,400; he got $700, put up the rest himself, and was off to New York. There he enrolled in the American Academy of Dramatic Arts, where his classmates included Joseph Schildkraut and Edward G. Robinson.

Powell got his first role, a walk-on in "The Ne'er-Do-Well," in 1912, and in 1913 got a supporting role in "Within the Law," which was successful enough to keep him employed for two years on tour. William Powell was on the New York stage in 1912, but it was ten years before his film career began. In 1924 he went to Paramount Pictures, where he was employed for the next seven years. During these years he played in a number of interesting films, but stardom was elusive. He did attract attention with *The Last Command* (1928) as Leo, the arrogant film director. Stardom finally came to Powell with his role as Philo Vance in *The Canary Murder Case* (1929), where he investigated the death of Louise Brooks, "the Canary."

Unlike many silent actors who were not English speaking (Emil Jannings) or had very feminine voices (John Gilbert, for example), sound boosted Powell's career.

> John Gilbert was a silent screen matinee idol, often paired up with Greta Garbo, his off-screen lover; but he had such a high, effeminate voice that he was basically a flop in talking pictures. Gilbert died of heart failure at age 39.

FORGOTTEN MOVIE STARS OF THE 30's, 40's, and 50's

Powell had a rich and sophisticated, urbane voice and his stage training and comic timing greatly aided his introduction to sound pictures. However, disappointed with the type of roles he was getting at Paramount, in 1931 he switched to Warner Brothers. He was again disappointed with his parts and made his last appearance as Philo Vance in *The Kennel Murder Case* (1933). In 1934 Powell went to MGM, where he was teamed with Clark Gable – the King of Hollywood - and Myrna Loy in *Manhattan Melodrama* (1934). While Philo Vance made Powell a star, another detective, Nick Charles, made him famous. He received an Academy Award nomination for *The Thin Man* (1934) and starred in the Best Picture winner for 1936, *The Great Ziegfeld*. Powell could play any role with authority, whether in a comedy, thriller or drama. He received his second Academy Award Nomination for *My Man Godfrey* (1936).

His first picture with Jean Harlow was *Reckless* (1935) and they clicked off-screen as well as on-screen, and soon after became engaged. While he was filming *Double Wedding* (1937) on one MGM sound stage, Harlow became ill on another and finally went to the hospital, where she died. Her death greatly upset both Powell and Myrna Loy, and Powell was away from the set for six weeks to deal with his sorrow. After that he traveled and did not make another MGM film for a year. He eventually made five sequels to *The Thin Man*, with the last one filmed in 1947. He received his third Academy Award nomination for his work in *Life with Father* (1947). After that, his screen appearances became fewer and his last role was in 1955 as a supporting player in *Mister Roberts*.

> With all the great stars in *Mister Roberts* – Henry Fonda, James Cagney, and Jack Lemmon – it is easy to forget that Powell played the ship's doctor.

FORGOTTEN MOVIE STARS OF THE 30's, 40's, and 50's

In the years that followed, Powell received many film offers, but was happy in retirement. On March 5, 1984, Powell died of heart failure in Palm Springs, California, at the age of 91, some thirty years after his retirement.

Recognition

William Powell received three Oscar nominations for Best Actor in a Leading Role but was never a winner. Those films were:

- ✓ *The Thin Man* - 1934
- ✓ *My Man Godfrey* – 1936
- ✓ *Life with Father* – 1947

Powell was also awarded the New York Film Critics Circle Award for Best Actor for two 1947 films: *Life with Father* and *The Senator Was Indiscreet*. Powell has a star on the Hollywood Walk of Fame at 1636 Vine Street.

William Powell and Myrna Loy as Nick and Nora Charles in *The Thin Man* series.

FORGOTTEN MOVIE STARS OF THE 30's, 40's, and 50's

My Favorite William Powell Films

1. The Thin Man Series – 1934-1947

William Powell and Myrna Loy, this time with their dog Asta, in *The Thin Man* series.

The Thin Man series may be considered the most successful film series in movie history, certainly the most successful up to that point in time. *The Thin Man* covered six total films and focused on the relationship between retired New York City police detective Nick Charles (William Powell) and his rich society wife (Myrna Loy) as they are called upon to solve a murder in each of the stories. The vibe between the two stars is wonderful, and their relationship is more equivalent to that of a modern day couple than other films of the time – equal partners who live to help while one-upping each other as they attempt to solve the crime. This is an absolute treasure of a film series, not to be missed by anyone who considers himself or herself a fan of classic movies.

FORGOTTEN MOVIE STARS OF THE 30's, 40's, and 50's

> About the only thing in the entire series that does not hold up that well today is Nick's overreliance on alcohol at any and all times of the day, as if to say, "drunks are really funny." Perhaps we have learned a lot about alcohol abuse and alcoholism over the years.

The first two films are particularly outstanding and while the others were a bit repetitive, are still worth a look today. Regarding their chemistry, Myrna Loy once declared: "it wasn't a conscious thing. If you heard us talking in a room, you'd hear the same thing. He'd tease me, and there was a sort of blending which seemed to please people."[9] Some 80 years later, we are still pleased.

The Thin Man – 1934

In the original film, nominated for four Academy Awards including Best Picture, one-time detective Nick Charles returns to New York with his new wife Nora and their dog, Asta. Nick re-connects with many of his old cronies, several of whom are eccentric characters as well as guys he has sent up the river.

He's also approached by Dorothy Wynant – Maureen O'Sullivan - whose inventor father Clyde Wynant is suspected of murdering her stepmother. Her father had left on a planned trip some months before and she has had no contact with him.

---

[9] From the jacket of the DVD of *Song of the Thin Man,* 1947

FORGOTTEN MOVIE STARS OF THE 30's, 40's, and 50's

Nick isn't all that keen on resuming his former profession but, encouraged by wife Nora, who thinks this all very exciting, he agrees to help out. He discovers a number of suspects, investigates the case, and solves the murder, announcing the identity of the killer at a dinner party for all of the suspects.

> Most people think that the Thin Man is a reference to Nick Charles, since William Powell is the star and was relatively thin. However, the real story is that the Thin Man is actually Clyde Wynant, who is referred to at several points as a thin man. But the name "Thin Man" stuck through the remainder of the series. Also, the film was shot in 12 days by noteworthy director W.S. Van Dyke.

After the Thin Man - 1936

In this first sequel, made in 1936, Nick and Nora Charles are returning to the West Coast by train and learn as they are summoned to dinner by Nora's family that the philandering husband of Nora's cousin Thelma has been missing for three days. Nick and Nora reluctantly decide to help out, round up the usual suspects, and solve the crime. The case takes a twist when Charles is shot and Thelma is accused of murder. Several other murders occur but eventually Nick gathers everyone into the same room to reveal the identity of the killer.

As always, Nora doesn't scold, doesn't nag, and looks far too pretty in the morning, while Nick whips up scrambled eggs at 3 a.m. The film features a top-notch supporting case, and you will be really surprised to find the identity of the murderer.

FORGOTTEN MOVIE STARS OF THE 30's, 40's, and 50's

Another Thin Man – 1939

Another Thin Man introduces baby Nick, Jr. into the cast. The case begins back in New York where the Charles family, including Nick, Jr. arrives for a weekend with a Long Island industrialist who fears someone wants to kill him.

Unfortunately, he is right. Nick is among the suspects, Asta the dog runs off with what might be the murder weapon, and Nora has her own ideas about the case and sneaks off to a nightclub without Nick to look for clues.

A birthday party for Nick, Jr. includes several of Nick's former criminal friends, including Dum-Dum, Wacky, Creeps, and Fingers. Eventually Nick identifies the killer. A good supporting cast includes Virginia Grey, Otto Kruger, C. Aubrey Smith, Ruth Hussey, Nat Pendleton, Sheldon Leonard, and Patrick Knowles. And none other than Shemp Howard of the Three Stooges plays (naturally) a character named Wacky.

> Shemp Howard was actually one of the original Three Stooges in vaudville, but he left the group before they started making those two-reel shorts in the early 1930's. However, he returned when his younger brother, Curly, suffered a stroke in 1947 and remained a Stooge until his own fatal heart attack in 1955. I guess once a Stooge, always a Stooge. Nyuk, Nyuk!

FORGOTTEN MOVIE STARS OF THE 30's, 40's, and 50's

Shadow of the Thin Man – 1941

A jockey who threw a race is murdered in the locker room at the racetrack. With that, Nick and Nora are off to the races on another case of murder, mayhem, mirth, and martinis – not necessarily in that order. Lots of false leads abound in this fourth entry in the series, involving gambling and possible racketeering. Highlights include a visit to the local wrestling arena and dinner at Mario's Grotto where, no matter what the person wants to order, the waiter insists on sea bass.

As usual, other murders take place, but in the end, Nick gathers all the suspects into a room and identifies the killer. As always, the supporting cast is terrific and features Barry Nelson, Donna Reed, Sam Levene, Louise Beavers, and Alan Baxter.

The Thin Man Goes Home – 1945

It is at this point that the series begins to get a bit weary and repetitive but is still worth a look. In this fifth entry in the series, Nick and Nora leave Nick, Jr. in boarding school, grab Asta, and head to Nick's hometown of Sycamore Springs to visit his parents. Nick's father, a prominent local physician, has always been a bit disappointed with Nick's choice of profession in particular and his lifestyle in general. With Nick's arrival, however, the townsfolk, including several of the local criminal element, are convinced that he must be there on a case despite his protestations that he's just there for rest and relaxation. When someone is shot dead on his parents' doorstep, however, Nick finds himself working on the case whether he wants to or not. Needless to say, by the end of the film, Nick's father is proud of his son. Another excellent supporting cast features Harry Davenport, Lucille Watson, Gloria De Haven, Leon Ames, and Donald Meek, an actor whose last name fits perfectly with most of his movie roles.

FORGOTTEN MOVIE STARS OF THE 30's, 40's, and 50's

Song of the Thin Man – 1947

In the final entry in the series, made 13 years after the original, a bandleader is killed and Nick and Nora must investigate the crime. Nick and Nora Charles are asked by Phil Brant and Janet Thayar, who have just eloped, to help them after band leader Tommy Drake is killed at a society dance which Nick and Nora also attended on the S.S. Fortune. The police are looking to arrest Brant for the murder, and while he claims he's innocent, Nick isn't too keen on having him around and turns him over to the police.

As they look into the case, Nick and Nora learn that bandleader Drake wasn't very well liked and, as always, there are actually several people who benefited from his death and could be considered suspects.

Drake owed money to loan shark Al Amboy, and Janet's father disliked Brant and may have set him up. Drake's girlfriend may have been having a fling with clarinetist Buddy Hollis, and he and Drake had a fist fight on stage during the festivities. Nick arranges for another party on the same boat where Nora notices something quite peculiar about one of the guest's jewelry.

As always, the suspects are rounded up and Nick identifies the real murderer at the end. A very good supporting cast includes Keenan Wynn, Dean Stockwell, Leon Ames, Gloria Graham, and Jayne Meadows (television pioneer Steve Allen's wife).

> The act of rounding up all the suspects so that Nick Charles can identify the real killer was a common feature in all of the Thin Man movies.

2. My Man Godfrey – 1936

Carole Lombard and William Powell (both on the right) in a scene from *My Man Godfrey*. This scene occurs early in the film, where (supposed) forgotten man Powell meets the goofy Bullock family.

> The tall, attractive woman on the left in the picture is actually Gail Patrick, who went on to become the executive producer of the Perry Mason television series with Raymond Burr.

This screwball comedy really showcases the talents of William Powell as Godfrey and Carole Lombard as Irene Bullock. In the depths of the Depression, a party game brings dizzy socialites Irene Bullock and her sister Cornelia to the city dump where they meet Godfrey, a derelict. It seems they are on a scavenger hunt and need a "forgotten man" to win the game. After rebuking Cornelia, Godfrey accepts the offer of the more sincere and humble Irene to be her forgotten man. Upon winning the contest, Irene hires Godfrey as the family butler.

FORGOTTEN MOVIE STARS OF THE 30's, 40's, and 50's

He finds the three Bullock women – mother and two sisters - to be the epitome of idle rich, and nutty as a proverbial fruitcake. Soon, the dramatizing Irene is in love with her 'protégé'...who feels strongly that a romance between servant and employer is out of place, regardless of that servant's mysterious past. As it turns out, Godfrey is anything but poor, but instead was a rich man planning on drowning himself in the river because of his feelings of worthlessness until he made friends with other forgotten men and observed their courage and nobility as opposed to the worthlessness of the Bullocks.

Powell and Lombard play off each other well as Godfrey and Irene in this wonderful screwball comedy. For this movie to be a success, Powell must be believable as a rich man, a derelict, and a butler, and he is convincing in all three roles. An excellent supporting cast includes Gail Patrick, Eugene Pallette, Alan Mowbray, and Mischa Auer.

Note that although Powell was divorced from Lombard, he insisted that she play the role of Irene, according to Robert Osborne of TCM. [10]

> Lombard had a very tragic ending to her life. She died in a plane crash over Las Vegas, Nevada in 1942 while returning from a war bonds rally in Indiana. She was 33 at the time of her death and married to Clark Gable.

---

[10] The reference to William Powell insisting on the casting of Carole Lombard as Irene Bullock was mentioned by TCM host Robert Osborne in his introduction of the film on December 8, 2011.

FORGOTTEN MOVIE STARS OF THE 30's, 40's, and 50's

3. Manhattan Melodrama – 1934

Manhattan Melodrama is the story of two friends – William Powell and Clark Gable – who end up on the opposite site of the law. Powell is the district attorney and Gable is the gangster, who grew up as boyhood friends in an orphanage but go their separate ways as adults, still maintaining their friendship even though they love the same woman, Myrna Loy. Loy ends up leaving Gable and marrying the straight-as-an-arrow district attorney Powell. Powell faces ethical decisions when he must decide whether or not to send Gable to the electric chair for his crimes.

This was Powell's first starring role in a major motion picture. In addition to strong performances by the three leads, this film is most notable as the movie John Dillinger saw at the theater the night he was murdered - he liked gangster movies - on July 22, 1934.

> As he was leaving the Biograph Theater in the Lincoln Park area of Chicago, escorted by the "Woman in Red," Dillinger was gunned down by FBI agents under the direction of Melvin Purvis.

4. The Kennel Murder Case - 1933

Anyone watching William Powell as the suave detective Philo Vance in four movies could predict that he would be outstanding in the role of Nick Charles. In this fourth and last

FORGOTTEN MOVIE STARS OF THE 30's, 40's, and 50's

Philo Vance movie with Powell, he is accompanied by his prize-losing Scottish terrier as he investigates the locked-room murder of a prominent and much-hated collector whose broken Chinese vase provides an important clue. The collector and his brother end up being murdered on the same night, and suspects include many of the residents of the apartment building where they live. Vance is called on by the police sergeant (Eugene Pallette) to help solve the murder.

This film has many of the elements of *The Thin Man* series that began a year later in 1934 – a suave detective who is one step ahead of the police, lots of suspects, and even a dog! What is missing is Nora Charles and the wonderful banter between Powell and Myrna Loy that made the latter series so special. A good supporting cast also includes Mary Astor and Ralph Morgan, whose brother Frank Morgan played the Wizard in the *Wizard of Oz*.

Other good William Powell films include the following:

- *The Great Ziegfeld*
- *Life with Father*

William Powell was an outstanding screen performer who is today remembered best for his role as Nick Charles in *The Thin Man* series. He was a suave and debonair gentleman with an exceptional flair for both drama and comedy.

FORGOTTEN MOVIE STARS OF THE 30's, 40's, and 50's

Myrna Loy – 1905-1993

Best known as Nora Charles from the Thin Man series, you could say that the best words to describe Myrna Loy were classy and elegant. She appeared first in silent films but hit her zenith in talkies. Myrna Loy was a huge star in the 1930's and 1940's and continued making films and television appearances into the early 1980's.

Loy started in films as a vamp but was best at playing witty, urbane, professional women who could go toe to toe with their male counterparts. She also did a great deal of work for charities, the war effort during World War II, and women's organizations throughout her long life. While she is best known for playing Nora Charles in the Thin Man series, Myrna Loy had a number of other notable roles during her acting career of almost six decades and was a true Hollywood star.

FORGOTTEN MOVIE STARS OF THE 30's, 40's, and 50's

My favorite Myrna Loy films are the following:

- *The Thin Man Series*
- *The Best Years of Our Lives*
- *Cheaper by the Dozen*
- *Mr. Blandings Builds His Dream House*

Biography

Myrna Williams, later to become Myrna Loy, was born on August 2, 1905 in Radersburg, Montana. Her father was a rancher, banker, and real estate developer and the youngest person ever elected to the Montana State Legislature at that time. Later on her family moved to Helena where she spent her youth.

At the age of 13, Myrna's father died of influenza and the rest of the family moved to Los Angeles, where they had visited a number of times previously. Myrna was educated in L.A. and the Westlake School for Girls where she caught the dancing and acting bug. She started at the age of 15 when she appeared in local stage productions in order to help support her family. Some of the stage plays were held in the now famous Grauman's Theater in Hollywood. Mrs. Rudolph Valentino happened to be in the audience one night and after that, she managed to pull some strings to get Myrna some parts in the motion picture industry.

Her first film was a small part in the production of *What Price Beauty?* (1925). Later she appeared the same year in *Pretty Ladies* (1925) along with Joan Crawford. She was one of the few stars – male or female - that would start in the silent movies and make a successful transition into the sound era. In the silent films, Myrna would generally appear as an exotic femme fatale.

FORGOTTEN MOVIE STARS OF THE 30's, 40's, and 50's

> Later, in the sound era, she would achieve her more typical image as a married, refined, wholesome character.

Unable to land a contract with a major studio, she continued to appear in small, bit roles, nothing that one could really call acting. Her first appearance as a Warner Brothers contract player was *The Caveman* (1926) where she played a maid. Although she was typecast over and over again as a vamp, Myrna continued to stay busy with small parts. Finally, in 1927, she received star billing in *Bitter Apples* (1927). After that, however, she returned to the usual smaller roles. Myrna seemed to take any role that would give her exposure and showcase the talent she felt was being wasted, even if it meant playing one vamp after another.

Finally her contract ran out with Warners and she signed with MGM where she got two meaty roles. One was in the *The Prizefighter and the Lady* (1933), and the other as Nora Charles in *The Thin Man* (1934) with William Powell. As good as William Powell was, most film experts agreed that the Thin Man series would never have been successful without Myrna in the role of Nora Charles. Her witty perception of situations gave moviegoers the impression that no one – criminals, cops, or even her husband - could pull a fast one over on the bright, not-to-be-taken lightly Mrs. Charles.

> After *The Thin Man* (1934), Myrna would appear in five more films in that series between 1934 and 1947.

FORGOTTEN MOVIE STARS OF THE 30's, 40's, and 50's

Myrna Loy was extremely popular with movie audiences during this time period. She was popular enough that, in 1936, she was named Queen of the Movies and Clark Gable the King in a nationwide poll of movie goers. She continued to make films through the 40s and 50s, including perhaps her next best role – in *The Best Years of Our Lives* - but the roles were few and far between. She did star in a couple of good films during that time – *Cheaper By the Dozen* and *Mr. Blandings Builds His Dream House*.

> To be mentioned in the same sentence as Clark Gable was quite an achievement in 1936. Gable was known as the King of Hollywood at that time, even though he did not make *Gone with the Wind* until three years later.

However, by the 1960's the parts had all but dried up as producers and directors looked elsewhere for fresher (frankly younger) talent. In 1960 she appeared in *Midnight Lace* (1960) with Doris Day and Rex Harrison and was not in another film until 1969 in *The April Fools* (1969). In the 1970's, she appeared mostly in TV movies, not theatrical productions. Her last film was in a made for television 1981 film called *Summer Solstice* (1981). By the time Myrna passed away, on December 14, 1993, at the age of 88, she had appeared in 129 motion pictures.

In her later years, she assumed an influential role as Co-Chairman of the Advisory Council of the National Committee Against Discrimination in Housing. In 1948 she became a member of the U.S. National Commission for UNESCO, the first Hollywood celebrity to do so.

> UNESCO is a specialized agency of the United Nations (UN). Its purpose is to contribute to peace and security on earth by promoting international collaboration through education, science, and culture in order to further universal respect for justice, the rule of law, and human rights.

Recognition

Myrna Loy was never nominated for an Oscar but did receive a much-deserved honorary Oscar for her career achievements in 1991. She also received career achievement awards from the Los Angeles Film Critics Association in 1983 and from the National Board of Review in 1979.

Myrna Loy has a star on the Hollywood Walk of Fame at 6685 Hollywood Boulevard.

As another form of recognition, in 1921, Myrna Loy posed for Harry Winebrenner's statue titled "Spiritual," which remained in front of Venice High School throughout the 20th century and can be seen in the opening scenes of the 1978 film *Grease*. The statue was vandalized several times, and at one point was removed from display. However it has been rebuilt using bronze, and is on display again, surrounded by some thorny rosebushes to protect it.[11] So Myrna Loy lives on at her alma mater, Venice High School.

---

[11] Wikipedia article on Myrna Loy, based on a story in the *L.A. Times* newspaper.

FORGOTTEN MOVIE STARS OF THE 30's, 40's, and 50's

Copy of "Spiritual," designed by teacher (not artist) Harry Winebrenner. Loy was a student at Venice High School when she posed for this statute.

My Favorite Myrna Loy Films

1. The Thin Man Series – 1934-1947

William Powell and Myrna Loy

FORGOTTEN MOVIE STARS OF THE 30's, 40's, and 50's

William Powell and Myrna Powell in a scene from a *Thin Man* movie. This type of screwball adult comedy with husband and wife as equals was quite novel and refreshing for Hollywood.

> And no one ever did it better before or after, than William Powell and Myrna Loy.

The Thin Man Films are discussed in the section on William Powell. Suffice it to say that the series would never have been anywhere near as successful without Myrna Loy. She matches Powell step for step in every film, and assists him – whether he likes it or not – in solving the murders, often placing herself in peril in the process.

She was always beautiful, always glamorous, yet down to earth enough to hold her own with the likes of Nick's friends like Dum Dum, Wacky, Creeps, and Fingers. And when she became a mother in the third film, it added a new perspective to the series.

Finally, I like the notion that while Nick seemed not to be able to exist without a martini in his hand, it never seemed quite as important to Nora.

> If you really closely compare the difference between the Philo Vance films with William Powell, which were basically OK, and the *Thin Man* series, which was terrific, the major difference is the addition of Myrna Loy in the latter series.

2. The Best Years of Our Lives - 1946

Myrna Loy shares a dramatic moment with husband Frederick March and daughter Teresa Wright. They are undoubtedly discussing whether or not Wright is better off with her current boyfriend or with unhappily married but likeable guy Dana Andrews.

In this film, previously discussed under the entries on Dana Andrews and Teresa Wright, Myrna Loy plays the wife of banker Frederick March and mother of Wright. Perhaps the most touching scene in the movie is at the very beginning, where March surprises his two grown kids and his wife with his return from WWII. If you don't get a tear in your eyes watching this scene, you are not really a very emotional individual. Again, Loy is the wife that every married G.I. would want to come home to.

> The scene I mentioned is the one that is always shown from this film – the two kids on either side of the doorway watching their parents meet and embrace for the first time in years. A truly memorable motion picture scene.

FORGOTTEN MOVIE STARS OF THE 30's, 40's, and 50's

Loy empathizes with her daughter's problems in loving a married man, tries to help Andrews readjust to civilian life, recognizes the changes in her husband, and generally helps out where needed. And in the scene where Wright tells her mom and dad that she is jealous of them because they always loved each other and never had any problems, Loy responds by saying that she can't count the number of times she told her husband she hated him. (But of course, she adds she didn't really mean it and they always worked things out.) Loy's performance is appealing and extremely heartfelt. She is part of a wonderful ensemble cast that features March, Andrews, Wright, Harold Russell, Virginia Mayo, and even composer/piano player Hoagy Carmichael, who composed "Stardust" among other songs.

3. Cheaper By the Dozen – 1950

Here's a picture of the dozen in *Cheaper by the Dozen*, with Myrna Loy and Clifton Webb heading the cast. Count them, there are a dozen in this picture.

FORGOTTEN MOVIE STARS OF THE 30's, 40's, and 50's

Cheaper By the Dozen is based on the real-life story of the Gilbreth family, following the family from Providence, Rhode Island, to Montclair, New Jersey, and detailing the amusing anecdotes found in large families – 12 to be exact. Frank Gilbreth, Sr., (Clinton Webb) was a pioneer in the field of time and motion studies, and often used his family as guinea pigs (with amusing and sometimes embarrassing results). Like many dads, he resisted popular culture, railing against his daughters' desires for bobbed hair and makeup. Loy plays his wife Lillian, who supports him in his work yet is the driving force in keeping things together. The two leads are very good, and Jeanne Crain and Edgar Buchanan highlight a strong supporting cast.

4. Mr. Blandings Builds His Dream House - 1948

In a similar comedy vein as *Cheaper by the Dozen*, *Blandings* features Cary Grant and Myrna Loy as Jim and Muriel Blandings. The Blandings are city dwellers who live in New York in a tiny apartment. One day they decide to move to the country and find that buying, building, and living in their own home is easier said than done. Planning to purchase and "fix up" an old house, the couple contacts a real estate agent, who uses them to unload "The Old Hackett Place" in fictional Lansdale County, Connecticut. It is a dilapidated two hundred-year-old farmhouse.

Blandings purchases the property for more than the going rate for property in the area, provoking his friend/lawyer Bill Cole to chastise him for following his heart rather than his head. Of course, problems ensue, along with misunderstandings among the principal characters. Cary Grant and Myrna Loy are excellent as Jim and Muriel Blandings, along with a strong supporting case that includes Melvyn Douglas as their friend Bill Cole, plus Reginald Denny and Louise Beavers.

FORGOTTEN MOVIE STARS OF THE 30's, 40's, and 50's

> If this film reminds you of a more modern film, it is probably *The Money Pit*, with Tom Hanks.

> Louise Beavers was an African-American actress who got all the maid/housekeeper roles that Hattie McDaniel from *Gone with the Wind* did not get. Beavers was the maid in one of my favorite films, *Reap the Wild Wind*.

Myrna Loy was a symbol of classy elegance in the movies of the 1930's and 1940's. She was also a pioneer for female involvement in civic activities and volunteerism. Because of *The Thin Man* and *The Best Years of Our Lives*, I believe she is an excellent choice for this book.

FORGOTTEN MOVIE STARS OF THE 30's, 40's, and 50's

Ronald Colman – 1891-1958

When I said that Barbara Stanwyck, John Garfield, Ronald Colman, and Susan Hayward were probably the best actors on my list of 25 forgotten stars, I am not exaggerating at all when it comes to Ronald Colman. He was perhaps the finest actor of his generation, and an outstanding leading man of the 1930's and 1940's. He is certainly best known for his beautiful, melodic speaking voice.

While Colman was a star in silent movies, the move to talking pictures only added to his stature as an actor. This was directly in contrast with an actor he resembled – John Gilbert – who was an even bigger star in silent films but faded quickly when talkies came into being because of his high, effeminate voice.

FORGOTTEN MOVIE STARS OF THE 30's, 40's, and 50's

> Ronald Colman starred in some of the greatest films of that era, including *A Tale of Two Cities, Random Harvest, The Prisoner of Zenda, The Light That Failed,* and *Lost Horizon.*

My Favorite Ronald Colman Films

My favorite Ronald Colman films are the following:

- *A Tale of Two Cities*
- *The Prisoner of Zenda*
- *The Talk of the Town*
- *Lost Horizon*

Biography

Ronald Charles Colman was a British leading man of primarily American films, one of the great stars of what is often considered the Golden Age of movies in the 1930's and 1940's. Raised in Ealing, England, the son of a successful silk merchant, he attended boarding school in Sussex, where he first discovered amateur theatre. He was supposed to attend Cambridge and become an engineer, but his father's death cost him the financial support necessary for him to continue his education.

Colman instead joined the London Scottish Regionals, an army territorial force. There he found an escape from office work, as well as new camaraderie with his fellow soldiers. He also began to take part in amateur theatricals, performing a variety of roles with the Bancroft Dramatic Society.

FORGOTTEN MOVIE STARS OF THE 30's, 40's, and 50's

At the outbreak of World War I Colman was sent to France. Seriously wounded at the battle of Messines--he was gassed--he was discharged from military service scarcely two months after shipping out for France.

> Many of the male stars of this era seem to have served in the military and actually participated in a war.

Upon his recovery he tried to enter the consular service, but a chance encounter got him a small role in a London play. He dropped other plans and concentrated on the theatre, and was rewarded with a succession of increasingly prominent parts. He made extra money appearing in a few minor films, and in 1920 set out for New York in hopes of finding greater fortune there than in an England still recovering from the effects of the war. After two years of impoverishment he was cast in a Broadway hit, "La Tendresse."

Director Henry King spotted him in the show and cast him as Lillian Gish's leading man in his first film, *The White Sister* (1923). His success in the film led to a contract with Samuel Goldwyn, and his career as a Hollywood leading man was underway. Colman became a very popular star of silent films, in romances and adventure films.

The coming of sound made his extraordinarily beautiful speaking voice even more important to the film industry. He played sophisticated, thoughtful characters of integrity with enormous ease, and swashbuckled expertly when called to do so in films like *The Prisoner of Zenda, A Tale of Two Cities, Random Harvest*, and *The Lost Horizon*. A decade later he received an Academy Award for his splendid portrayal of a tormented actor in *A Double Life* (1947). Much of his later career was devoted to "The Halls of Ivy," a radio show that was transferred to television in 1954.

He continued to work until nearly the end of his life, which came in 1958 after a brief lung illness. Colman was survived by his second wife, actress Benita Hume, and their daughter Juliet Benita Colman.

> "The Halls of Ivy" was a TV comedy that featured Colman as William Todhunter Hall, the president of a small Midwestern college, and his wife, Victoria, a former British musical comedy star who sometimes felt the tug of her former profession. It followed their interactions with students, friends, and college trustees.

Recognition

Ronald Colman received an Oscar for Best Actor in a Leading Role for his performance in *A Double Life* (1948). He was nominated for three other Best Actor Oscars for the following films:

- *Condemned* – 1930
- *Bulldog Drummond* – also 1930
- *Random Harvest* – 1943

Colman won a Golden Globe for Best Motion Picture Actor for *A Double Life*.

He has two stars on the Hollywood Walk of Fame – one for motion pictures at 6801 Hollywood Boulevard, and one for television at 1625 Vine Street.

FORGOTTEN MOVIE STARS OF THE 30's, 40's, and 50's

My Favorite Ronald Colman Films

1. A Tale of Two Cities – 1935

Ronald Colman, Elizabeth Allen, Edna Mae Oliver, and Reginald Owen in *A Tale of Two Cities*.

The definitive version of this adaptation of the Charles Dickens' novel stars Ronald Colman as Sydney Carton in perhaps his most famous role. The film takes place in the late 18th century, just after England has lost its American colonies and just before the French Revolution. The seeds of revolution are burning in Paris as the French upper class completely overindulges while the poor are starving.

A young French nobleman, Charles Darnay, disgusted by the treatment of the masses by the French nobility, including his own family, relocates to London because he can no longer tolerate the injustices he sees. As he arrives, he is falsely accused of being a traitor and stands on trial in London for treason. There, he is defended by the alcoholic Sydney Carton (Colman), who has squandered his life in pursuit of drinking. Carton discovers how Darnay was falsely accused and is successful in getting an acquittal.

FORGOTTEN MOVIE STARS OF THE 30's, 40's, and 50's

At the trial, Carton is introduced to Darnay's lady friend (and future wife) Lucie Manette, who Carton immediately falls in love with and recognizes as a true treasure. Carton rededicates his life to nobler purposes – even when she marries Darnay – and vows that if he can ever repay her kindness toward him, he will do it, even if it means giving up his life in the process.

Years pass, and the French Revolution has begun. Reason has gone by the wayside, replaced by lunatics like the evil Madame DeFarge, who are willing to sacrifice anyone of means to the guillotine. Darnay, living in London, learns that his former tutor has been accused of treason and returns to Paris to try to free him – a noble but not very smart move, given the attitude of the people in charge toward any aristocrat.

Of course, when he arrives in France, Darney is accused of treason and placed on trial, where it appears that he will be freed until the intervention of Madame Defarge. Darnay's family, including his friend Carton, travels to France to attempt to free him, but is unsuccessful.

The only thing that can be done is for Sydney to fulfill his promise, and he does so without the French knowing, by substituting himself in place of Darney in prison and taking Darnay's place at the guillotine. In the final scene, he explains to a newly found seamstress friend, also headed to the guillotine, how he can be so calm when he is about to die with the immortal line:

> "It is a far, far better thing that I do, than I have ever done; it is a far, far better rest that I go to, than I have ever known."

FORGOTTEN MOVIE STARS OF THE 30's, 40's, and 50's

Colman is simply brilliant in the role of Sydney Carton, first as the alcoholic cynic, next as the caring individual whose object of his love marries another man while he suffers in silence and carries on, and finally, as the most noble man of all, who substitutes his life for another for the benefit of that man's wife and daughter.

You simply cannot watch the ending of this movie without choking up, and that is due completely to the performance of Ronald Colman as Sydney Carton.

This is one of those movies where, no matter how many times I see it, the ending gets to me. Others would be *It's a Wonderful Life, Les Mis,* including the new version, and – I have to admit – *An Affair to Remember*, when Cary Grant sees the portrait of Deborah Kerr in her anteroom. And of course, *Pride of the Yankees*, where Gary Cooper as Lou Gehrig tells the Yankee fans that "today, I am the luckiest man on the face of the earth," in spite of the fact that we know he is dying of ALS, more commonly called Lou Gehrig's disease.

An outstanding supporting cast includes Elizabeth Allen as Lucie, Donald Woods as Darnay, Basil Rathbone, Reginald Owen, Henry B. Walthall, H.B. Warner, Blanche Yurka as Madame Defarge (a terrific performance), and Edna Mae Oliver, a great character actress who practically steals the movie as Lucie's friend and governess. If you see only one version of *A Tale of Two Cities*, please make sure it is this one.

(Next Page) Ronald Colman as Sydney Carton and Isabel Jewell, as his new-found seamstress friend, as they prepare to be executed at the guillotine. She is afraid and marvels at Carton's lack of fear as he prepares for his death.

FORGOTTEN MOVIE STARS OF THE 30's, 40's, and 50's

2. The Prisoner of Zenda - 1937

Douglas Fairbanks, Jr. and Ronald Colman in the climactic scene from *The Prisoner of Zenda*. (In just a few minutes, Fairbanks will jump out the window into the river after uttering the famous line, "He who fights and runs away may live to fight another day." However, in spite of that line, no sequel to this film was ever made.)

FORGOTTEN MOVIE STARS OF THE 30's, 40's, and 50's

The Prisoner of Zenda is a classic swashbuckler, and again this version is the definitive film version of the adventure novel by Anthony Hope. An Englishman on holiday in the kingdom of Ruritania happens to be a distant cousin and an identical look alike to the soon-to-be-coronated King of Ruritania, Rudolph V. He is spotted by advisors to the king and is asked to impersonate the king when the rightful monarch is drugged and kidnapped by his enemies, most notably Michael (Raymond Massey). Reluctantly, he agrees.

Moreover, he is asked to risk his life by filling in for the would-be king just before his impending coronation. If Rudolf V isn't present at the ceremony, he will forfeit the crown to his younger brother. Complications ensue when Princess Flavia, the king's betrothed, begins to notice a "personality change" in her fiancé. It seems that the real king was something of a spoiled brat while the Englishman, also named Rudolph (Rassendyll), acts more like a king than the real king. (Sounds a bit like *The Man in the Iron Mask*.)

There are complications, plots, and counter-plots, among them the schemes of Michael's mistress Antoinette de Mauban, and those of his dashing but villainous henchman Rupert of Hentzau (Douglas Fairbanks, Jr.), and Rassendyll (Colman) falling in love with Princess Flavia. In the end, the King is restored to his throne; but the lovers, as duty requires, must part forever.

Ronald Colman is again simply brilliant in the double role of king and common man in this swashbuckler. He carries off both parts with equal aplomb and has us wishing that the fake king could somehow become the real king.

A truly outstanding cast includes Raymond Massey as Michael, Douglas Fairbanks, Jr. as Rupert, Mary Astor, Madeleine Carroll, a young David Niven, and C. Aubrey Smith.

FORGOTTEN MOVIE STARS OF THE 30's, 40's, and 50's

> While Douglas Fairbanks, Jr. is the real villain of the film, he does not die but instead escapes by diving from the castle into the river – a scene repeated in 1965's *The Great Race* with Ross Martin in a similar role. This is because, according to Robert Osborne of TCM, a sequel was planned with Fairbanks' character, Rupert of Hentzau, becoming the lead in the sequel. But no sequel was ever made, and we are instead left with the incorrect impression that something was left on the cutting room floor.

The basic premise of this film – an average Joe substituting for the head of state because of an uncanny resemblance to the head of state – might also remind you of a more modern film, *Dave*, with Kevin Kline and Sigourney Weaver (another favorite.)

3. The Talk of the Town – 1942

Jean Arthur, professor Ronald Colman, and Cary Grant in a scene from *Talk of the Town*.

FORGOTTEN MOVIE STARS OF THE 30's, 40's, and 50's

This outstanding comedy, which received seven Oscar nominations, stars Cary Grant, Jean Arthur, and Ronald Colman. Grant plays Leopold Dilg, an innocent man but a social activist who is wrongly accused of a crime he did not commit – arson at the factory where he works, coupled with murder, since the foreman also apparently died in the fire. To avoid what seems like a certain conviction and execution, Dilg breaks out of jail and takes refuge in the first house he can find, which happens to be owned by his former school mate, Nora, played by the wonderful Jean Arthur.

Nora's houseguest, just arriving for the summer, is a legal scholar played by Ronald Colman, who teaches law at the state university and has come to town for the summer to write a book. Dilg poses as the gardener, and the three begin a real friendship, especially the two men. Colman knows all about the law and its principles but has no real experience in applying it, while layman Dilg is the practical man whose only concern is fairness and accuracy in using laws.

The three stars make this film. The banter between Colman's high mindedness and Grant's more practical approach is outstanding, as is Jean Arthur's performance as the landlord who tries to keep pace and keep Dilg from being detected.

4. Lost Horizon – 1937

FORGOTTEN MOVIE STARS OF THE 30's, 40's, and 50's

(Previous page). Ronald Colman and H.B. Warner discuss the virtues of Shangri-La in a scene from *Lost Horizon*.

In this 1937 classic, directed by Frank Capra, British diplomat Robert Conway (Colman) and a small group of civilians crash land in the Himalayas, and are rescued by the people of the mysterious, Eden-like valley of Shangri-la. Protected by the mountains from the world outside, where the clouds of World War II are gathering, Shangri-la provides a seductive escape for the world-weary Conway. Conway and his cohorts, played by Edward Everett Horton, John Howard, and Thomas Mitchell, experience this idyllic life without care or concern but also long for their homeland. They are caught in a struggle about whether to remain in Shangri-la or try to return to their homeland.

Conway really learns to love Shangri-La while his younger brother (John Howard), does nothing but plan for his escape. Compounding the decision is that residents of the valley grow old at an extremely slow pace, so that one's life seems endless. When Conway asks the leader if the people in Shangri-la are happy, he replies that the inhabitants are ruled by moderation and therefore learn to be happy as a result.

Colman is perfectly cast as the British diplomat who experiences the wonders of this paradise but also balances that against the desire to return to home and country and his regular responsibilities. Jane Wyatt plays the female lead, a school teacher who makes it even more difficult for Colman to leave; they fall in love although she explains why she will never leave Shangri-La. The cast also includes H.B. Warner and Sam Jaffe as leaders of Shangri-la. But it is Colman's performance that is the key to this film, and he was never better than as a man trying to balance the ideal with the practical.

FORGOTTEN MOVIE STARS OF THE 30's, 40's, and 50's

As I indicated, Colman was an outstanding actor with a beautifully resonant voice. He was nominated for four Oscars and was awarded one. He may have uttered more great lines than anyone else in film history. Ronald Colman was a forgotten star who truly deserves a place in this book.

FORGOTTEN MOVIE STARS OF THE 30's, 40's, and 50's

Kathryn Grayson – 1922-2010

I will tell you right up front that I enjoy musicals, especially the classic ones from the 1950's; as a result, Kathryn Grayson is one of my favorites. She had a beautiful singing voice, was very attractive, a decent enough actress to make movies, and made a number of top-notch movie musicals in the 1940's and 1950's with stars like Gene Kelly, Frank Sinatra, Mario Lanza, and Howard Keel. I must admit that my favorites were probably the ones she made with Keel, including *Showboat* and the classic Cole Porter musical, *Kiss Me Kate*. Both musicals were wonderful on stage, and just as good as movies. Grayson had that rare quality of a voice that was good enough to sing opera but also lent itself well to Broadway show tunes and movie musicals.

FORGOTTEN MOVIE STARS OF THE 30's, 40's, and 50's

Kathryn Grayson lived well into the 21st century, passing away in 2010 at the age of 88. Grayson often played parts in which she was a real prima donna but was apparently very easygoing and easy to work with in real life, except in her dealings with Mario Lanza, which you will hear about later.

My favorite Kathryn Grayson films are the following:
- *Kiss Me Kate*
- *Showboat*
- *The Toast of New Orleans*
- *Anchors Aweigh*
- *The Desert Song*

Biography

Kathryn Grayson was born Zelma Kathryn Elisabeth Hedrick in Winston-Salem, North Carolina on February 9, 1922, the daughter of Charles E. Hedrick and Lillian Grayson Hedrick. Charles was a building contractor-realtor. Early in Kathryn's life, the Hedrick family moved to St. Louis, Missouri, where she was discovered singing on the empty stage of the St. Louis Municipal Opera House by a janitor.

> I am not sure how one gets discovered by a janitor, but who am I to question this?

He introduced her to Frances Marshall of the Chicago Civic Opera, who gave the twelve-year-old girl voice lessons until she was signed by RCA Red Seal records at the age of 15. At that time, she was being trained to sing opera.

However, her opera career was cut short when she was seen and heard by Louis B. Mayer and was signed by MGM to a contract without even the formality of a screen test. She was then given acting lessons and had to pose for countless publicity photos. Kathryn, a coloratura soprano, made her first film in 1941, a "B" picture called *Andy Hardy's Private Secretary*. Her unusual combination of looks, a beautiful singing voice, and genuine acting talent brought her official stardom in 1945 in *Anchors Aweigh* with Gene Kelly and Frank Sinatra. A major star while at MGM, Grayson also made films at Warner Brothers and Paramount Studios.

Grayson's most memorable roles came in the late 1940's and early 1950s. They were *Show Boat* (1951), where she played Magnolia, opposite Ava Gardner and Howard Keel; and *Kiss Me Kate* (1953), playing actress Lilli Vanessi, who portrayed Katherine in the movie's "show within a show."

> If you are not familiar with *Kiss Me Kate*, it is basically a musical version of Shakespeare's play, "Taming of the Shrew." But unlike Shakespeare, it had lots and lots of singing and dancing, of course.

In 1953 she left MGM, then made only one film, *The Vagabond King* (1956), at Paramount. She was paired with Mario Lanza a few times, but the two never got along, supposedly due mostly to Lanza's hot temper and alcohol abuse.

Grayson switched to television in the mid-1950's and tended to take on more dramatic roles. Her roles on television included "Playhouse 90" and "General Electric Theater." She made her opera debut in 1960 performing "Madame Butterfly," "La Traviata," and "La Boheme" and in 1983 starred in "Orpheus in the Underworld" for Opera New England.

FORGOTTEN MOVIE STARS OF THE 30's, 40's, and 50's

On stage, Kathyrn Grayson scored triumphs in such stage musicals as "The Merry Widow" for which she was nominated for the Sarah Siddons Award. She toured in "Naughty Marietta," "Rosalinda," "Show Boat," "Kiss Me Kate" and "Camelot" and in 1983 a departure as Miss Tweed in "Something's Afoot."

Not surprisingly, she and Howard Keel toured extensively in "Man of La Mancha" and appeared together in Las Vegas. This began a string of highly successful appearances for her and Keel in Las Vegas. In 1982 Miss Grayson received rave reviews for her first all-dramatic stage performance in Lucille Fletcher's "Night Watch." In 1987, again in a departure, she starred in the much-acclaimed British farce "Noises Off."

From 1988 through 1997 Grayson toured in her one-woman show, "An Evening with Kathryn Grayson." She was offered the title role in the 1996 Albert Brooks film *Mother*, but declined the part because she thought the character was "brain dead;" Debbie Reynolds got the part instead. In 1996 and 1997 she appeared with Van Johnson in "Love Letters" with great success. This prompted them to tour in their own production "Red Sox and Roses." She continued to work well into her senior years as a teacher of voice. Grayson gave Master Classes and taught private voice lessons. She passed away in 2010 at the age of 88.

> Van Johnson's trademark was that he almost always wore red socks. Hence the name, Red Sox and Roses. I have no idea if he was a Boston Red Sox fan, but he was from New England.

FORGOTTEN MOVIE STARS OF THE 30's, 40's, and 50's

Recognition

Kathryn Grayson has a star on the Hollywood Walk of Fame at 1600 Vine Street. She received numerous non-film awards but no major movie awards. Let's face it, you are not going to get a lot of formal recognition from making movie musicals.

My Favorite Kathryn Grayson Films

1. Kiss Me Kate – 1953

Kathryn Grayson and Howard Keel in costume as their Shakespearian characters in *Kiss Me Kate*. For most of this film, they are fighting!

FORGOTTEN MOVIE STARS OF THE 30's, 40's, and 50's

This top-notch musical features Kathryn Grayson as Lilli Vanessi and Howard Keel as her ex-husband Fred Graham in a movie within a movie version of Shakespeare's "Taming of the Shrew." Fred and Lilly are a divorced pair of actors who are brought together by famed songwriter Cole Porter. (Ron Randall actually plays Cole Porter in the opening scene of this motion picture.)

Porter has written a musical version of the Shakespearean play which he is calling "Kiss Me Kate." Of course, talking Lilli into playing the co-lead with her ex-husband is quite a task, and in most cases, the couple seems to act a great deal offstage like the characters they play onstage - fighting. Meanwhile, Fred has a new girlfriend, dancer Lois Lane, (Ann Miller), who plays Kate's sister Bianca in the play and is really in love with one of Kate's suitors in the play. Got it so far?

The relationship between Fred and Lilli changes – from bad to good to bad to good and so on – frequently during rehearsals, on opening night before the curtain goes up, and even on stage on opening night in ways that relate to the actual story in the stage play. In turn, what happens on stage has an effect on the emotional whims of the two leads.

Thrown into the mix of further subplots are Tex Callaway, Lilli's on-again/off again cattle baron fiancé who wants to marry Lilli and take her back to his cattle ranch in Texas, and two gangsters who have come to the theater to help their boss collect on a gambling debt from Fred (one that he knows nothing about) and who won't leave the backstage area or in some cases even the stage itself, in order to protect their boss' new investment (Fred).

All the experts thought Porter was washed up at this time, but he proved he had one more great Broadway show in him.

FORGOTTEN MOVIE STARS OF THE 30's, 40's, and 50's

> Cole Porter is one of America's greatest songwriters. A list of his hits includes:
>
> - *Night and Day*
> - *I Get a Kick Out of You*
> - *Easy to Love*
> - *What Is This Thing Called Love?*
> - *Love for Sale*
> - *De-Lovely*
> - *Begin the Beguine*
> - *Just One of Those Things*
> - *Anything Goes*

As usual with musicals, the success depends on the spark between the two leads, and Grayson and Keel are perfect as the on again/off again couple; they genuinely seem to alternate between loving and hating each other, exactly what the plot requires, and their singing voices are just spectacular. Each one can be humble or arrogant depending on how the other sets them off. Add to this a Cole Porter score (how could you go wrong there?) featuring songs like "Wunderbar," "Brush Up Your Shakespeare," and "So in Love." Toss in a great supporting cast that includes Ann Miller, Bob Fosse, and Bobby Van as dancers, and James Whitmore and Keenan Wynn as the two dumb but hilarious gangsters, and you have a brilliant version of this top-notch musical.

> If you want a real example of a show stopping musical number, look no further than James Whitmore and Keenan Wynn singing "Brush up Your Shakespeare." Watching two incompetent hoods singing this tribute to the great English bard is a treasure and very funny to boot.

FORGOTTEN MOVIE STARS OF THE 30's, 40's, and 50's

2. Showboat – 1951

Kathryn Grayson as Magnolia and Howard Keel as Gaylord Ravenal in happier moments.

This is the 1951 version, and the best and most cinematic rendering (with a $2 million plus budget), of the Jerome Kern/Oscar Hammerstein musical *Showboat*, about the adventures of Captain Andy (Joe E. Brown) and his family and friends as they take their showboat down the Mississippi River in the early 1900's, performing musical shows in every town where they stop.

The "Cotton Blossom," owned by the Hawks family, is the showboat where everyone comes for great musical entertainment in the South. Julie Laverne (Ava Gardner) and her husband (Robert Sterling) are the stars of the show. After a snitch who was spurned by Julie tells the local police that Julie (who's half African-American) is married to a white man, the two stars are forced to leave the showboat. In the South, interracial marriages were still forbidden at that time.

FORGOTTEN MOVIE STARS OF THE 30's, 40's, and 50's

Magnolia Hawks (Kathryn Grayson), Captain Andy Hawks' daughter, becomes the new showboat attraction and her leading man is Gaylord Ravenal (Howard Keel), a gambler. The two instantly fall in love and marry, without Mrs. Hawks's approval. Magnolia and Gaylord leave the "Cotton Blossom" for a whirlwind honeymoon and settle in Chicago, where Ravenal becomes a successful gambler, at least initially.

Magnolia soon faces the realization that gambling means more to Gaylord than anything else. She confronts Gaylord with an ultimatum and after he gambles away their fortune, he leaves her - not knowing she is pregnant, but believing that she will return to a more secure situation back on the Cotton Blossom, where she of course returns to.

Meanwhile, Julie has turned into a down-on-her-luck singer whose husband has left her. As a result, she becomes in essence a drunk and a prostitute. Years pass, Magnolia is raising her five-year-old daughter on the Cotton Blossom, and Gaylord has regained his luck as a successful riverboat gambler. One day, he meets Julie on a gambling ship, and she tells Ravenal that he deserted his wife and daughter just when he was most needed. Of course, he knows nothing of having a daughter, and is bowled over when learning that fact.

Realizing that family now means more to him than anything, he returns to the Cotton Blossom and is reunited with Magnolia and his daughter. Julie can only watch from the riverbank, knowing that at least she has had a part in her friend Magnolia's happiness. Another excellent musical and certainly a real tear jerker, Grayson and Keel are paired up for the first time as husband and wife. They exhibit a real chemistry in this film, and Grayson's character's naiveté is a perfect match for the more experienced, worldly Ava Gardner as Julie.

FORGOTTEN MOVIE STARS OF THE 30's, 40's, and 50's

An excellent supporting cast includes Joe E. Brown as Captain Andy, Agnes Moorehead as his wife, William Warfield, Robert Sterling, and Marge and Gower Champion as performers on the Cotton Blossom.

And the songs are of course, unforgettable, and include "Make Believe," "Ol' Man River," "Bill," and "Can't Help Lovin' That Man of Mine." While Grayson and Keel are the two leads and very good, the real surprise of this movie is Ava Gardner, whose performance as the star Julie is really the best performance in the film.

> Although Magnolia uses the older Julie as a mentor in this film, in reality Kathryn Grayson and Ava Gardner were both born in 1922. They were both 29 when this movie was made.

> In the stage versions I have seen of this musical, Captain Andy tends to be the central character. However, in this film version at least, the main characters are clearly Magnolia, Julie, and Ravenal. I guess when you are appealing to a wider movie audience, youth and good looks win out over character.

3. The Toast of New Orleans – 1950

(Next page) Kathryn Grayson and Mario Lanza in a publicity photo from *The Toast of New Orleans*. In spite of this pic, apparently there was no love loss between these two on the set of the movie, most likely because of Lanza's temper.

FORGOTTEN MOVIE STARS OF THE 30's, 40's, and 50's

The director of an opera is looking for a male baritone singer to match up with his brilliant but difficult soprano. Kathryn Grayson plays the snooty opera singer who is introduced to a simple, rough-and-tumble fisherman in the Louisiana bayous, played by Mario Lanza, but this fisherman can not only sing, but has an opera-quality voice – happens all the time, right? Grayson's agent lures him away to New Orleans to teach him to sing opera, but comes to regret this rash decision when the singers fall in love. David Niven plays the manager/agent and J. Carroll Naish and Rita Moreno are also featured prominently in the cast.

This is not a great musical by any stretch of the imagination, but it does bring together two operatic-quality voices in Kathryn Grayson and Mario Lanza. And while they are not great acting talents – especially Lanza – they are decent enough for a musical.

FORGOTTEN MOVIE STARS OF THE 30's, 40's, and 50's

> The most interesting fact about this movie is that Grayson, the prima donna soprano in the film, was in real life a pleasure to work with and very easygoing and cooperative on the set, while Lanza, the easy-going fisherman, was extremely self-centered and a real prima donna on the set. I guess that is why they call it acting!

4. Anchors Aweigh – 1945

Kathryn Grayson and Gene Kelly at a lunch counter in a scene from *Anchors Aweigh*. Once they really get to know each other, they fall in love – of course.

FORGOTTEN MOVIE STARS OF THE 30's, 40's, and 50's

Two sailors, one naïve (Clarence Doolittle – Frank Sinatra), the other (Joe Brady- Gene Kelly) experienced in the ways of the world, are on liberty in Los Angeles, the setting for this movie musical. Kelly, the one experienced in the ways of the world, has his heart set on spending time with his girl, but that doesn't work out. So instead he tries to find a date for Sinatra, the one who is inexperienced in the ways of the world.

> How about that for acting! Frank Sinatra playing a shy guy inexperienced in the ways of the world? That is not the Frank Sinatra I remember!

Just as they are getting started, they meet a little boy named Donald who has run away from home to join the Navy. Taking him back home, they meet his Aunt Susan (Grayson), who is quite a bit younger and more attractive than they were led to believe. Right away, Clarence (Sinatra) develops a crush on Susan and asks Joe (Kelly) for help in getting a date with her. Joe tells Susan that he knows a big-time music producer and that he can get her an audition with him. Of course, Joe doesn't really know any big-time music producer, and to complicate matters, he is beginning to fall for Susan himself. Everything ends up just fine when Clarence finds a girl from his home town of Brooklyn and Joe and Susan fall in love.

The three leads – Grayson, Kelly, and Sinatra – are all very good and work well together in this movie. Plus, this is the film where Kelly dances with Jerry Mouse from Tom and Jerry of cartoon fame in a spectacular combination of live action and animation, especially for 1945. The supporting cast includes Jose Iturbi and a young Dean Stockwell as Donald.

FORGOTTEN MOVIE STARS OF THE 30's, 40's, and 50's

> Gene Kelly and Frank Sinatra were always a great combination in a movie. Kelly could really dance and also sing, and Sinatra could really sing and also dance. They played in three films together – *On the Town, Anchors Aweigh*, and *Take Me Out to the Ball Game*. *On the Town* is one of the best movie musicals ever, and the other two aren't bad either. Although I will never figure out why Kelly was always cast as the experienced playboy while Sinatra was the shy and retiring one around girls.

5. **The Desert Song – 1953**

Kathryn Grayson and Gordon MacRae in a scene from *The Desert Song*.

FORGOTTEN MOVIE STARS OF THE 30's, 40's, and 50's

The Desert Song is an operetta with music by Sigmund Romberg and book and lyrics by Oscar Hammerstein II, Otto Harbach and Frank Mandel. It was inspired by the 1925 uprising of the Riffs, a group of Moroccan freedom fighters, against French colonial rule.

Sheik Yousseff poses as a friend of the French while secretly plotting to overthrow them. Opposing Yousseff are the Riffs, whose masked leader, The Red Shadow, is Paul Bonnard, a professor who is studying the desert, and whose attacks on the supply trains intending to bring supplies to Sheik Yousseff keep the Riff villages in food. Foreign Legion General Birabeau arrives to conduct an investigation, accompanied by his daughter, Margot. Birabeau hires Bonnard to tutor her, and she is attracted to a Legionnaire captain, Claud Fontaine. While the general, Bonnard and Fontaine pay a visit to Yousseff, an American newspaper man, Benji Kidd, discovers a secret way in and out of Yousseff's palace, with the aid of Azuri, a dancing girl in love with Bonnard. Bonnard is forced to resume his role as the Riff leader, and kidnap Margot until he can convince her of Yousseff's treachery. But Yousseff's men attack the Riff camp and take Margot prisoner. After the final battle, the French General and his soldiers realize that The Red Shadow and the Riffs were actually on their side and helped in preventing an uprising. Paul reveals that The Red Shadow is dead, and Margot is distraught until he reveals to her (in song, of course) that Paul Bonnard and The Red Shadow are one and the same individual.

> Because of the constant tensions in the Middle East, this musical is almost never performed today. Too bad, because while the plot is fairly dopey, it does contain some great Sigmund Romberg music.

FORGOTTEN MOVIE STARS OF THE 30's, 40's, and 50's

In spite of the silly plot (where it takes an American professor to lead the Arabs against the evil sheik), it's hard to dislike a movie musical starring Gordon McRae as The Red Shadow and Kathryn Grayson as Margot, and especially hard to dislike them when they have a nice Sigmund Romberg score featuring songs like "The Desert Song," "One Alone," and the rousing "Riff Song," one of the best show stopper songs you can imagine, to work with. A good supporting cast features the always enjoyable Raymond Massey as the evil Sheik Yousseff, Steve Cochran, and Dick Wesson, as the unnecessary comic relief in this movie. Grayson, as always, is beautiful and sings wonderfully also. And Ray Collins (Lt. Tragg on the "Perry Mason" series), plays Kathryn Grayson's father, General Birabeau.

> Ray Collins keeps popping up a lot in this book, proving he did more than just play Lt. Tragg on "Perry Mason."

As I hope I have shown, Kathryn Grayson was a beautifully talented performer who combined good looks, reasonable acting ability, and an outstanding soprano voice into a successful motion picture career. She is one of the two individuals in this book whose contributions were primarily in musicals, and the other person – Howard Keel - is next.

Howard Keel – 1919-2004

Many people will only remember Howard Keel for his role as Clayton Farlow on the long-running television show, *Dallas*. But Howard Keel was much more than that. He has been called the John Wayne, Errol Flynn, and Clark Gable of movie musicals,[12] and rightfully so. Keel was a perfect leading man for the movie musicals of the 1950's – tall at 6'4", handsome, brawny, a good actor, and a wonderful baritone voice.

For example, he really looked like a mountain man in *Seven Brides for Seven Brothers*. Although his acting career ventured beyond musicals, he is best known among movie fans for a series of musicals that included *Seven Brides for Seven Brothers, Kiss Me Kate, Kismet, Showboat, Calamity Jane*, and *Annie Get Your Gun*. Quite a resume in my book!

---

[12] IMDB page on Howard Keel.

FORGOTTEN MOVIE STARS OF THE 30's, 40's, and 50's

My favorite Howard Keel films include the following:

- Seven Brides for Seven Brothers
- Kiss Me Kate
- Showboat
- Kismet
- Calamity Jane
- Annie Get Your Gun

Biography

Born Harold Clifford Keel in rural Gillespie, IL, in 1919, his childhood was rather unhappy. Keel's father was a hard-drinking coal miner – not surprising, given the location in Illinois coal country - and his mother a stern, repressed Methodist homemaker. When Howard was 11 his father died, and the family moved to California soon after.

> It was not unusual for coal mining families in Illinois to move to California at that time, seeking a better life.

As a young adult, he initially earned his living as an automobile mechanic, but soon found work during WWII at Douglas Aircraft – a defense contractor - in Los Angeles. His naturally talented but untrained voice was discovered by the staff of his aircraft company, and soon he was performing at various venues for the company's clients.

Keel was inspired to sing professionally one day while attending a Hollywood Bowl concert. He quickly advanced through the musical ranks from singing waiter to music festival contest winner to guest recitalist. Imagine having Howard Keel sing to you while you are eating your steak!

FORGOTTEN MOVIE STARS OF THE 30's, 40's, and 50's

In 1946 Oscar Hammerstein II "discovered" him during John Raitt's understudy auditions for the role of Billy Bigelow in Broadway's "Carousel." He was cast on sight and his future was set. Keel managed to understudy Alfred Drake as Curly in "Oklahoma!" as well, and in 1947 took over the male lead in the London production, with great success.

British audiences took to the charismatic singer and he remained there as a concert vocalist while making his non-singing film debut in the British crime drama *The Hideout* (1949). MGM, which was looking for an answer to Warner Bros.' Gordon MacRae, sought him out, and he returned to the U.S.

> Most of the best Broadway musicals made into movies in the 1950's starred either Howard Keel or Gordon MacRae. MacRae starred in *Oklahoma!*, *Carousel*, and *The Desert Song* during that period. Keel was in most of the rest. While MacRae was good, Howard Keel was even better – more rugged, much taller, and a better actor.

Changing his stage moniker to Howard Keel, he became a star with his first role, as sharpshooter Frank Butler opposite Betty Hutton's Annie Oakley in the popular musical *Annie Get Your Gun* (1950). From then on he was showcased in many of MGM's biggest and most classic extravaganzas, such as *Show Boat* (1951), *Calamity Jane* (1953), *Kiss Me Kate* (1953) and (his favorite) *Seven Brides for Seven Brothers* (1954) at the top of the list.

Kismet (1955) opposite Ann Blyth would be his last, as the nation's passion for movie musicals was beginning to run its course. Plus, rock and roll was appearing on the scene.

Beginning in 1960, the brawny Keel moved effortlessly into rugged but routine action movies and appeared in such films as *Armored Command* (1961), *Waco* (1966), *Red Tomahawk* (1967) and *The War Wagon* (1967), the last one starring John Wayne and featuring Keel as a wisecracking Native American, believe it or not.

In the 1970s he kept his singing voice alive by returning full force to his musical roots. Some of his summer stock and tour productions, which included "Camelot," "South Pacific," "Seven Brides for Seven Brothers," "Man of La Mancha," and "Show Boat," reunited him often with such former MGM leading ladies as Kathryn Grayson and Jane Powell.

Keel also worked up a Las Vegas nightclub act with Grayson in the 1970s. But Keel was introduced to a new generation of Americans when he replaced Jim Davis as the upstanding family patriarch of the nighttime soap drama "Dallas" in 1978 after Davis' untimely death. As Clayton Farlow, Miss Ellie's second husband, he enjoyed a decade of steady work. In later years he continued to appear in concerts. As a result of this renewed fame, he landed his first solo recording contract with "And I Love You So" in 1983. Married three times, he died in 2004 at the age of 85 of colon cancer, survived by his third wife, three daughters and one son.

Recognition

Howard Keel received a lifetime achievement award from the Ft. Lauderdale International Film Festival in 2000 for musical cinema achievements. He received the King Vidor Memorial Award in 2001 from the San Luis Obispo International Film Festival. He was nominated as Outstanding Actor in a Supporting Role in 1988 for his role as Clayton Farlow by Soap Opera Digest Awards. Again, no Oscar nominations for musical performers.

FORGOTTEN MOVIE STARS OF THE 30's, 40's, and 50's

Howard Keel has a star on the Hollywood Walk of Fame at 6253 Hollywood Boulevard.

My Favorite Howard Keel Films

   1. Seven Brides for Seven Brothers – 1954

Jane Powell and Howard Keel in a publicity photo from *Seven Brides for Seven Brothers*. It's easy to see why Keel was cast in this film – he actually looks like a rugged mountain man.

Adam Pontipee is the oldest of seven brothers who live on a ranch/farm in 1850's Oregon. The movie begins with Adam going into town with the sole purpose of finding himself a wife - before returning home that night. He convinces Milly, a waitress/cook who makes the best beef stew in town, to marry him that same day, much to the chagrin of some of the townspeople. When they return to his home in the country, then and only then does she discover he has six brothers - all living in his cabin.

FORGOTTEN MOVIE STARS OF THE 30's, 40's, and 50's

Expected to be essentially the maid for the family, Milly instead sets out to reform the uncouth siblings, who are anxious to get wives of their own. Then, after reading about the Roman capture of the Sabine women – a story of ancient Rome immortalized in the painting by Peter Paul Rubens - Adam develops an inspired solution to his brothers' loneliness – they will kidnap the six best-looking single women in town and bring them back to the ranch as wives. Of course, they do just that, and just as they are crossing the mountains to return home, an avalanche closes off the only road from the town to their home until spring, leaving the families of the girls heartbroken.

When Milly finds out about this, she is angry beyond belief, and puts all the blame squarely on Adam. An angry Adam leaves in a huff, deciding to spend the winter alone in the brothers' cabin away from Milly and the rest of the world. In the end, everything turns out all right for Adam, Milly, and the brothers and their girls.

Seven Brides for Seven Brothers is simply a terrific movie musical, in fact one of the best movie musicals ever made. There are several reasons for this:

1. The performances of Jane Powell as Milly and especially Howard Keel as Adam, are noteworthy. Keel, with his full beard (shaven off early in the movie), moustache, and 6'4" frame, is a perfect Adam.
2. The songs are very good.
3. The dancing, in particular the dancing of the six younger brothers and their ladies, is really outstanding. The dance number during the scene where the entire town is building a barn is one of the best dance scenes in movie history.

FORGOTTEN MOVIE STARS OF THE 30's, 40's, and 50's

> This particular scene is often shown in specials on American musicals. If you have not seen it, you are really missing something. It was choreographed by famed Broadway director and choreographer Michael Kidd.

Keel's wonderful baritone voice and solid acting is a key to the success of this movie. An outstanding supporting cast includes Russ Tamblyn as the youngest Pontipee, Jeff Richards and Tommy Rall as two of the other brothers, and some wonderful female dancers including the gorgeous Julie Newmar and the talented Ruta Lee. This film won an Oscar for Best Musical Score for a musical picture, and rightly so. If they had an Oscar for best dancing, it would have won that also.

2. Kiss Me Kate - 1953

Kathryn Grayson and Howard Keel in a scene from Cole Porter's *Kiss Me Kate*. It seems that this divorced couple can't get along onstage or off stage.

FORGOTTEN MOVIE STARS OF THE 30's, 40's, and 50's

I described the plot of *Kiss Me* Kate in the previous chapter on Kathryn Grayson. Fred and Lilly are a divorced pair of actors who are brought together by Cole Porter, played by Ron Randall, who appears only in the first scene. Porter has written a musical version of "The Taming of the Shrew," called "Kiss Me Kate." Of course, offstage, the couple seem to act a great deal like the characters they play – Petruchio and Katherine; in other words, they fight constantly.

A fight on the opening night threatens the production, as well as two thugs – not the brightest bulbs on the planet - who have the mistaken idea that Fred owes their boss money and insist on staying next to him all night – onstage or off!

Adding to the confusion is that Lilly's future husband – Tex Callaway – is planning to marry her right after the show and take her back to his Texas ranch. Of course, it is a musical, so you can guess which guy Lilly ends up with at the end of the film – the Texas rancher or Fred, her soul mate.

The music in this movie is simply sensational – just what you would expect from a score written by the great Cole Porter. It features songs like "Wunderbar," "So in Love," "Another Op'nin, Another Show," and "Always True To You in My Fashion," among others. The key to the movie is the interaction between the two leads, and Kathryn Grayson and Howard Keel are perfect; they really work well together in romantic times, as well as in the scenes where they hate each other. And they both sing beautifully and with gusto.

A really strong supporting cast includes Ann Miller, Bob Fosse, Tommy Rall, Bobby Van, and Willard Parker. Miller, Fosse, Rall, and Van were all famous dancers – in fact, Bob Fosse became a choreographer and director and directed the Oscar-winning film *All That Jazz*, which won four Academy Awards in 1979.

FORGOTTEN MOVIE STARS OF THE 30's, 40's, and 50's

And the two thugs, Lippy and Slug, played by Keenan Wynn and James Whitmore, practically steal the movie. Their performances in general are outstanding, and their rendition of "Brush up Your Shakespeare" is the show stopping number in this musical. But it is the performances of the two leads that carry the day. This film is a must see for all lovers of musicals.

It is interesting to note that neither Grayson nor Keel do much if any dancing in this film or in fact any of their films. But unlike stars like Gene Kelly, Frank Sinatra or even Fred Astaire, they were singers, not dancers. And when you have dancers like Ann Miller, Bob Fosse, Bobby Van, and Tommy Rall in this cast, you don't need to have the two leads do any dancing at all. At least I don't think so.

> As I indicated earlier, after a great career, everybody thought Cole Porter was pretty much washed up in the late 1940's. But he proved the critics wrong, in 1948, with *Kiss Me, Kate*. It was by far his most successful Broadway show, running for 1,077 performances in New York and 400 in London.
>
> The production won the Tony Award for best musical (the first Tony awarded in that category), and Porter won for best composer and lyricist. In the first movie based on Cole Porter's life – *Night and Day* - Cary Grant played Porter. This was certainly a miscasting, as Porter was gay and very effeminate looking, and Cary Grant was, well, Cary Grant.

FORGOTTEN MOVIE STARS OF THE 30's, 40's, and 50's

3. Showboat – 1951

Keel and Grayson

I have already discussed this film in the section on Kathryn Grayson. Suffice it to say that, as the romantic lead, Howard Keel adds a lot to the movie as the Mississippi gambler recruited for the Show Boat.

As in *Kiss Me Kate*, Howard Keel and Katherine Grayson as Gaylord Ravenal and Magnolia work extremely well together. You can tell from their performances that they genuinely like each other, and this comes off in their songs. *Showboat* features some really great music, including "Make Believe," "Can't Help Lovin' Dat Man," "Bill," and of course "Ol' Man River," an ode to the Mississippi River. And an outstanding supporting cast features Ava Gardner, Joe E. Brown, Agnes Moorehead, Robert Sterling, Marge and Gower Champion, and William Warfield, who sings "Ol' Man River." Special mention should go to Ava Gardner as the doomed Julie, who turns in an unbelievably good performance and a very sympathetic portrayal of this character.

4. Kismet - 1955

Howard Keel as Hajj, the poet, in *Kismet*. The cast also included Vic Damone, Ann Blyth, and Dolores Grey.

Like a tale spun by Scheherazade, *Kismet* follows the remarkable and repeated changes of fortune that engulf a poor poet, Hajj, played by Howard Keel. It all happens in one incredible day when Kismet (Fate) takes a hand. The film takes place in ancient Baghdad and involves Hajj's efforts to become wealthy through taking advantage of fate. Trying to get rich, Hajj ends up having to talk his way out of all kinds of trouble several times; meanwhile, his beautiful daughter (Ann Blyth) meets and falls in love with the young Caliph (Vic Damone). In the end, in spite of all his efforts, Hajj comes to realize that you really cannot control fate.

FORGOTTEN MOVIE STARS OF THE 30's, 40's, and 50's

Keel makes the most of a role that is probably designed for an older man.

> Keel was only 35 when he made this movie, and his character has a grown daughter, played by the beautiful Ann Blyth, who was actually 27 at the time. But thanks to a good Hollywood makeup artist, Keel was able to pull it off.

Keel makes the most of the role and as always, sings beautifully, especially the opening number and theme of the musical, "Fate." The supporting cast includes Dolores Grey, Monte Woolley, Sebastian Cabot, and Mike Mazurki (below), who always played tough guys like Moose Malloy in *Murder, My Sweet*. The film also features several memorable songs such as "Stranger in Paradise" (one of my favorites), "And This Is My Beloved," and "Baubles, Bangles, and Beads."

This film is not up to the standards of the previous three Howard Keel movies, but still worth viewing.

Mike Mazurki

FORGOTTEN MOVIE STARS OF THE 30's, 40's, and 50's

On the previous page is a picture of Mike Mazurki, who seemed to always play tough guys in films in the 1940's and 1950's and was 6'5" and a former professional wrestler. Actually, Mazurki in real life was very intelligent, ranked #1 in his graduating class at Manhattan College with a B.A. degree, and was well read. But you can certainly see why he got all those tough guy parts in movies. I can hear the director saying, "We need a mean-looking guy for this part – Call Mike Mazurki!"

5. Calamity Jane - 1953

Howard Keel and Doris Day singing up a storm in *Calamity Jane*. This scene is from the very end of the film. I have seen pictures of the real Calamity Jane, and she looks nothing like Doris Day. And I don't mean that in a good way!

If you like the more famous *Annie Get Your Gun*, you will probably like *Calamity Jane* almost as much. Substitute Doris Day as Calamity Jane for Betty Hutton as Annie Oakley, and they have a somewhat similar theme – women of the West who can hold their own against men but are grown-up tomboys who realize they need to also become ladies in order to get their men. (My apologies to the Feminists, I am just describing the basic plot of the two films.)

FORGOTTEN MOVIE STARS OF THE 30's, 40's, and 50's

Calamity Jane is set in Deadwood, Dakota Territory; the town, of course, is largely the home of men, where Indian scout Calamity Jane is as hard-riding, boastful, and handy with a gun as any man; quite an overpowering personality. But the army lieutenant she favors (played by Phillip Carey) doesn't really appreciate her finer qualities. One of Jane's boasts – that she can get a famous actress from Chicago, Adelaid Adams, to entertain the boys from South Dakota, brings her to the Windy City to recruit the star for the Golden Garter stage. Not knowing what Ms. Adams looks like, Calamity Jane thinks that Adams' maid is really Adelaid Adams, and the maid does not tell her otherwise; so Calamity Jane brings back the maid to Deadwood instead of the real Adelaid Adams.

Arriving in Deadwood, the maid eventually confesses to Jane that she is a phony, but the boys in town hear her sing and like her anyway. The rest of the film finds the two women becoming good friends while vying for the affections of the lieutenant as well as Jane's good buddy and rival, Wild Bill Hickok (Howard Keel). The two women end up with the guys they were destined to end up with, and all's well that ends well in Deadwood, at least for the time being. As you may remember, Wild Bill Hickok was eventually shot and killed in a card game in Deadwood.

This is really Doris Day's film, but Keel acts up a storm as Wild Bill Hickok with enough singing and bravado to appease his fans. He looks and acts like a musical Wild Bill Hickok would act and is perfect in the part. Unlike *Annie Get Your Gun*, there is only one really good song in this movie, "Secret Love," sung beautifully by Doris Day; it won the Oscar for Best Original Song, and rightly so.

And now that I have teased you, here is a picture of the real Calamity Jane – not exactly a double for Doris Day!

FORGOTTEN MOVIE STARS OF THE 30's, 40's, and 50's

I imagine that the real Calamity Jane did not sing nearly as well as Doris Day, either.

6. Annie Get Your Gun - 1950

Betty Hutton and Howard Keel as the leads in *Annie Get Your Gun* – Betty as Annie Oakley, and Howard as her rival and true love, Frank Butler.

FORGOTTEN MOVIE STARS OF THE 30's, 40's, and 50's

The story is a fictionalized version of the life of Annie Oakley (1860–1926), who was a sharpshooter from Ohio, and her husband, Frank Butler. When the travelling Buffalo Bill's Wild West Show visits Cincinnati, Ohio, Frank Butler (Keel), the show's handsome, womanizing star, challenges anyone in town to a shooting match. Foster Wilson, a local hotel owner, doesn't appreciate the Wild West Show taking over his hotel, so Frank gives him a side bet of one hundred dollars on the match. Annie Oakley (Hutton) enters and shoots a bird off a woman's hat while it is still being worn, and then explains her simple backwoods ways to Wilson with the help of her siblings. When Wilson learns she's a brilliant shot, he enters her in the shooting match against Frank Butler.

While Annie waits for the match to start, she meets Frank Butler and falls instantly in love with him, not knowing he will be her opponent. At the shooting match, Annie finds out that Frank is the "big swollen-headed stiff" from the Wild West Show. She wins the contest, and Buffalo Bill and Charlie Davenport, the show's manager, invite Annie to join the Wild West Show. Annie agrees because she loves Frank even though she has no idea what "show business" is.

Over the course of working together, Frank falls in love with the plain-spoken, honest, tomboyish Annie. But her ability to shoot, coupled with her obvious candor at all times, angers Frank enough that he quits the show. Of course, they all get back together at the end, with Annie and Frank tying the knot.

In his first starring Hollywood musical, Howard Keel makes an excellent Wild West musical hero; he is handsome, strapping, and has a great voice. But the film really belongs to Betty Hutton as Annie Oakley. She is simply outstanding in this role – effervescent, outgoing, and completely unflappable, and Keel complements her very well. (Although rumors persist to this day that everyone in the cast found Hutton difficult to get along with.) And the songs are simply outstanding, including

FORGOTTEN MOVIE STARS OF THE 30's, 40's, and 50's

"There's No Business Like Show Business," "Anything You Can Do, I Can Do Better," "Doin' What Comes Natur'lly," "I Got the Sun in the Morning and the Moon at Night," "You Can't Get a Man With a Gun," "The Girl That I Marry," and "I'm an Indian Too." An excellent supporting cast includes Louis Calhern as Buffalo Bill Cody, J. Carroll Naish as Chief Sitting Bull, Edward Arnold, and Keenan Wynn.

To summarize, Howard Keel was really the top male musical star of the 1950's, as one can see from the six films featured above. He had a long Hollywood and stage career, and appeared in such dramatic roles as St. Peter (*The Big Fisherman*) as well as the aforementioned Clayton Farlow from TV's "Dallas." But it is his musicals from the 1950's that we will always remember him for, and rightly so. He was the rare combination of good looks, bravado, masculinity, and a beautiful singing voice and acting talent that is rarely found in the past or present.

FORGOTTEN MOVIE STARS OF THE 30's, 40's, and 50's

Tyrone Power – 1914-1958

Tyrone Power was clearly one of the biggest stars of this era, featured in many swashbuckling movies as well as many other films, including westerns, dramas, and even a courtroom thriller. I was originally not going to include him in this book because I felt he did not meet one of my key criteria – I felt he was still too well known today to be included in the book. In fact, several people who knew I was writing this book just assumed that Tyrone Power would automatically be included, and I said probably not. However, since that time, others have convinced me that his being too well known today is not a problem (apparently most people under 40 have never heard

FORGOTTEN MOVIE STARS OF THE 30's, 40's, and 50's

of <u>him</u> either, including my older daughter, a huge movie fan), so I have reconsidered and included him.

Power, part of a famous acting family dynasty that included his grandfather and father, appeared in many outstanding films between the late 1930's and his untimely death of a heart attack in 1958 at the age of 44. He starred in many classic films, including *The Mark of Zorro, Jesse James,* and *The Razor's Edge,* among others. He was featured in so many swashbuckling roles because of his extremely handsome features, but always sought better roles that he was finally able to achieve in the late 1940's and 1950's. He is a forgotten star who truly should be remembered by movie fans of today.

> All you need to know about how popular Power was, is to understand that in the movie *Jesse James*, Tyrone Power played Jesse James and icon Henry Fonda played his brother, Frank James.

My favorite Tyrone Power films are the following:

- *The Mark of Zorro*
- *Jesse James*
- *Nightmare Alley*
- *Witness for the Prosecution*
- *The Sun Also Rises*
- *The Black Swan*
- *The Razor's Edge*
- *Captain from Castile*

Biography

Tyrone Power was one of the great romantic adventure film stars of the mid-twentieth century, and the fourth Tyrone

FORGOTTEN MOVIE STARS OF THE 30's, 40's, and 50's

Power of four in a famed acting dynasty reaching back to the eighteenth century. His great-grandfather was the first Tyrone Power (1795-1841), a famed Irish comedian. His father, known to historians as Tyrone Power Sr., but to his contemporaries as either Tyrone Power or Tyrone Power the Younger, was a huge star in the theatre (and later in silent films) in both classical and modern roles. His mother, Patia Riaume, was also a Shakespearean actress as well as a respected dramatic coach.

Tyrone Edmund Power Jr. (also called Tyrone Power III) was born in his mother's hometown, Cincinnati, Ohio, in 1914. Because young Tyrone was a frail, sickly child, the family moved to the warmer climate of southern California. After his parents' divorce, he and his sister Anne returned to Cincinnati with their mother. There he attended school while developing an obsession with acting after appearing in school plays. Although raised by his mother, he also corresponded with his father, who encouraged his son's acting dreams. He was an uncredited performer in his father's stage production of "The Merchant of Venice" in Chicago when his father died in his arms in 1931.

> His father suffered a heart attack in December 1931, dying in his son's arms onstage. That definitely inspired the younger Power to follow in his father's footsteps and become an actor.

Unbelievably handsome even by Hollywood standards, Power early on struggled to find work in Hollywood. He appeared in a few small roles, then went East to do stage work. A screen test led to a contract at 20th Century Fox in 1936, and he quickly progressed to leading roles. Within a year or so, he was one of Fox's leading stars, playing in contemporary and period pieces with ease. Most of his roles were colorful without much depth of charactter, and his swordplay was more praised than his dialogue. He served in the Marine Corps in World War II as a pilot.

After the war, he got his best reviews for an atypical part as a downward-spiraling con-man in *Nightmare Alley* (1947). Although he remained a huge star, much of his post-war work was unremarkable. He continued to do notable stage work and also began producing films. Following a stirring performance in Billy Wilder's *Witness for the Prosecution* (1957), Power began production on *Solomon and Sheba* (released in 1959 with Yul Brynner in the role of Solomon). Halfway through shooting, he collapsed during a swordfighting scene with actor and good friend George Sanders and died of a heart attack before reaching the hospital.

Power was only 44 years old at the time of his death.

> The filmmakers used some of the long shots that Tyrone Power had filmed before his death, and an observant fan can even see him in some of the scenes, particularly in the middle of the duel.

Recognition

Power received a Bambi Award (German film festival awards for international excellence) in 1952. He also has a star on the Hollywood Walk of Fame at 6747 Hollywood Boulevard.

My Favorite Tyrone Power Films

FORGOTTEN MOVIE STARS OF THE 30's, 40's, and 50's

1. The Mark of Zorro - 1940

Tyrone Power and his enemy Basil Rathbone in a scene from *The Mark of Zorro*, with Power playing Don Diego Vega and of course, Zorro.

The first and perhaps best sound version of the Zorro story starred Tyrone Power as the man in the black mask (not the iron mask). Set in 1820's California, the son of a California nobleman comes home from Spain to find his native land under a villainous dictatorship. Don Diego Vega (Power) decides on a course of action that will achieve results while not hurting his family.

On the one hand he plays the useless fop whom no one could suspect of taking any action at all, while on the other he is the masked avenger Zorro, saving California from the dictator, whose lieutenant is Captain Esteban, played by Basil Rathbone. (Rathbone plays basically the same role as he did in *The Adventures of Robin Hood*, as Guy of Gisborne in that film.) Linda Darnell plays the love of his life, Lolita Quintero,

FORGOTTEN MOVIE STARS OF THE 30's, 40's, and 50's

who is in love with the dashing Zorro but finds the effeminate Diego Vega completely unappealing. Of course, after a series of adventures, Zorro drives out the villains and restores order and democracy to Southern California.

In spite of the fact that Power did not look one bit Hispanic, he is very dashing and effective in the role. Handsome, daring, athletic, and witty, he is the epitome of a hero in this landmark swashbuckler. A strong supporting cast includes Gale Sondergaard and Eugene Pallette.

> Basil Rathbone was actually an excellent fencer; yet he always lost his on-screen swordfights because he was the villain. He often ended up coaching the actors playing the good guys.

2. Jesse James – 1939

Tyrone Power as Jesse James and Henry Fonda as Frank James in quieter times during *Jesse James*.

FORGOTTEN MOVIE STARS OF THE 30's, 40's, and 50's

As the film opens, the railroads are squeezing farmers off their land, including the Great Plains and Missouri. When a railroad agent kills their mother, Frank and Jesse James get their revenge by taking up robbing banks and trains. While the railroads and the law consider them to be villains, the public regards them as heroes.

This movie definitely develops the case that the James brothers were well intentioned but misguided rather than mean outlaws – not necessarily true if you read the non-fictional accounts of the James brothers. In reality Jesse was a rather brutal killer, including murdering innocent people.

The motion picture follows the triumphs, tribulations, and problems of the James brothers and their friends, and the end of Jesse: When Jesse finally retires, his erstwhile friend Robert Ford shoots him in the back to get the reward money.

This movie is very effective because of the pairing of Tyrone Power as Jesse James and Henry Fonda as his brother Frank. They receive almost equal screen time, with Jesse as the central figure and Frank as his loyal brother and best friend. Power and Fonda play off each other very well, and Fonda went on, of course, to make a number of westerns throughout his long career. Power is very effective playing a good but misunderstood Jesse James.

This movie's supporting cast includes Nancy Kelly, Randolph Scott (a Forgotten Star), Henry Hull, Brian Donlevy, Donald Meek, Jane Darwell, and John Carradine as Bob Ford, Jesse's friend, who shoots him in the back for the reward money.

By the way, a sequel titled *The Return of Frank James*, followed, starring Fonda. In the sequel Frank tracks down the Ford brothers while attempting to clear his name and the name of his brother.

3. Nightmare Alley – 1947

FORGOTTEN MOVIE STARS OF THE 30's, 40's, and 50's

In one of those "the jig is up" moments, two-timing Stan (Tyrone Power) is caught by our buddy - strongman Mike Mazurki - while his two lady friends Zeena (Joan Blondell – furthest left) - and Molly (Coleen Gray – right of Joan Blondell) – look on. I told you Mazurki always played heavies!

Tyrone Power was always seeking roles where he could demonstrate his acting ability as opposed to his skills as a swashbuckler. He found just such a role in *Nightmare Alley*, a morbid but compelling post-World War II drama centered around the more sleazy aspects of carnival life. Ambitious carnival barker Stan Carlisle (Power) introduces the act of mentalist Zeena (Joan Blondell), who is assisted by her drunken and barely functional husband Pete. Power carries on a romance with Zeena as well as with another circus performer, Molly, played by Coleen Gray. When Stan accidentally provides Pete with a bottle of wood alcohol instead of gin, Pete dies and leaves Zeena without a partner for her act. Her act revolves around a code between the mentalist

FORGOTTEN MOVIE STARS OF THE 30's, 40's, and 50's

and her sidekick to fool the audience, and Stan convinces her to take him on as her partner and teach him the code. She does, and Zeena's new act is better than ever.

Eventually, Stan marries Molly and the two of them strike out for greener pastures using the code, this time with con man Stan as the mentalist and Molly as his assistant. They are performing in the best nightclubs and making lots of money, but it just isn't good enough for Stan. He sets upon a scheme – with the help of a local psychologist – to fleece really wealthy people out of their money by attempting to establish contact with dead relatives.

All is going well until Stan's callous plan to con a millionaire by conjuring up the man's dead daughter (a plan that Molly cannot go along with) backfires and leaves him running from the law. Stan and Molly end by separating, with Stan now wanted by the police and fleeced out of $150,000 by the even more conniving psychologist. Molly returns to circus life while Stan becomes an alcoholic drifter, winding up at Molly's carnival playing the lowest form of carnival life – the "Geek," a job seemingly only taken by alcoholic crazy people.

> Tyrone Power relished parts like this, where he was able to play more than just a handsome swashbuckler. He is a real rascal in this film.

This no-holds-barred, highly original drama shows a morbid but fascinating look at carnival life. Power moves from a low-level but ambitious carnival barker to a top-notch mentalist, only to fall to the lowest form of carnival life as the Geek. He is charming as always, but also manipulative, and at the same time vulnerable in a way that Power was never seen before or after. An outstanding supporting cast features Gray, Blondell,

FORGOTTEN MOVIE STARS OF THE 30's, 40's, and 50's

Helen Walker as the psychologist who is even shrewder than Power, and ex-pro wrestler Mike Mazurki as the carnival strongman.

> This film is a must see for anyone who thinks that Power never played anything but heroes and swashbucklers. He is anything but a hero in this film.

4. Witness for the Prosecution – 1957

Leonard Vole (Tyrone Power) pleads with Charles Laughton to take his murder case while another attorney, played by Henry Daniell, looks on. Then Vole takes the witness stand later on in *Witness for the Prosecution*. He looks very worried in both pictures – after all, he is on trial for murder.

FORGOTTEN MOVIE STARS OF THE 30's, 40's, and 50's

This film adaptation of an Agatha Christie novel features an all-star cast including Tyrone Power, Charles Laughton, Elsa Lanchester, and Marlene Dietrich. When seemingly innocent Leonard Vole is arrested for the sensational murder of a rich, middle-aged widow that he had befriended, the famous barrister Sir Wilfrid Robarts (Laughton) agrees to appear on his behalf. Sir Wilfrid, recovering from a near-fatal heart attack, is *supposed* to be on a "diet" of lighter food and easier court cases. This one turns out to be anything but easy.

His housekeeper (Lanchester) is trying to protect his health, but Wilfred proves a difficult patient. And the lure of the criminal courts is too much for him, especially when the case is as difficult as this one is: Vole's only alibi witness is his wife, the calm and coldly calculating Christine Vole (Marlene Dietrich), whom Vole married while stationed in Germany during World War II. Sir Wilfrid's task becomes even more impossible when Christine agrees to be a witness not for the defense but for the prosecution. The trial moves forward to a spellbinding conclusion, with Sir Wilfrid postponing his cruise for at least one more legal defense.

FORGOTTEN MOVIE STARS OF THE 30's, 40's, and 50's

This film is one of the best courtroom dramas ever made, primarily because of an outstanding script and terrific performances by the three leads. Laughton has never been better as the cranky but brilliant defense attorney who senses there is something wrong with this case but cannot put his finger on it. Dietrich is simply outstanding as the wife who has more than a few tricks up her sleeve. And Power is very good in an offbeat role for him – a complete nebbish in all appearances; we believe he is innocent, but is he telling the truth? The final 30 minutes of the film are completely spellbinding, with twists and turns galore. An outstanding, mostly English supporting cast includes Henry Daniell, Torin Thatcher, Una O'Connor, and a young Ruta Lee.

> The film includes one of the great movie lines of all time, uttered by a gypsy woman whom Laughton encounters - "I'll give ya somethin' to dream about, Mister. Wanna kiss me, ducky?"

Witness for the Prosecution was the last film Tyrone Power made. He died a year later while filming *Solomon and Sheba*.

5. The Sun Also Rises - 1957

with Ava Gardner

FORGOTTEN MOVIE STARS OF THE 30's, 40's, and 50's

(Previous page) An older, more mature Tyrone Power consoling the love of his life, played by Ava Gardner, in a taxi in *The Sun Also Rises*.

This motion picture, based on the Hemingway novel of the same name – the first of Hemingway's great novels – centers around the lives of a group of disillusioned, hedonistic American expatriates living in Paris around and after the end of World War I. American journalist Jake Barnes (Power) and his friends, principally fellow writer Robert Cohn (Mel Ferrer), spend their free time at cafes and bars. Jake has a special interest in his ex-fiancée, Lady Ashley (Ava Gardner). Barnes was injured during World War I and was left impotent as a result, apparently causing the strain in their relationship. As we learn, Gardner plays an alcoholic as well as a collector of men.

Jake runs into an old writer buddy (Eddie Albert). The two of them go fishing in Spain before deciding to attend the bullfights and annual running of the bulls in Pamplona. There, they meet up with a group that includes Lady Ashley, Cohn (smitten with Lady Ashley) and Lady Ashley's new fiancé, Scotsman Mike Campbell (Errol Flynn), and the five friends spend their time drinking, fighting each other, and attending the bullfights, where Lady Ashley meets and goes on vacation with a 22 year old bullfighter. Of course, that affair does not work out, and it appears that Power and Gardner will be reunited at the end of the flick.

The film is definitely autobiographical in nature, with the story demonstrating the lives of the American expatriates living in Paris after the War who came to be known as the Lost Generation. Power campaigned for better parts toward the end of his career, and this was definitely one of them. Power, Gardner, and especially Errol Flynn are outstanding in this film version of the Hemingway novel. It was the last really

FORGOTTEN MOVIE STARS OF THE 30's, 40's, and 50's

good role for Flynn, who was pretty much washed up at this time from a lifetime of overindulgence.

> "The Lost Generation" was a term coined by author Gertrude Stein and included Hemingway, John Steinbeck, T.S. Elliott, F. Scott Fitzgerald, and John Dos Passos, among others.

6. The Black Swan – 1942

Dashing Tyrone Power in a duel in *The Black Swan*.

After England and Spain make peace, former brigand Sir Henry Morgan (Laird Cregar) is named Governor of Jamaica in 1674. He soon announces that the era of the pirate is over and asks his former captains to give up their ways and sail for the good of England. Not every pirate agrees, however, and one in particular, Captain Leech (George Sanders), refuses to give up his pirate ways. Leech does accept an offer, however, from English aristocrat Roger Ingram, who provides him with sailing information in an attempt to unseat the newly appointed Governor by aligning himself with the unrepentant pirates.

When Morgan is unable to stop the actions of his old shipmates, he is suspected of still being allied with them. In an effort to thwart Ingram's plans and aid his friend Morgan, former pirate Captain Jamie Waring (Power) kidnaps Lady Margaret Denby, the previous governor's daughter and fiancée of Ingram, in an effort to get to the bottom of things. Naturally, Waring and Lady Denby (Maureen O'Hara) fall in love, and things work out for England and those on the side of good.

Power is excellent in his typical swashbuckler/leading man role, and is especially good as a pirate who fights for the cause of England. He is surrounded by a wonderful supporting cast that includes Maureen O'Hara, Laird Cregar, George Sanders, Thomas Mitchell, and Anthony Quinn, among others.

7. The Razor's Edge – 1946

Tyrone Power and the beautiful Gene Tierney, from a scene early on in *The Razor's Edge*.

FORGOTTEN MOVIE STARS OF THE 30's, 40's, and 50's

This first and best film version of the W. Somerset Maugham novel about a young man trying to discover the meaning of life featured an all-star cast including Tyrone Power, Gene Tierney, John Payne, Herbert Marshall, Clifton Webb, and Ann Baxter. Webb was nominated for an Oscar for Best Supporting Actor for this film, and Baxter won an Oscar as Best Supporting Actress. The basic plot of the melodrama centers around Power, a disenchanted World War I veteran who leaves his home in Chicago to travel around the world to find the meaning of life – sounds like the 1960's! He and his fiancée, Tierney, agree to rekindle their love after he has "found himself" and determined what he wants to do with the rest of his life. Ten years later he resurfaces, affecting the lives of everyone around him. Most of the movie takes place in Paris, with Power and Tierney playing the leads and the others playing key supporting roles as relatives or friends.

This film is another effort by Power to remove himself from swashbuckler roles and prove that he could act, and he is excellent in the role of the disenchanted veteran who must travel the world to find meaning in life.

8. Captain from Castile - 1947

Power on right

FORGOTTEN MOVIE STARS OF THE 30's, 40's, and 50's

(Previous page). Several of the stars from *Captain from Castile* – from left to right, Lee J. Cobb, Jean Peters, Caesar Romero, and Tyrone Power as the Captain from Castile. Romero plays explorer Hernando Cortez.

> Cobb had a distinguished career as a supporting actor and was the most hardened juror in the Henry Fonda version of *Twelve Angry Men*. He was also the union boss in *On the Waterfront*. Cobb was nominated for Oscars for Best Supporting Actor for *On the Waterfront* and again for *The Brothers Karamazov*, but did not win for either movie.

Captain from Castile is an exciting adventure tale about the first Spanish expedition to Mexico under the leadership of Hernando Cortez. In Spain in 1518, young landlord Pedro De Vargas (Tyrone Power) offends his sadistic neighbor De Silva, who just happens to be an officer of the Inquisition, by aiding a servant of De Silva's to escape to freedom.

As an officer, De Silva is able to imprison Vargas' father, mother, and sister and kills the sister when the family refuses to declare themselves as heretics. After that, Vargas seeks revenge against the man who killed his innocent sister. Forced to flee after he believes he has killed De Silva, Pedro, friend Juan Garcia (Lee J. Cobb), and adoring servant girl Catana (Jean Peters) flee Spain for Cuba and join Hernando Cortez' (Caesar Romero) first expedition to Mexico. Arriving in the rich new land, Cortez decides to switch from exploration to conquest because of the wealth he sees.

FORGOTTEN MOVIE STARS OF THE 30's, 40's, and 50's

Embroiled in continuous adventures and a romantic interlude, Pedro almost forgets he has a deadly enemy, De Silva, until the latter reappears as an emissary of the Spanish king. Then Vargas must decide whether to honor his family or hold to the promise he made to the expedition's priest about not seeking revenge against his enemies.

Captain from Castile is an excellent movie, more of an adventure flick than a swashbuckler, although there are a few swordfights as one would expect in a Tyrone Power film. As always, Power is noble, gallant, and surprisingly human in the lead as the Captain. Jean Peters plays his love, Catana, in her first film, and Caesar Romero is excellent as the explorer Cortez. A strong supporting cast includes Lee J. Cobb, Alan Mowbray, John Sutton as De Silva, and Thomas Gomez.

> Watch for Jay Silverheels (Tonto in the "Lone Ranger" television show with Clayton Moore as the Lone Ranger) as the servant whose life is saved by Vargas.

Tyrone Power made any number of good flicks throughout his career. Other good Tyrone Power films include the following:

- *Son of Fury*
- *Rawhide*
- *Pony Soldier*
- *The Black Rose*
- *In Old Chicago* – his mother's cow started the Chicago fire!
- *Alexander's Ragtime Band*
- *The Eddy Duchin Story*

FORGOTTEN MOVIE STARS OF THE 30's, 40's, and 50's

The more one looks at Tyrone Power, the more one realizes what a talent he was. He was effortless in swashbuckling roles but equally good in dramatic parts that allowed him to demonstrate his acting ability. The films listed above are just a sample of the many good films he made. It is really a shame that he passed away at the age of 44, just when he was beginning to demonstrate a real talent for acting.

This is one forgotten star who should never be forgotten.

FORGOTTEN MOVIE STARS OF THE 30's, 40's, and 50's

Jean Simmons - 1929-2010

Jean Simmons was an English beauty and versatile actress who became a star in films at the age of 19. She played in a variety of parts and always appeared to be appropriate for that role, whether it was as a noble Roman, a Salvation Army worker, a religious zealot, a western heroine, a devious villainess, or the wife of a slave in ancient Rome. She handled herself well in almost every part she ever played in her almost six decade career in movies. In fact, in her obituary in the *New York Times*, the newspaper stated that her talent often exceeded the roles she played.

Simmons was a bit younger than most of the stars in this book. Her heyday was in the 50's and 60's, but a good number of her best roles were in movies in the 50's.

FORGOTTEN MOVIE STARS OF THE 30's, 40's, and 50's

My favorite Jean Simmons films are the following:

- *Spartacus*
- *Guys and Dolls*
- *Elmer Gantry*
- *Angel Face*
- *The Robe*
- *The Big Country*

Biography

Jean Merillyn Simmons was born January 31, 1929, in Crouch End, London to Charles Simmons and his wife, Winifred (Loveland) Simmons. She moved into acting through her early training as a dance student. As a 14-year-old, she was selected by her school to play Margaret Lockwood's precocious sister in *Give Us the Moon* (1944), and she went on to make a name for herself overseas in such major British productions as *Caesar and Cleopatra* (1945), *Great Expectations* (1946) (as the spoiled, selfish Estella), *Black Narcissus* (1947) (as a native beauty), *Hamlet* (1948) (playing Ophelia and earning a Best Supporting Actress Oscar nomination), *The Blue Lagoon* (1949) and *So Long at the Fair* (1950), among others.

In 1950, at the age of 21, she married British actor Stewart Granger. Jean came to Hollywood in the early 1950s after her contract was sold to Howard Hughes, a practice not uncommon at the time. Hughes tried unsuccessfully to have an affair with the newly-married Simmons, a not unusual action for Hughes.

> It seems as if Hughes had or tried to have affairs with about half the women in this book.

FORGOTTEN MOVIE STARS OF THE 30's, 40's, and 50's

Spurned by Simmons, Hughes took his revenge by refusing to lend Jean to director William Wyler, who wanted her to star in *Roman Holiday*, the film that would bring Audrey Hepburn an Oscar and make her a star. And, according to Granger, when Ms. Simmons refused to sign a seven-year contract with RKO, the studio Hughes had bought in 1948, he threatened "to put her in three lousy productions that would ruin her career." As it turns out, one of those movies, *Angel Face* (1952), a film noir directed by Otto Preminger and co-starring Robert Mitchum, was actually an excellent film – one of my choices below - featuring a solid performance by Simmons, playing one of the movies' most beautiful killers. She had to do four pictures for Hughes; after that experience, she never signed a contract with a studio again.

> Howard Hughes was one of the most colorful characters of the 20th century. He was a business magnate, investor, aviator, aerospace engineer, film maker, and philanthropist. He was one of the wealthiest people in the world, and also very strange.

In her first movie after her contract with Hughes ended — *Young Bess* (1953) at MGM — Ms. Simmons starred as the spirited and headstrong young woman who would become queen of England. *Young Bess* was the first American movie in which Ms. Simmons played opposite Granger.

In 1953, Jean Simmons also played the determined title character in *The Actress*, an MGM film based on Ruth Gordon's autobiographical play, "Years Ago." Then she slipped quietly into supporting roles of women who were subordinate to strong men. For example, she was the noble Roman who walked to her death with Richard Burton in *The Robe* (1953), when she refused to abandon her Christian faith. In *The*

FORGOTTEN MOVIE STARS OF THE 30's, 40's, and 50's

Egyptian (1954), set 13 centuries before Christ, she was the shy tavern maid who secretly loved the film's hero, a physician. As *Desiree* (1954), she was mistress to Marlon Brando's Napoleon. And she was excellent in musicals as the strait-laced Sergeant Sarah Brown of the Save-a-Soul Mission, who was charmed by Brando's Sky Masterson in *Guys and Dolls* (1955).

> In *Guys and Dolls*, she employed her own singing voice and earned her first Golden Globe Award.

Simmons divorced the reportedly-abusive Granger in 1960 and almost immediately married writer-director Richard Brooks, who cast her as Sister Sharon opposite Burt Lancaster in *Elmer Gantry* (1960), a memorable adaptation of the Sinclair Lewis novel and a starring role for Simmons. That same year she co-starred with Kirk Douglas in Stanley Kubrick's *Spartacus* (1960), perhaps her most famous role, and played a would-be home wrecker opposite Cary Grant in *The Grass Is Greener* (1960).

> Most movie fans will say their favorite Stanley Kubrick film is *2001: A Space Odyssey*, but my favorite Kubrick flick is *Spartacus*. I guess I like films about ancient Rome better than futuristic movies about outer space filled with all kinds of symbolism that I can't understand.

FORGOTTEN MOVIE STARS OF THE 30's, 40's, and 50's

Off the screen for a few years, she was excellent in a brilliant performance as the mother in *All the Way Home* (1963), a literate, tasteful adaptation of James Agee's "A Death in the Family." After that, however, as she neared 40, she found quality projects somewhat harder to come by, and took work in lesser films such as *Life at the Top* (1965), *Mister Buddwing* (1966), *Divorce American Style* (1967), *Rough Night in Jericho* (1967), and *The Happy Ending* (1969) (a Richard Brooks film for which she was again Oscar-nominated, this time as Best Actress).

Jean continued making films well into the 1970s. In the 1980s she mainly appeared in TV mini-series, such as "North and South" (1985) and "The Thorn Birds" (1983). Jean made a comeback to films in 1995 in *How to Make an American Quilt* (1995) co-starring Winona Ryder and Anne Bancroft, and more recently played the elderly Sophie in the English version of Hayao Miyazaki's *Howl's Moving Castle* (2004). She died in 2010 at the age of 80.

Recognition

Unlike most of the forgotten stars in this book, Jean Simmons performed in an era – the 1950's and after – where movie stars received a lot more recognition than they did previously. You can tell by the amount of well-deserved acknowledgement she received during her long career.

Jean Simmons was nominated for two Oscars: Best Actress in a Leading Role for *The Happy Ending* in 1970 and for Best Actress in a Supporting Role, for *Hamlet* in 1949. She won an Emmy Award for Outstanding Supporting Actress in a Limited Series or Special for "The Thorn Birds" in 1983 and was nominated for an Emmy for Outstanding Guest Actress in a Drama Series for her performance in "Murder, She Wrote" in 1989.

She won Golden Globes for Best Actress in a Musical Comedy for *Guys and Dolls* in 1956 and a special Golden Globe for Most Versatile Actress in 1958. Simmons was nominated for a Golden Globe for *The Thorn Birds* (1984), *The Happy Ending* (1970), *Elmer Gantry* (1961), *Home Before Dark* (1959), and *This Could Be the Night* (1958). She also won an award from the Venice Film Festival as Best Actress for her performance in *Hamlet* in 1949. She received many other nominations for her work from organizations such as BAFTA, the Screen Actors Guild, and the Laurel Awards.

My Favorite Jean Simmons Films

1. Spartacus – 1960

Slave girl Jean Simmons serving wine to Crassus (Lawrence Olivier) and Batiatus (Peter Ustinov) in *Spartacus*. Ustinov is the owner of the gladiator training center where Spartacus (Kirk Douglas) and Varinia (Simmons) first meet and fall in love. This scene takes place before the slaves revolt.

FORGOTTEN MOVIE STARS OF THE 30's, 40's, and 50's

The 1960 Stanley Kubrick classic is certainly one of the best of the epic-type films, ranking right up there with *Ben Hur* and *Lawrence of Arabia*. It tells the story of a Thracian slave who led a slave revolt against the Roman empire in 73 B.C. This uprising took place just when Rome was reaching its heyday and was quite a shock to the new empire. But the movie's theme of freedom fighting against tyranny is a universal theme that has never been illustrated better. It is one of my 10-15 all-time favorite movies.

In 73 BC, a Thracian slave named Spartacus is captured and sent to the gladiatorial training school run by Lentulus Batiatus (Peter Ustinov). There he sees men being treated like animals in the arena as sport for the wealthy Romans who happen to be passing by on their journey to and from Rome.

After his friend Draba (played by Woody Strode) is brutally slain when he refuses to kill Spartacus in the arena for the sport of four visiting Romans, Spartacus and his fellow gladiators overpower the guards and claim their freedom. Then, Spartacus leads a revolt designed not to merely create havoc but to actually obtain freedom for the gladiators. The uprising soon spreads across Italy involving thousands of slaves (reportedly 70,000 according to recent books).

Spartacus' plan is to acquire sufficient funds to hire ships from Silesian pirates who could then transport them from Brandisium in the south of Italy to other lands not under the control of the Roman Empire at that time. The Roman Senator Gracchus (Charles Laughton) schemes to have Marcus Publius Glabrus, Commander of the garrison of Rome, lead an army against the slaves who are living on Vesuvius. When Glabrus is defeated, his mentor, Senator and General Marcus Licinius Crassus (Lawrence Olivier) is greatly embarrassed and leads his own army against the slaves.

FORGOTTEN MOVIE STARS OF THE 30's, 40's, and 50's

Spartacus and the thousands of freed slaves successfully make their way to Brandisium only to find that the Silesians have abandoned them – there are no ships waiting to take them away from Italy. They then turn north and must face the might of Rome. Of course, they are no match for the best legions in the Roman army. Those who did not die in battle are crucified by Rome as a warning to anyone else planning to rebel against Rome. However, on the cross Spartacus achieves his goal as he sees his baby son being escorted by his wife to their freedom.

Everything about this film is wonderful. The cast features Kirk Douglas as Spartacus, Jean Simmons as his wife Varinia, Charles Laughton, Lawrence Olivier, Peter Ustinov in his Oscar-winning performance as the owner of the gladiator training school, Tony Curtis, John Ireland, Woody Strode as the gladiator who refuses to kill Spartacus in the arena, John Gavin, Charles McGraw, and many others. The movie is very inspirational, the plot very interesting, and the battle scenes exceptional.

Kirk Douglas and Jean Simmons make an exceptional pairing as husband and wife, realizing that their time together must be meaningful because it is likely to be short lived. Jean Simmons has Lawrence Olivier, Peter Ustinov, and Kirk Douglas all vying for her, and I can easily understand why.

> In reality, Spartacus wanted to cross over the Alps and make his escape into central Europe, but he could not convince his followers to make that journey. If they had, thousands of them would have likely survived. But the prospect of crossing the Alps to get into Europe was too daunting a task for his followers, so they remained in Italy instead.

FORGOTTEN MOVIE STARS OF THE 30's, 40's, and 50's

2. Guys and Dolls - 1955

Left to right. The quartet of Marlon Brando, Jean Simmons, Frank Sinatra, and Vivian Blaine in *Guys and Dolls*. Sinatra and Blaine were terrific in their roles, Simmons very good in hers, and Brando okay as Sky Masterson, a part that should have been played by Gene Kelly.

Guys and Dolls is an outstanding musical about Damon Runyon-type characters in New York City who are gamblers in search of a spot for their illegal gambling game (the Guys) and the "Dolls" who they are matched up with, for better or for worse. Nathan Detroit (Frank Sinatra) has been engaged forever to singer Miss Adelaide (Vivian Blaine), and all she wants to do is give up her singing career at the local nightclub, get married to Nathan, buy a house in the suburbs with a picket fence, and raise a bunch of kids. Nathan prefers a long courtship, which has now been going on about 20 years.

FORGOTTEN MOVIE STARS OF THE 30's, 40's, and 50's

Sky Masterson (Marlon Brando), the best of the gamblers, against his better judgment falls for the straight-laced Salvation Army recruiter Sergeant Sarah Brown (Simmons) in a seemingly impossible match, based on her distaste for gambling and his lack of reverence. He bets Detroit that he can take Sarah Brown on a date to Havana, Cuba. Another bet requires him to convince a group of gamblers who are only interested in finding a location for their next crap game, to attend the mission meeting. It seems he has promised Sister Sarah a group of sinners for her next meeting.

Overall, this is one of my favorite musicals. The music by Frank Loesser is terrific, the production values and costumes are great, and the dancing outstanding. It includes some of my favorite songs from musicals – "Luck Be a Lady Tonight," "Sit Down You're Rocking the Boat," "Adelaide's Lament," "Guys and Dolls," and "If I Were a Bell" – and the production numbers are first rate throughout. Sinatra and Blaine are both outstanding, Jean Simmons is very appealing as Sarah Brown – you can see that she could be both a Salvation Army bell ringer as well as a real "doll" – and Brando is OK as Sky Masterson.

Actually, Brando has a decent singing voice and is overall at least satisfactory, but the part should have been played by Gene Kelly, who unfortunately was not available at the time – he was under contract to another studio, MGM, who would not release him to make this film.

> This film must have been a real challenge for the director, because it featured stars with two completely different acting styles. Brando, the method actor, wanted about 40 takes for every scene before he got comfortable, while Sinatra was known for his insistence on trying to do every scene in one take.

As I indicated, Jean Simmons won a Golden Globe award for her performance in this movie.

3. Elmer Gantry – 1960

Jean Simmons as lay preacher Sister Sharon in *Elmer Gantry*.

Elmer Gantry is an outstanding motion picture that won all kinds of awards, including Best Picture and Best Actor at the Oscars. The film is about a fast talking, hard drinking traveling salesman (Burt Lancaster as Elmer Gantry) who always has a story and a hip flask to entertain cronies and customers alike. He is immediately taken with Sister Sharon Falconer (Jean Simmons), a lay preacher whose hellfire and damnation revivalism has attracted quite a following and press coverage.

FORGOTTEN MOVIE STARS OF THE 30's, 40's, and 50's

Gantry uses his own quick wit and knowledge of the bible to become an indispensable part of Sister Sharon's road show troop but soon finds that his past catches up with him in the form of Lulu Bains (Shirley Jones), now a prostitute. While Gantry seeks and eventually gets forgiveness from Sharon, tragedy strikes when she finally manages to get out of her revivalist tent and open a permanent church.

Elmer Gantry was a huge hit and won Oscars for best actor (Lancaster), best supporting actress (Shirley Jones), and best writing. But Jean Simmons is the focal point as the enigmatic Sister Sharon, who is spellbinding yet very vulnerable in her role. And who knew that Shirley Jones, the sweetheart from *Oklahoma* and *Carousel*, could act like that? An outstanding supporting cast includes Arthur Kennedy as a member of the press, Dean Jagger, Hugh Marlowe, and singer Patti Page.

> Here's an "OOPS" in this picture. At one point, Elmer Gantry refers to Christ's miracle of feeding the 5,000 with five fishes and two loaves of bread. According to the Gospels, it was five bread loaves and two fishes.

4. Angel Face - 1952

Simmons and Mitchum

FORGOTTEN MOVIE STARS OF THE 30's, 40's, and 50's

(Previous page) Robert Mitchum and Jean Simmons in an early scene from *Angel Face*. Watch out for her!

When Mrs. Tremayne is mysteriously poisoned with gas, ambulance driver Frank Jessup (Robert Mitchum) meets her refined but sensuous stepdaughter Diane (Jean Simmons), who quickly pursues and infatuates him. Under Diane's seductive influence, Frank is soon the Tremayne chauffeur; but he begins to suspect lurking danger under her surface sweetness. When he shows signs of pulling away, Diane schemes to get him in so deep via marriage that he'll never be able to leave.

This is Jean Simmons' first American movie and an outstanding example of film noir. She is paired with Mitchum, the perfect male film noir star, and the combination is very successful. Is she sweet and innocent, or a monster under that veneer? A good cast includes Herbert Marshall as her father, Leon Ames, and Mona Freeman.

5. The Robe - 1953

Richard Burton and Jean Simmons as star-crossed lovers in *The Robe*.

FORGOTTEN MOVIE STARS OF THE 30's, 40's, and 50's

This big-budget Hollywood religious spectacle stars Richard Burton and Jean Simmons as the noble and dedicated Romans who become Christians and Victor Mature as Burton's Greek slave Demetrius. Marcellus (Burton) is a tribune in the time of Christ. He is in charge of the group that is assigned to crucify Jesus. Drunk, he wins Jesus' homespun robe after the crucifixion. However, upon his return to Rome, he is tormented by nightmares and delusions after the event.

Hoping to find a way to live with what he has done, and still not believing in Jesus, he returns to Palestine to try and learn what he can of the man he killed. Simmons, as Diana, is his fiancée and then wife, and both are encouraged to become Christians by the Greek slave Demetrius (Mature). Forced to choose between Rome and Christianity by the new Roman emperor, the crazy Caligula, they choose the path of Christianity, which unfortunately brings them the utter distaste of the new emperor.

An excellent biblical movie, this movie features three top stars in the lead roles. Simmons is perfectly cast as the beautiful, noble Roman Diana, who is in search of something more. Mature is outstanding as the Greek slave who finds Christianity. Frankly, Burton is somewhat stilted in the lead as Marcellus. An excellent supporting cast features Jay Robinson as Caligula (how he failed to win an Oscar as Caligula is unbelievable), Michael Rennie in one of his several roles as the disciple Peter, Dean Jagger, and Richard Boone of "Have Gun Will Travel" television fame, where he played Paladin, as Pontius Pilate.

> Jay Robinson returned as Caligula in *Demetrius and the Gladiators*. Truly, one of the worst Roman emperors but a great performance.

6. The Big Country - 1958

Jean Simmons and Chuck Connors in a scene from *The Big Country*. Believe it or not, Simmons actually prefers handsome, smart, and gentle Gregory Peck over the brutish Chuck Connors. This is Chuck Connors just before his days as *The Rifleman*.

The Big Country is a sprawling 1958 western with a terrific cast in a story about two bull-headed ranchers fighting for decades over water rights. Retired, wealthy sea captain James McKay (Gregory Peck) arrives in the vast expanse of the West to marry fiancée Pat Terrill (Carol Baker). McKay is a man whose values and approach to life are a mystery to the ranchers, and ranch foreman Steve Leech (Charlton Heston) takes an immediate dislike to him. Pat is spoiled, selfish and controlled by her wealthy father, Major Henry Terrill (Charles Bickford).

FORGOTTEN MOVIE STARS OF THE 30's, 40's, and 50's

The Major is involved in a ruthless civil war over water rights for cattle, against a rough clan led by Rufus Hannassey (Burl Ives). The land in question is owned by Julie Maragon (Jean Simmons) and both Terrill and Hannassey want it. After all, access to water was a key factor in owning cattle in the Old West.

McKay quickly decides on a conciliatory approach designed to have both men compromise to get what they want; for that, he is unjustly branded a coward by most, including his fiancée Pat Terrill.

As it turns out, he is much more attracted to Julie (Simmons) who, like him, simply cannot understand why men would fight to the death over water rights. Only she seems to understand why it would be better to negotiate a settlement that satisfies everyone rather than fighting about it.

A series of adventures takes place, including Julie willing to marry the brutish son of Hannassey (Chuck Connors in a good role). In the end, the two ranchers do indeed fight to the death, and after they kill each other, the audience is left with the feeling that perhaps reason will take over.

The Big Country is one of those sprawling, bigger than life westerns with simply an outstanding cast, including Gregory Peck, Jean Simmons, Charlton Heston, Carol Baker, Chuck Connors, Charles Bickford, and Burl Ives, as the meanest man west of the Pecos – this is the same Burl Ives who recorded Christmas songs like "Holly Jolly Christmas!" Peck has the lead and is his usual effective self, with Simmons in a part that demonstrates depth of character.

Everyone in the cast was good, with standout performances from Peck, Ives (Oscar winner for Best Supporting Actor), Connors, and Bickford.

FORGOTTEN MOVIE STARS OF THE 30's, 40's, and 50's

> This film was made just before Chuck Connors was cast in his most famous role, as TV's "Rifleman." Connors was originally a baseball player and played for my favorite team, the Chicago Cubs and their minor league club, the L.A. Angels. He was discovered while playing baseball for the Angels. Had the Cubs never sent him to the minors, he might never have been a star. (That's the Cubs for you – recognizing talent, even if it's not baseball talent!)

Jean Simmons was an English beauty whose film career included a variety of roles in different types of films. She was nominated for two Oscars and won two Golden Globe awards. Her career extended well into the 1990's.

She certainly deserves a place in this book.

FORGOTTEN MOVIE STARS OF THE 30's, 40's, and 50's

Jean Arthur – 1900-1991

Jean Arthur was a wonderful star of some great romantic comedies and serious dramas in the 1930's and 1940's. She was not what you would call drop-dead gorgeous, but instead blonde and cute. But her main asset was a wonderful squeaky but at the same time appealing voice that came to fruition in a variety of wonderful roles during that time period. Her career actually began during the silent film era of the 1920's and continued for the next 30+ years in movies and television. She even had her own TV show in 1966 that lasted for only 11 weeks, but she did not perform in movies or TV after that.

FORGOTTEN MOVIE STARS OF THE 30's, 40's, and 50's

Jean Arthur worked with some of the best male stars in the world at the time, including Cary Grant, Gary Cooper, John Wayne, James Stewart, Ronald Colman, Joel McRae, and Alan Ladd, and always held her own in that company.

For my money, she did her best work in romantic comedies and Frank Capra-type uplifting dramas.

My favorite Jean Arthur films – and there were many to choose from – are the following:

- *Mr. Deeds Goes to Town*
- *Mr. Smith Goes to Washington*
- *You Can't Take It with You*
- *Talk of the Town*
- *The More the Merrier*
- *The Plainsman*
- *Shane* – as in "Come back, Shane!"

Biography

Jean Arthur was born Gladys Georgianna Greene in upstate New York, 20 miles south of the Canadian border, in 1900. She was discovered by Fox studios while doing commercial modeling in the early 1920's. Following her screen debut in a bit part in John Ford's *Cameo Kirby* (1923), she spent several years playing unremarkable roles as an ingénue or leading lady in silent films, mainly comedy shorts and cheaply-made westerns. With the arrival of sound she appeared in movies whose quality was only slightly better than that of her past silent films. Her career bloomed with her appearance in Ford's *The Whole Town's Talking* (1935), in which she played opposite Edward G. Robinson, with Robinson in a dual role as a notorious gangster and his lookalike, a weak and timid clerk. This film showcased her flair for romantic comedy that she mastered in later roles.

FORGOTTEN MOVIE STARS OF THE 30's, 40's, and 50's

> I did not realize that Jean Arthur was in silent films, but it makes sense. After all, she was born in 1900, which would have made her 27-28 when the first talkies appeared.

The turning point in her career came when she was chosen by Frank Capra (she made three top-quality films with Capra) to star with Gary Cooper in the classic social comedy *Mr. Deeds Goes to Town* (1936). Here she rescued the hero from greedy human vultures who plot to separate him from his wealth. In Capra's masterpiece *Mr. Smith Goes to Washington* (1939), she again rescued a besieged hero (James Stewart), protecting him from a band of manipulative and cynical politicians and their cronies.

> Manipulative and cynical politicians and their cronies – I see nothing has changed in the 75+ years since this flick was made.

For her performance in George Stevens' *The More the Merrier* (1943), in which she starred with Joel McCrea and Charles Coburn, she received a Best Actress Academy Award nomination, but the award went to Jennifer Jones in *The Song of Bernadette*. (Coburn, incidentally, won for Best Supporting Actor for this film). She appeared in a number of other quality films during this period of time, from the mid 1930's through about the mid 1940's.

FORGOTTEN MOVIE STARS OF THE 30's, 40's, and 50's

Jean's career began waning toward the end of the 1940s, partly because by then she was in her late 40's, and in those days, similar to today, leading ladies just did not have as much staying power as leading men.

She starred with Marlene Dietrich and John Lund in Billy Wilder's fluff about post-World War II Berlin, *A Foreign Affair* (1948). Thereafter, Arthur returned to the screen just once, again for George Stevens but not in comedy. She starred with Alan Ladd and Van Heflin in Stevens' western classic *Shane* (1953), playing the wife of a besieged settler (Heflin) who accepts help from a secretive gunman (Ladd) in the settler's effort to protect his farm. It was her silver-screen swansong.

In 1966 she starred as a witty and sophisticated lawyer, Patricia Marshall, a widow, in the TV series "The Jean Arthur Show" (1966). Her time was apparently past, however; the show ran for only 11 weeks. She also taught acting classes at the university level after her retirement.

In spite of her outgoing, bubbly personality onscreen, off screen Arthur was known as a reclusive woman. News magazine *Life* observed in a 1940 article: "Next to Greta Garbo, Jean Arthur is Hollywood's reigning mystery woman." As well as recoiling from interviews, she avoided photographers and refused to become a part of any kind of publicity. This was quite different from her typical on-screen roles, where she generally played extroverted characters.

She died in 1991 at the age of 91. By the way, her stage name came from two of her greatest heroes – Joan of Arc and King Arthur.

> And her favorite leading man was – Gary Cooper.

FORGOTTEN MOVIE STARS OF THE 30's, 40's, and 50's

Recognition

Jean Arthur received an Oscar nomination for Best Actress in a Leading Role for *The More the Merrier* in 1943. She has a star on the Hollywood Walk of Fame at 6333 Hollywood Boulevard.

My Favorite Jean Arthur Films

1. Mr. Deeds Goes to Town – 1936

Gary Cooper and Jean Arthur in a publicity still from *Mr. Deeds Goes to Town*. Gary Cooper plays eccentric millionaire Longfellow Deeds. Arthur is the newspaper columnist who at first thinks he is strange but comes to believe in him and what he stands for.

FORGOTTEN MOVIE STARS OF THE 30's, 40's, and 50's

This movie is a real treasure, a timeless screwball comedy made during the depression era and directed by Frank Capra, that reminds us all of the values that are really important in life. Longfellow Deeds – Gary Cooper - lives in a small town in the East (Mandrake Falls, Vermont), leading a very modest and unpretentious kind of life - including playing the tuba in the town band.

When a relative dies and leaves Deeds a fortune, Longfellow picks up his tuba and moves to the big city – New York - where he becomes an instant target for everyone from the greedy opera committee looking for money to the daily newspaper in search of a story because of his naiveté and lack of concern for material possessions.

Deeds outwits them all until Babe Bennett – Jean Arthur - comes along. Babe is a hot-shot reporter who figures the best way to get close to Deeds and get her story is to pose as a damsel in distress. At first, she leads him on solely to get her story, then eventually realizes he really is not a publicity hound but a nice guy who really does not need a lot of money to be happy.

Ultimately, however, Deeds is put on trial by his own lawyers and financial people for wanting to give his money away. They want him institutionalized because they say he is mentally incompetent (after all, what person in his/her right mind would want to give their money away?).

At the trial, Deeds at first refuses to stand up for himself. As a result, things are going really badly for him until he is forced at last by the presiding judge to defend his sanity. Then we find out who is really "pixilated," Deeds or the Mandrake Falls Faulkner sisters and the greedy lawyers, with Babe believing in Deeds throughout the trial.

FORGOTTEN MOVIE STARS OF THE 30's, 40's, and 50's

This is clearly a classic Gary Cooper movie – a regular guy forced to defend himself against the power of greed – but Jean Arthur is also outstanding and completely believable as the reporter who at first is only out for a story until she finds the real inner beauty of the seemingly wacky Mr. Deeds.

This is the film that made a star out of Jean Arthur, and one can easily see why. She is really cute but also very likeable in this role. A good supporting case includes George Bancroft, Lionel Stander, Douglass Dumbrille, and H.B. Warner. You might get "pixilated" from watching this comedy classic, which won an Oscar for Best Director for Capra and was nominated to several others, including Cooper for Best Actor and the film for Best Film.

2. Mr. Smith Goes to Washington – 1939

James Stewart and Jean Arthur share a taxi in *Mr. Smith Goes to Washington*. He is obviously happy about being a new Senator.

FORGOTTEN MOVIE STARS OF THE 30's, 40's, and 50's

The governor of an unnamed Western State has to pick a replacement to the U.S. Senate for the recently deceased senator from that state. He appoints naive and idealistic Jefferson Smith (James Stewart), leader of the Boy Rangers, to be the new senator. Upon arriving at the Senate, Smith is reunited with and taken under the wing of the state's senior senator/presidential hopeful, best friend of his deceased father and Smith's childhood hero, Senator Joseph Paine (Claude Rains).

In Washington, however, Smith discovers many of the shortcomings of the political process. He is deemed a bumpkin by the press as his earnest goal of a national boys' camp in his state leads to a conflict with the state political boss, Jim Taylor (Edward Arnold). Taylor first tries to corrupt Smith and then later attempts to destroy Smith through a completely false conflict of interest scandal against him. Smith has worked closely with Senator Paine's secretary, Clarissa Saunders (Jean Arthur) in developing the bill, and she comes to realize that Smith is in fact not a country bumpkin but rather the type of bright and honest individual who should be in the Senate.

But Senator Paine stands aside while Taylor and his crew of crooks come up with phony evidence of an apparent conflict of interest against Smith – they produce fraudulent evidence that Smith actually owns the land he is proposing for the camp and will profit enormously from the camp. Believing in him, Saunders talks Smith into launching a filibuster to postpone the appropriations bill until he can prove his innocence on the Senate floor just before the vote to expel him from the Senate.

Nearly broken by the news that the machine is overcoming his efforts to prove his innocence, Smith still vows to press on until people believe him, but eventually faints from sheer exhaustion on the floor of the Senate. Overcome with guilt,

FORGOTTEN MOVIE STARS OF THE 30's, 40's, and 50's

Paine leaves the Senate chamber and attempts to commit suicide by shooting himself. When he is stopped, he bursts back into the Senate chamber, loudly confesses to the whole scheme, and vehemently affirms Smith's innocence, to the delight of all.

> The most famous scene in this movie – the one shown all the time – is where James Stewart, exhausted from his filibuster, is holding and sifting through all the letters supporting his efforts. Arthur is in the gallery in this scene, rooting him on. When he finally faints from exhaustion, we think all is lost – but that is not necessarily the case.

This is truly one of the great Frank Capra comedy dramas, and James Stewart (Oscar nominee for Best Actor) has never been better than in this role as the heroic Senator Jefferson Smith. Jean Arthur is very capable as the woman who thinks of him as a bumpkin but comes to realize he is a lot more than that. A truly superb supporting cast includes Claude Rains, Edward Arnold, Thomas Mitchell, Guy Kibbee, Eugene Paulette, Beulah Bondi, and Harry Carey (the actor, not the baseball announcer) as the Senate President. The theme of honesty versus political corruption is just as prominent today as it was when this film was made in 1939 – maybe more so.

3. **You Can't Take It with You – 1938**

Next page. Director Frank Capra, Lionel Barrymore, and Jean Arthur on the set of *You Can't Take It with You*. Barrymore is the patriarch of the family and Arthur his granddaughter in this wonderful comedy.

FORGOTTEN MOVIE STARS OF THE 30's, 40's, and 50's

This Oscar-winning picture (Best Picture and Best Director for Frank Capra) from 1938 is an absolutely wonderful comedy that features Jean Arthur, James Stewart, and an all-star supporting cast of character actors in madcap roles.

Stenographer Alice Sycamore (Jean Arthur) is in love with her boss Tony Kirby (James Stewart), who is the vice-president of the powerful company owned by his greedy and heartless father Anthony P. Kirby (Edward Arnold). Kirby Sr. is organizing a monopoly in the trade of munitions, and needs to buy one last house owned by Alice's grandfather Martin Vanderhof (Lionel Barrymore) in a twelve block area in order to complete the project. However, Martin is the patriarch of an anarchic and eccentric family where the members are not fixated on making money.

Martin's daughter (Spring Byington) is a wacky playwright who has never sold a play and who uses her cat as a paperweight for her plays. His son in law (Samuel S. Hinds) makes fireworks in the basement; why? Because he never grew up. Alice's sister (a young Ann Miller) is a dancer with no talent, and her husband (Dub Taylor) is an ex-Alabama

FORGOTTEN MOVIE STARS OF THE 30's, 40's, and 50's

football player who plays Chopin on the xylophone. When Tony proposes to Alice, she states that it would be mandatory to introduce her simple and lunatic family to the snobbish Kirbys, and Tony decides to pay a surprise visit to Alice and her relatives one day before the scheduled dinner party, to catch them as they really are. Big mistake!

There is an inevitable clash of classes and lifestyles, the Kirbys spurn the Sycamores, and the entire party is arrested and placed in jail for illegally making fireworks, In court, the elder Kirby realizes how much Vanderhof really possesses – friends – compared to how little he himself possesses (money) because, after all, you can't take it with you. Because of the embarrassment, Alice breaks with Tony, changing the lives of the Kirby family. Martin decides to bow to pressure and sell to Kirby, but as in any Frank Capra movie, you know that good will prevail and the seemingly heartless person will end up saving the day.

This outstanding film demonstrates that you can in fact make a terrific comedy without the cheap tricks employed in most romantic comedies today. Everybody in this wacky film is just outstanding, with the two leads – Arthur and Stewart – as the straight ones in the group. While they are excellent in their parts, they are probably outdone by the members of the cast in the zanier roles. Additional supporting cast members include Mischa Auer as a wacky dance instructor, Eddie Anderson (Rochester on the Jack Benny Show), Donald Meek, and H.B. Warner.

> Lionel Barrymore could easily have been nominated for an Oscar for this movie but was not. He did win an Academy Award in 1931 as Best Actor for *A Free Soul*.

FORGOTTEN MOVIE STARS OF THE 30's, 40's, and 50's

> The idea of Ann Miller as a dancer who can't dance is certainly preposterous. In real life, Ann Miller was an outstanding dancer who partnered with Fred Astaire, Gene Kelly, Mickey Rooney, and others in a number of big musicals, including *Easter Parade, On the Town,* and *Kiss Me Kate*.

Here is Ann Miller- center- in a scene from *On the Town*, dancing with Betty Garrett, Frank Sinatra, Jules Munshin, Vera-Ellen, and Gene Kelly, about three sailors on a 24-hour pass in New York City.

This film is as relevant today as it was when it was made in 1938. When the tax collector shows up unexpectedly at the Vanderhof house and demands that Martin pay several years' worth of back taxes, Martin proudly says, "Why should I?" "Well, to support Congress, the President, and the Supreme Court," replies the tax collector. "Not with my money!" Replies Vanderhof, showing that politics was a mess even in 1938.

4. The Talk of the Town - 1942

Three great stars – Cary Grant, Ronald Colman, and Jean Arthur – in a scene from *The Talk of the Town*.

This outstanding comedy, which received seven Oscar nominations, stars Cary Grant, Jean Arthur, and Ronald Colman. Grant plays Leopold Dilg, an innocent man but a social activist who is wrongly accused of a crime he did not commit – arson at the factory where he works, coupled with murder, since the foreman also apparently died in the fire. To avoid what seems like a certain conviction and execution, Dilg breaks out of jail and takes refuge in the first house he can find, which happens to be owned by his former school mate, Nora, played by Jean Arthur. Nora's houseguest, just arriving for the summer, is a legal scholar, played by Ronald Colman, who teaches law at the state university and has come to town for the summer to write a book. Dilg poses as the gardener, and the three begin a real friendship, especially the two men. Colman knows all about the law and its principles but has no real experience in applying it. Layman Dilg is the practical man whose only concern is fairness and accuracy in applying the law. A series of adventures follows, with the three of them involved together in resolving what Dilg must do to clear himself and regain his good name.

FORGOTTEN MOVIE STARS OF THE 30's, 40's, and 50's

Even with Cary Grant and Ronald Colman in this film, it is actually Jean Arthur whose performance makes the film memorable. She is in most every scene with Grant and Colman, has the most screen time of the three, and really is the one who holds the film together. She acquits herself very well as the landlady who has one invited guest and another unexpected one and must balance what she knows about Grant so as not to disclose his real identity. She needs to show both a serious and comedic side in this movie, and she does.

> The banter between Grant and Colman, and their realization that both of them have excellent points to make about "the law," really makes this movie shine.

The Talk of the Town was nominated for seven Academy Awards but did not win any. *Mrs. Miniver* and *Pride of the Yankees* were the big Oscar winners that year.

5. The More The Merrier – 1943

Jean Arthur with one of her renters, Benjamin Dingle (Charles Coburn), in *The More the Merrier*.

FORGOTTEN MOVIE STARS OF THE 30's, 40's, and 50's

This delightful romantic comedy was made during the height of World War II, when there was a severe housing shortage, especially in Washington, D.C. with all the government jobs available. Connie Milligan (Jean Arthur) rents an apartment. Believing it to be her patriotic duty, she offers to sublet half of her apartment, fully expecting a suitable female tenant. What she gets instead is mischievous, middle-aged Benjamin Dingle (Charles Coburn). Dingle talks her into subletting to him, and then he promptly meets Sergeant Joe Carter (Joel McCrea), who has no place to stay while he waits to be shipped out overseas shortly. Dingle solves the problem by subletting half of his half to the young, irreverent Carter - creating a situation tailor-made for comedy and romance.

When Connie finds out about the new arrangement, she orders them both to leave, but she is forced to relent because she has already spent their rent money. Joe and Connie are of course attracted to each other, though she is engaged to well-paid government bureaucrat Charles J. Pendergast (Richard Gaines). It seems that Connie's mother married for love, not security, and Connie is determined not to repeat her mistake. But Dingle happens to meet Pendergast at a business luncheon and does not think he is a suitable mate at all for the delightful and perky Connie. He decides that Joe would be a better match for his landlady. The rest of the film involves a series of adventures related to mistaken identity, whether or not McCrea's character is a spy, and related escapades.

> Government bureaucrats never seem to fare well in these films. I was a government bureaucrat for over 25 years, and can personally attest to the fact that we are wonderful and exciting people, not at all dull.

Jean Arthur again is terrific as the perky but stable landlady who is trying to help the country while not making the same mistakes her mother did. McCrea is a suitable leading man and Coburn is really good as the mischievous Mr. Dingle. Look for former *Tarzan* Bruce Bennett as an FBI agent in this film. Jean Arthur received her only Best Actress Oscar nomination for this film, but she lost out to Jennifer Jones for *The Song of Bernadette*. Charles Coburn, however, did win an Oscar for Best Supporting Actor as the irrepressible Mr. Dingle.

> And the film was nominated for Best Picture but lost out to a fairly good film of its own merit – *Casablanca*. You may have heard of it.

6. The Plainsman - 1936

Gary Cooper as Wild Bill Hickok and Jean Arthur as Calamity Jane in a scene from *The Plainsman*. I have seen pictures of Calamity Jane, and she did not look anywhere near that good. In fairness, Hickok was not exactly Gary Cooper handsome either.

FORGOTTEN MOVIE STARS OF THE 30's, 40's, and 50's

Made in the same year as *Mr. Deeds Goes to Town*, this western classic again teams up Gary Cooper and Jean Arthur, in this case Cooper as Wild Bill Hickok and Arthur as the woman who loves him, Calamity Jane. At the end of the Civil War, Bill Hickok, Buffalo Bill, and others with an adventurous spirit are looking to the West as the next great frontier to settle. At the same time, the manufacturers of repeating rifles find a profitable means of making money by selling the weapons to the North American Indians in the West, using the front man John Lattimer to sell the guns to the Cheyenne, Sioux, and other tribes. The assassination of President Lincoln only serves to fuel their greed.

While travelling in a stagecoach with Calamity Jane, William "Buffalo Bill" Cody, and Buffalo Bill's young wife Louisa Cody (who plan to settle down in Hays City, Kansas and manage a hotel), Wild Bill Hickok finds the guide Breezy wounded by arrows; Breezy tells Hickok that the Indians are attacking a fort using repeating rifles. Hickok meets Gen. George A. Custer, who assigns Buffalo Bill to guide a troop with ammunition to help the fort. Meanwhile, the Cheyenne kidnap Calamity Jane, forcing Hickok to expose himself to rescue her. Back at the Cheyenne camp, Calamity Jane must either tell the Indians where Buffalo Bill and the troops are located, or they will kill the man she loves. Of course, she cannot bear to witness the execution of Bill Hickok, and that action leads to several battles with the Cheyenne and Sioux Indians. Custer's last stand and the shooting of Hickok in Deadwood, South Dakota are also part of the film.

The Plainsman is an excellent western primarily because of the pairing of the always stalwart Gary Cooper as Hickok and Jean Arthur as Calamity Jane. While she certainly does not look like the real Martha Jane Canary, who became known as Calamity Jane, Arthur is believable as the rough and tough frontier woman with a soft spot for Wild Bill. Cecil B. DeMille

FORGOTTEN MOVIE STARS OF THE 30's, 40's, and 50's

directed this flick, which pretty much guarantees great scenery, lots of action, a good plot, and its fair share of dopey dialogue. But it is a good western nonetheless. The movie also features James Ellison in a very good performance as Buffalo Bill, Charles Bickford as the villain Lattimer, Helen Burgess as Louisa, and a cameo role for Gabby Hayes as the scout Breezy.

> If you are looking for a sympathetic portrayal of the plight of the Native American, this is NOT your movie. Try *Devil's Doorway* (see Robert Taylor section of this book) instead.

7. Shane – 1953

An older and more mature Jean Arthur with Alan Ladd in her last feature film, *Shane*. She is the good frontier wife married to hard working Van Heflin, but there is also a definite attraction to the drifter, Shane, played by Alan Ladd in his most famous role. ("Come back, Shane").

FORGOTTEN MOVIE STARS OF THE 30's, 40's, and 50's

This is one of the great westerns of all time, and Alan Ladd's signature role, as Shane, a drifter who manages to hook up with a group of settlers attempting to build a future through farming and growing crops as opposed to raising cattle. This was a common theme in many westerns, even including the musical *Oklahoma!* A drifter/gunman named Shane rides into a conflict between cattleman Ryker and the settlers, like the Starretts (Van Heflin and Jean Arthur), whose land Ryker wants. The last thing that Shane wants is trouble, but he decides to stay and help the settlers in their fight against overwhelming odds with the ranchers. Shane is eventually forced to take a stand when the cattlemen force him into a situation where he can no longer back away but must stand and fight. When Shane (surprising the ranchers) beats up Ryker's man Chris, Ryker then tries to buy him off. Of course, that does not work either, and Shane and Joe Starrett are forced to take on the whole Ryker crew. Ryker sends to Cheyenne for truly evil gunslinger Wilson (Jack Palance), supposedly even faster with a gun than Shane. There is also definitely some developing chemistry between Shane and Joe's wife Marian Starrett.

When the Ryker crew continues to harass and kill the settlers, Shane decides that peaceful co-existence is just not going to work. He decides he must personally clear out all the guns from the valley before he can ride off, with the Starretts' son Joey hollering "Shane ... Shane ... Come Back!" That leads to the inevitable fight to the finish between Shane and Wilson (Jack Palance, a really mean guy in this film).

This terrific western has a number of good themes – peaceful settlers against cattle ranchers, a gunman who wants to give up that life, the value of a hard working but more mundane existence versus an exciting life, the ability to turn one's life around, and even a woman's attraction to her solid hardworking husband versus the excitement of a gunman.

FORGOTTEN MOVIE STARS OF THE 30's, 40's, and 50's

Alan Ladd has never been better in the role of a guy whose actions speak louder than his words – another typical western theme. Van Heflin is excellent as the solid farmer trying to make a life for his family through hard work. And Jean Arthur is a lot more than the wife who cooks, cleans, and manages the house. The supporting cast is wonderful – Jack Palance, Edgar Buchanan, Elisha Cook, Jr., Ben Johnson, and child star Brandon De Wilde as Joey Starrett, whose utterance of "Come Back, Shane" is of course legendary.

Overall, Jean Arthur was a good actress whose distinctive voice made her a very popular star in the 1930's and 1940's. She was equally versatile in comedies and dramas and was matched up with some of Hollywood's premier stars of that era, especially her pairings with Gary Cooper and James Stewart. My guess is that she would have had even a longer career had she been born about ten years' later; she was already in her late 30's when she began hitting her stride – a rather old age for leading ladies in those days.

Unlike many stars of today, she was a lot more than mere window dressing or eye candy in her roles and as such, deserves to be remembered.

FORGOTTEN MOVIE STARS OF THE 30's, 40's, and 50's

Gail Russell – 1924-1961

If you are a fan of John Wayne, as I am, you are probably familiar with Gail Russell, even if you did not know it. She was a particular favorite of Wayne's and starred with him in a couple of really good films – The *Angel and the Badman* and *Wake of the Red Witch*. They remained good friends for the rest of her life. Unfortunately, her problems with alcohol cost her the complete stardom that she probably would have otherwise received, and led to her untimely death at age 36 caused most likely by her addiction to alcohol. The combination of her beauty plus a certain fragility was actually quite appealing. Unfortunately that frailty continued off screen with her addiction and death at such an early age. While the sheer number of her films was not impressive, the quality of her performances and her ability to light up the screen in those films was definitely worth noting.

FORGOTTEN MOVIE STARS OF THE 30's, 40's, and 50's

My favorite Gail Russell films are:

- *The Angel and the Badman*
- *Wake of the Red Witch*
- *The Uninvited*
- *Seven Men from Now*

Biography

Gail Russell was born in my hometown, Chicago, Illinois on September 21, 1924. She remained in the Windy City until her parents moved to California when she was 14. She was an above average student in school and upon graduation from Santa Monica High School was signed by Paramount Studios. Her mother had convinced her to take a screen test during her high school days, and Paramount executives apparently liked what they saw.

Because of her rare beauty, Gail was to be groomed to be one of Paramount's top stars. Unlike many starlets who had considerable experience on the stage, she was very shy with virtually no acting experience to speak of, but her beauty was so apparent that the studio figured they could work with her on her acting skills by way of an acting coach that Paramount employed.

Gail's first film came at the age of 19 when she had a small role as Virginia Lowry in *Henry Aldrich Gets Glamour* (1943). It was her only role that year. The following year she appeared in her first quality motion picture, *The Uninvited*, with Ray Milland.

> It was also apparently the first time Gail used alcohol to steady her nerves on the set. As it turned out, not a good move.

FORGOTTEN MOVIE STARS OF THE 30's, 40's, and 50's

The Uninvited was a horror story very well done for its day and importantly also a profitable one for the studio. Her third film co-starred Gail and Diana Lynn in *Our Hearts Were Young and Gay* (1944). The film was based on a popular book of the time, and the film was even more popular than the book.

In 1945, Gail appeared in *Salty O'Rourke* (1945), a story about crooked gamblers involved in horse racing. Although she wasn't a standout in the film, Gail worked well as part of the supporting cast. Later that year, Gail appeared in *The Unseen* (1945), another story about a haunted house and starring Joel McCrea. Gail played Elizabeth Howard, a governess of the house in question. The film turned a profit, but was not the hit that executives hoped for. In 1946, Gail was again teamed with Diana Lynn for a sequel to *Our Hearts Were Young and Gay* called *Our Hearts Were Growing Up* (1946). The plot centered around two young college girls getting involved with bootleggers. Unfortunately, the film was not anywhere near the caliber of the first film, and it failed at the box-office.

> If it had been a success, there might have been other entrees as the two women got older, leading to *Our Hearts Were on Medicare*.

With *Calcutta* in 1947, Gail bounced back in a more popular film which starred Alan Ladd. That same year, Gail was cast with John Wayne and Harry Carey – again, the actor, not the baseball announcer - in *The Angel and the Badman*. The western was a popular one with the public, and Gail shined in the role of Penelope Worth. Still later, Gail appeared in Paramount's all-star musical called *Variety Girl* (1947). The critics roasted the film, while the public turned out in droves to ensure its success at the box-office.

FORGOTTEN MOVIE STARS OF THE 30's, 40's, and 50's

Next came what I consider her best film, *Wake of the Red Witch* (1948), a seafaring adventure with John Wayne, who seemed to bring out the best in her.

After the releases of *Song of India* (1949), *El Paso* (1949), and *Captain China* (1950), Gail married Guy Madison, one of the up and coming actors in Hollywood.

> You may remember Guy Madison, whose most famous role was as Wild Bill Hickok, in the 1950's television series of the same name, with Andy Devine as his friend, Jingles Jones. "Hey, Wild Bill, wait for me!"

After *The Lawless* in 1950, Paramount decided against renewing her contract because of Gail's increasing drinking problems; she had been convicted of operating a motor vehicle while under the influence of alcohol. The studio didn't want its name mired with a movie star who couldn't control her drinking.. After *Air Cadet* in 1951, she disappeared from movie sets for the next five years while she attempted to get control of her life. She divorced Madison in 1954.

In 1956, Gail returned to the silver screen in *Seven Men from Now* (1956). It was a Randolph Scott western with Gail being cast in the role of Annie Greer. In 1957, Gail was fourth billed in *The Tattered Dress* (1957), a film which also starred Jeanne Crain and Jeff Chandler. The following year, she had a reduced part in *No Place to Land*. As you can tell, the roles were getting smaller and smaller.

FORGOTTEN MOVIE STARS OF THE 30's, 40's, and 50's

By now, the effects of her alcoholism had clearly taken its toll on her career and her health. She was again absent from the screen until 1961's *The Silent Call*. It was to be her last film. On August 26, 1961, Gail was found dead in her small studio apartment in Los Angeles, California. Death was attributed to malnourishment and a liver ailment caused by her addiction to alcohol. She was only 36 years old.

Recognition

Gail Russell has a star on the Hollywood Walk of Fame at 6933 Hollywood Boulevard.

My Favorite Gail Russell films:

1. **The Angel and the Badman – 1947**

John Wayne (the badman,) and Gail Russell (the angel) worked well together in this film. There was always good chemistry between these two in this movie and also in *Wake of the Red Witch*.

FORGOTTEN MOVIE STARS OF THE 30's, 40's, and 50's

Quirt Evens (John Wayne) is an all-around tough guy, maybe not a bad person but certainly with a checkered and criminal past. As the film begins, Quirt is wounded and on the run. He rides onto a farm owned by Quaker Thomas Worth and his family and promptly collapses from exhaustion.

The daughter, Penelope Worth (Gail Russell) immediately sees something of value in him, and personally takes charge of nursing Quirt back to health. During the recovery period, she explains to him the Quaker code of non-violence and what it means to her. It is clear that a romance is beginning to bud between Quirt and Penelope, in spite of her Quaker values and his reputation as a gunman.

After recovering, Quirt decides to stay on and help the family with chores as a farmhand. He actually helps end a feud peacefully between Thomas Worth and a neighbor over water rights, and is given a Bible at a Quaker gathering for his help in settling the dispute in a peaceful way. More and more, Quirt is torn between his violent past and the non-violent ways of the Quakers and the woman he has come to love.

The rest of the film demonstrates this struggle between Quirt attempting to begin a new life while being tempted by his past. Throughout this entire period, the local marshal – played by veteran western actor Harry Carey - warns Quirt that he is the wrong man for Penny and will inevitably wind up at the end of a rope. Quirt's old adversaries appear and cause a situation in which Penny is injured and clinging to life. Quirt decides to exact his revenge against the two gunmen.

In town, Quirt is about to draw down on the two gunmen when Penny and her family arrive in their wagon. No longer driven by revenge, Quirt surrenders his gun to Penny. As the villains prepare to gun down a now-unarmed Quirt, the town marshal appears and shoots both outlaws.

FORGOTTEN MOVIE STARS OF THE 30's, 40's, and 50's

After Quirt renounces lawlessness in favor of farming and rides off in the Worths' wagon with Penny, the marshal picks up Quirt's discarded weapon from the dust. He says he will hang it on his office wall - "with a new rope." He is now convinced that Quirt will settle down, and his days as a badman are over.

This black and white western features an excellent performance by John Wayne as the gunman attempting to redeem himself, guided by Russell, who is very good as the shy, devout Quaker girl. The attraction between the two stars helps make this film a much better than average western. A strong supporting cast includes Bruce Cabot – the romantic lead in the original 1933 version of *King Kong* – as an outlaw.

Harry Carey, actor

Harry Caray, Cub announcer

FORGOTTEN MOVIE STARS OF THE 30's, 40's, and 50's

2. Wake of the Red Witch – 1948

Ill-fated lovers John Wayne as Captain Ralls and Gail Russell as Angelique in *Wake of the Red Witch*.

Wake of the Red Witch is another John Wayne/Gail Russell film made one year after the successful *Angel and the Badman*. This unusual John Wayne vehicle – one that reminds me of *Reap the Wild Wind*, one of my favorite films - is full of all kinds of plot twists and is set in the East Indies in the 1860's. The focus of the film is the deadly rivalry between two men of the sea.

Ship's captain Ralls (John Wayne) carries a long-standing grudge against shipping magnate Mayrant Sidneye (Luther Adler). The reason for the animosity: Sidneye stole away Ralls' true love, Angelique (Gail Russell).

FORGOTTEN MOVIE STARS OF THE 30's, 40's, and 50's

The story of the love between Ralls and Angelique is told in a series of flashbacks by two of the supporting cast – Gig Young and Adele Mara. Revenge has warped Ralls to the point that sometimes he seems to be the heavy of the picture, as much as Adler, who is the real villain in the film.

Complications involving valuable pearls ensue before the offbeat climax, which finds Rails scuttling his own vessel, the Red Witch, as a means of getting even with Sidneye. The film's resolution – Ralls undertaking a dive for the pearls while Sidneye watches from the deck of the ship - is one of the strangest ever concocted for a Wayne picture.

The Wake of the Red Witch has a lot of similarities to *Reap the Wild Wind*, including a climactic underwater diving scene. Also, in both films the female character is the centerpiece of the film – in the previous film, Paulette Goddard, and in this movie, Gail Russell.

Wake represented the second screen teaming of John Wayne and Gail Russell, and as in the earlier film, they make an excellent romantic teaming. Gail Russell's character's fragility comes through very strongly in this film. She is perfectly cast for this flick.

> This film obviously had great significance for John Wayne, since he named his own production company – Batjac – after the name of the shipping company in this film. Wayne produced a number of films, including *The Alamo*, a good film but not a financial success.

3. The Uninvited – 1944

Ruth Hussey, Gail Russell, and Ray Milland in a scene from the eerie film, *The Uninvited*. Gail looks like she has just seen a ghost, and that is a definite possibility in this flick.

A brother and sister (Ray Milland and Ruth Hussey) move into an old seaside house on the English coast that has been abandoned for many years. Their original enchantment with the house diminishes as they hear stories of the previous owners and meet their daughter (Gail Russell, now a young woman) who lives as a neighbor with her grandfather. They also hear unexplained sounds during the night.

It soon becomes obvious to the brother and sister that the house is actually haunted. The reasons for the haunting and how they relate to the daughter, whom the brother (Milland) is falling in love with, prove to be a complex mystery. As they are compelled to solve it, the supernatural activity in the house increases to a frightening level.

FORGOTTEN MOVIE STARS OF THE 30's, 40's, and 50's

This is Gail Russell's first starring role, and at the age of 20, she acquits herself admirably as the young woman haunted by the mystery of the house where she grew up.

4. Seven Men From Now - 1956

An older (32) Gail Russell co-stars with Randolph Scott (the hero, naturally) and Lee Marvin (the villain, naturally) in the classy western produced by John Wayne's Batjac Productions and directed by Budd Boetticher, who directed many of Scott's westerns in the 1950's – (see the section on Randolph Scott).

Ex-sheriff Ben Stride (Scott) is tracking down the seven men who held up an Arizona Wells Fargo office and killed Stride's wife. Stride is tormented by the fact that his own failure to get re-elected as sheriff forced his wife to get a job, which resulted in her working in the express office on the day the office was robbed and she was murdered; thus, he feels responsible for her death. On his journey, Stride encounters a married couple, the Greers – played by Gail Russell and Walter Reed – heading west to California. He helps them free their wagon from the mud.

As they move on, they encounter two disreputable characters – Masters (Lee Marvin) and Clete (Don "Red" Barry), who know that Stride is looking for the express office robbers and the $20,000 in gold that they stole. The two ne'er-do-wells plan to let Stride lead them right to the bandits, then make away with the gold themselves. Of course, no Randolph Scott movie would be complete without some type of Indian threat, and in this case it comes from the Chiricahua Apache. Eventually we learn that Masters and Clete aren't the only ones with a plan– John Greer is also at least somewhat involved in the stolen gold. The entire crew moves toward the meeting place where the gold is to be exchanged for cash, with the inevitable shootings along the way.

FORGOTTEN MOVIE STARS OF THE 30's, 40's, and 50's

Gail Russell is perfect in her role as the dutiful wife accompanying her husband on their journey from out East to California. She is eight years older than in *The Wake of the Red Witch,* and while still beautiful, shows the same type of fragility as in earlier roles. And she probably looks a bit older than her 32 years, while still drawing the attention of most of the male cast.

The film is beautifully photographed, which certainly adds to its aura. A good supporting cast includes John Larch, John Beradino, and Stuart Whitman in a brief role as a cavalry lieutenant warning Stride and his party about the Chiricahua uprising.

In films like the four I mentioned, Gail Russell proved that she was a brunette beauty with a vulnerability that I found very attractive. It was unfortunate that her inner demons resulted in an all-too-brief movie career and early death at age 36.

FORGOTTEN MOVIE STARS OF THE 30's, 40's, and 50's

Lizabeth Scott - 1922-

Lizabeth Scott was very attractive, blonde, very sultry, and a darn good actress when given a good role. She specialized in playing bad or misunderstood females where, with a few exceptions, she generally ended up with the leading man and turning out all right. Also, she is the only star from this book who is still alive! In her movie roles, she was not above using her "charms" to get what she wanted. Like me, she is of Czech origin – another point in her favor. She was more of a Lauren Bacall type then a helpless heroine, and I find that to be very appealing in her roles. She certainly would have been an exact opposite of my previous star, Gail Russell, who was always very vulnerable in her roles. After completing her final major film role, Scott signed a recording contract with a subsidiary of RCA Victor Records and recorded an album in 1957. Simply titled *Lizabeth*, the tracks are a mixture of torch songs and playful romantic ballads – very fitting when you consider how well it matched her personality on screen.

> Humphrey Bogart referred to her as "Cinderella with a husky voice." I think that's a pretty good description. She co-starred with him in *Dead Reckoning*.

She did not make a ton of films – only 21 – and wasn't a terrific actress like a Barbara Stanwyck. But I always found her very alluring and sensual. You could never tell whether she was the good girl or the villainess at first and oftentimes not until the very end of the movie – but it was always a joy to watch her on screen. To put this in perspective, if you like Lauren Bacall but prefer blondes over brunettes, you will love Lizabeth Scott.

My favorite Lizabeth Scott films are the following:

- *Too Late for Tears*
- *I Walk Alone*
- *Dead Reckoning*
- *The Strange Love of Martha Ivers*
- *Pitfall*

Biography

Born Emma Matzo in 1922 in Scranton, Pennsylvania to Czechoslovakian parents, Lizabeth Scott studied at the Alvienne School of Drama in New York City. In late 1942, at

FORGOTTEN MOVIE STARS OF THE 30's, 40's, and 50's

the age of 20, she was making only a minimal living with a small Midtown Manhattan summer stock company when she got a job as understudy for Tallulah Bankhead in Thornton Wilder's play "The Skin of Our Teeth." However, Scott never had an opportunity to substitute for Bankhead because Miriam Hopkins was signed to replace Bankhead instead.

Scott then returned to her drama studies and also did some fashion modelling. Soon afterward, Scott was at the Stork Club when film producer Hal Wallis asked who she was, unaware that an aide had already arranged an interview with her for the following day. When Scott returned home, however, she found a telegram offering her the lead for the Boston run of "The Skin of Our Teeth." Since Scott could not turn down this opportunity, she sent Wallis her apologies and went on the road to Boston instead.

At the same time, film agent Charles Feldman saw a photograph of Scott in *Harper's Bazaar* magazine. He admired her natural beauty and took her on as a client. Scott made her first screen test at Warner Brothers, where she and Wallis finally met. Though the test was not that great, the producer recognized her potential and signed her to a contract when he moved from Warner Brothers to rival Paramount. Her film debut was in *You Came Along* (1945) opposite Robert Cummings.

Paramount publicity dubbed Scott "The Threat," in order to create an onscreen persona for her similar to Lauren Bacall or Veronica Lake. Scott's smoky sensuality and husky voice lent itself to the film noir genre and, beginning with *The Strange Love of Martha Ivers* (1946) starring Barbara Stanwyck, Kirk Douglas, and Van Heflin, the studio cast her in a series of noir thrillers. Film historian Eddie Muller has noted that no other actress has appeared in so many noir films, with more than three quarters of her 21 films qualifying as film noir, a natural for her looks and deep, sultry voice.

FORGOTTEN MOVIE STARS OF THE 30's, 40's, and 50's

Shortly after the second film, Wallis resigned and formed his own production company, releasing films primarily through Paramount; among other things, he sought good vehicles for Scott. Soon after, Lizabeth was paired with the duo of Burt Lancaster and Kirk Douglas in *I Walk Alone*, a film noir story of betrayal and vengeance. Scott plays a nightclub singer who provides sympathy and support to Lancaster, recently released from prison.

> If you seem to remember Burt Lancaster and Kirk Douglas being in many films together, you are right. These two friends were in seven films together, including *I Walk Alone*.

In *Dead Reckoning* (1947), Humphrey Bogart plays a wronged man (a noir hero), who struggles to learn the fate of a missing army buddy. Scott is the ex-girlfriend who knows more than she lets on, and uses her beauty and overall allure to keep him on and off track. Scott's next role was in a film noir gem called *Pitfall*. This drama details the fall from grace of an errant suburban husband and father (Dick Powell, also surprisingly effective in a number of film noir classics) at the hands of an alluring femme fatale played by Scott.

Her last really good film was *Too Late for Tears,* where she uses her considerable appeal to take advantage of her husband and also her partner in crime. In spite of her beauty, allure, and excellent acting skills, by the end of 1949 Scott had appeared in nine films, but hadn't achieved the level of stardom and clout that was needed in the studio system to influence the direction of her own career.

From 1950 on, she was never given an opportunity to reach much beyond her usual good girl gone wrong or femme fatale roles she had become known for. She continued to make films

FORGOTTEN MOVIE STARS OF THE 30's, 40's, and 50's

for Paramount, most of which are not particularly compelling. In 1955 Scott, who never married and was never really part of the Hollywood social set, sued Confidential Magazine over allegations concerning her sexual preferences. In 1957 her film career basically came to an end with her role in *Loving You*, Elvis Presley's second movie.

Since 1957 she has seldom been seen except for a few rare television appearances and an American Film Institute tribute to Hal Wallis. Her legacy lives because of her excellent performances in a number of film noir and related classics.

Recognition

Lizabeth Scott has a star on the Hollywood Walk of Fame at 1624 Vine Street.

My favorite Lizabeth Scott movies are the following:

1. Too Late for Tears – 1949

Murderess Lizabeth Scott confronts Don DeFore in a scene from *Too Late for Tears*.

Not her most famous role but perhaps her best one, Lizabeth Scott stars in a murder mystery of a woman who wants to

FORGOTTEN MOVIE STARS OF THE 30's, 40's, and 50's

strike it rich at any cost. A married couple (Lizabeth Scott and Arthur Kennedy) are driving on a secluded highway near Los Angeles one evening when a satchel containing $60,000 is suddenly thrown from a car into the back seat of their convertible. Knowing the money was not intended for them, the husband wants to turn the money into the police, but the wife wants to keep it for a while; they agree to have it checked at the railroad station until they decide what to do with it.

Soon, the wife is visited by a man (Dan Duryea) claiming to be a private detective, but is actually the man for whom the money was intended. He claims the money is his, but the wife wants to split it with him. Things take a definite turn when the husband is determined to turn the money into the police, and the wife decides to remove him, permanently. She conspires with the other man to murder him and make it look like he has run away to Mexico. But naturally, things begin to fall apart when yet another man, claiming to be a war buddy of the husband, shows up and believes that something is rotten in the state of Denmark.

I watched this film for the first time recently and loved it, especially Lizabeth Scott in the starring role. Scott is perfectly cast as the conniving wife who decides that this is her chance to become rich, and no one, not even her husband, is going to stop her. She seems naive but is actually way too much for any of the men who surround her to control – including her husband and newfound accomplice.

A stellar cast includes Arthur Kennedy as the husband, Dan Duryea as her accomplice, and Don DeFore as the supposed war buddy of her husband. But Lizabeth Scott is clearly at the core of the movie. Dan Duryea sums up the constantly double-crossing Scott when he utters the following line: "Don't ever get a heart. I like you just the way you are." This was a very good role for Lizabeth Scott, to be sure. One in which she was

FORGOTTEN MOVIE STARS OF THE 30's, 40's, and 50's

not the girl from the wrong side of the tracks who ends up on the right side of the tracks.

> Dan Duryea was one of those actors who was always the bad guy and who was always deliciously villainous or psycho villainous, whether it was in Westerns or modern day dramas. A pretty normal guy, he once said, "I chose to be the meanest s.o.b. in the movies... strictly against my mild nature, as I'm an ordinary, peace-loving husband and father." If I ever do a book on character actors, Dan Duryea will be in it.

2. I Walk Alone – 1948

Lizabeth Scott as the love interest but much, much more in *I Walk Alone*. That's ex-con and tough but good guy Burt Lancaster on the left and businessman but bad guy Kirk Douglas on the right. Definitely a

FORGOTTEN MOVIE STARS OF THE 30's, 40's, and 50's

film noir classic and a terrific performance by Burt Lancaster, as always!

Frankie Madison (Burt Lancaster) returns to New York after 14 years in prison. Fourteen years ago, he and his pal, Noll Turner (Kirk Douglas) made an agreement when the police were chasing them after they had committed a bootlegging crime – they weren't going to outrun the police in their truck, so one guy would jump out of the truck with the money and the other guy would take the rap and go to prison. When the guy in prison finally got out of jail, they would split everything 50/50 – whatever the guy who avoided prison made during that time, it would be split 50/50 when the guy who went to prison got out. Simple as that.

But trouble is on the way. Noll is now a wealthy nightclub owner, and Frankie is expecting him to honor their agreement when he was caught and Noll got away. But they completely differ on the meaning of the 50/50 split – basically, Noll is trying to cheat Frankie. Can Frankie, who knows only the strong-arm methods of Prohibition, win out against modern-day Big Business? It will be tough...even with the unlikely alliance of Noll's torch singer ex-girlfriend Kay (Lizabeth Scott), whom Noll introduces to Frankie in an effort to calm him down and also throw him off the track. Caught in the middle is the third member of the group, Dave (Wendell Corey) who was the bookkeeper in the original arrangement and Noll's accountant in the nightclub. Dave is torn between the guy he has worked for the past 14 years, and the guy who he knows is getting a raw deal. Of course, Frankie and Kay end up falling in love and working together to get what is rightfully Frankie's (and keep from getting murdered along the way) – while Noll, with the help of henchmen like Dan (our old buddy Mike Mazurki), has no plans to resume their former partnership. Noll decides he must eliminate Frankie, and the real drama begins.

FORGOTTEN MOVIE STARS OF THE 30's, 40's, and 50's

This film, a good thriller all around, is predictable at times but very stylish, gritty and keeps the viewer involved all the time. It's a "can't miss" for film noir fans. Lancaster is really good as the tough – one might call him brutish - but tender Frankie, whose methods that worked during prohibition just don't apply any longer. Matched against him is Douglas, who has learned all about big business and corporations but is as mean as they come when it comes to getting his own way. Scott is more than just a mere love interest and lends plenty of grit and support to the movie. And Scott is a match for both of them with her sultry but honest performance – she's no dumb blonde in this film!

> *I Walk Alone* was Burt Lancaster's fourth film. In the first two – *The Killers* and *Brute Force* – he also played convicts.

3. The Strange Love of Martha Ivers – 1946

Lizabeth Scott and Van Heflin discuss strategy in *The Strange Love of Martha Ivers*. Has Van Heflin ever been bad in a movie? I don't think so.

FORGOTTEN MOVIE STARS OF THE 30's, 40's, and 50's

Martha Ivers (Barbara Stanwyck) is the teenaged niece of a very autocratic, mean, wealthy aunt who owns most of the town. Ivers' teacher lives with them along with his son, Walter O'Neill (Kirk Douglas in his first movie). Sam Masterson (Van Heflin) is a friend from the wrong side of the tracks who is running away from home and pays a last visit to the home of his friend Martha before he leaves. As he is leaving, Martha, in a fit of rage while watching her aunt beat Martha's cat, kills her aunt with a poker stick, but the murder is blamed on an intruder. And that's the tale Martha, Walter, and Walter's father carry forward.

Eighteen years pass, and Sam happens to be driving through town when his car breaks down. He has not been back to his old stomping grounds in 18 years. Sam meets a girl waiting to take a bus out of town (Lizabeth Scott) and they hit it off really well. Sam finds out that Martha and Walter are unhappily married and that Martha is the richest person in town while Walter is the district attorney. When it turns out that Scott gets arrested for breaking parole, Sam goes to his old pal Walter and asks the District Attorney to get his new girlfriend off the hook. Walter says he will look into it, but suspects that Sam is going to blackmail him and Martha because Sam witnessed the murder that took place 18 years ago. So the rest of the movie is a cat and mouse game between the three principals (Sam, Walter, and Martha) with Walter and Martha not necessarily on the same side since they really can't stand each other. A dramatic conclusion awaits all four of the principals in this movie.

This is Lizabeth Scott's first major role, and while she is clearly a supporting player to the likes of Barbara Stanwyck, Kirk Douglas, and Van Heflin, she makes the most of it. She really holds her own in her one scene with the veteran actress Stanwyck and is once again the girl with the checkered past trying to get a break and change her life, tough yet vulnerable.

FORGOTTEN MOVIE STARS OF THE 30's, 40's, and 50's

Van Heflin is really the star of the movie and is excellent, Stanwyck is outstanding as always, and Douglas is very good in his first role as the alcoholic district attorney with a love/hate relationship with his wife. Judith Anderson plays Ivers' aunt and is very good in a small role.

> Van Heflin was an outstanding character actor who occasionally played the lead in films. He did it all – film noir, westerns like *Shane* and *3:10 to Yuma*, crime films, and even swashbucklers like *The Three Musketeers*. He won his only Oscar for *Johnny Eager*, with Robert Taylor in the lead.

4. Dead Reckoning – 1947

Not a scene from the movie, but Lizabeth Scott and Humphrey Bogart on the set of *Dead Reckoning* taking a break for tea. Bogey looks worried here.

Rip Murdock (Humphrey Bogart) and his pal Johnny Darke are en route to Washington to receive the Congressional Medal of Honor for heroism during World War II. Johnny, finding out that there will be considerable press coverage of the event,

FORGOTTEN MOVIE STARS OF THE 30's, 40's, and 50's

suddenly disappears and then turns up dead in the morgue of a Southern city. Rip learns that Johnny had been accused of murder of a friend's husband and sets out to investigate for himself. He can't believe his pal Johnny could possibly be a killer.

While investigating, he falls in love with Coral (Lizabeth Scott) whose husband is the one Johnny is supposed to have killed. He also crosses paths with a casino owner and his henchman, who are determined not to have him find out the truth, even if it means disposing of him. A series of double crosses ensues for the rest of the movie. What Rip has to determine is if Coral is really in love with him and trying to help him find the real murderer, or if she is involved in the killings of her former husband and Johnny.

> Of course, because it's femme fatale Lizabeth Scott, we can't be sure and have to wait to the end of the movie to find out.

Both Bogart and Scott are terrific in this excellent example of film noir. We know Bogie is on the level in his search to find his buddy's murderer, but is Scott? Her husky voice and overall sultriness only add to her charm as either a helpless female or a femme fatale. She easily reminds one of a young Lauren Bacall in this film. A good supporting cast includes Morris Carnovsky as the casino owner, Marvin Miller as his henchman, and Wallace Ford as a locksmith trying to help Rip and Coral with the "key" to unlocking the mystery.

Bogart was married to Bacall at this time, and Scott has a similar acting style to Bacall. (That was certainly no coincidence in casting her for this film.) Perhaps that is why there is such good vibes between the two in this flick.

FORGOTTEN MOVIE STARS OF THE 30's, 40's, and 50's

> The film is directed by John Cromwell, the father of actor James Cromwell (*Babe, L.A. Confidential, The Queen*, and many others.)

5. Pitfall – 1948

Lizabeth Scott and the shadow of Dick Powell in a publicity photo from *Pitfall*. Actually, he never tried to kill her. It's easy to see why the three male leads in this film easily fell for her.

The theme of this film should be: be happy with a boring life full of routine.

This film noir classic details the fall of an errant suburban husband and father named Johnny Forbes (Dick Powell, again surprisingly effective in another film noir classic) at the hands of an alluring female played by Lizabeth Scott. Powell plays a successful insurance executive, married to his high school

FORGOTTEN MOVIE STARS OF THE 30's, 40's, and 50's

sweetheart (Jane Wyatt), living out a comfortable but routine and boring existence in a Los Angeles suburb. He is restless and unfulfilled ("I feel like a wheel within a wheel within a wheel") when he receives what at first seems like a routine assignment to recover goods that have been bought with stolen money, a claim paid off by Powell's firm.

The items are traced to Mona Stevens (Scott), a model living in suburban Los Angeles. It seems that her boyfriend Smiley - now in prison but soon to be released – stole some goods belonging to Powell's company and gave them to his girl friend; now Powell has to go to Scott to get them back. Powell is attracted to her, and what starts out as innocent flirtation ends up in a short but passionate love affair.

Powell's journey into a daydream ends in tragedy as he becomes a prisoner in his own home. He kills Scott's just-released-from-jail boyfriend, who has been set on his trail by a jealous private investigator out to get Scott for himself (Raymond Burr, excellent as a pathetic thug who also covets Scott's sexual favors).

The principals are both excellent in this film. Dick Powell demonstrates once again his flair for film noir roles. Scott is very believable as the girl caught in the middle. While she has bad taste in men but is really a decent person trying to do the right thing, a series of events orchestrated by Burr prevents that from happening. Her sex appeal in this film is absolutely amazing.

Raymond Burr as MacDonald in his pre-Perry Mason days is exceptional as the thug private investigator who will do anything to get Scott as his girl friend. These days, an abusive nut case like MacDonald would have a restraining order placed on him. Jane Wyatt is fine as the wife whose loyalty is definitely tested to the limit in this movie.

FORGOTTEN MOVIE STARS OF THE 30's, 40's, and 50's

> Before he was television's Perry Mason, Raymond Burr was a character actor in films. He generally played the heavy and was usually a rather vicious bad guy, the kind who would beat up people for fun. His weight also seemed to fluctuate quite a bit – in *Pitfall*, he was definitely on the heavy side. But those thug roles all ended in 1958 when he became good guy Perry Mason, who won all his cases except one.

While Lizabeth Scott had a relatively small number of quality film roles, she had a unique ability to play the good girl gone wrong or the temptress with equal aplomb. And her sex appeal was definitely smoldering. She is the kind of female you would dream about meeting while you were out taking a walk through your neighborhood. But I don't seem to remember many females who looked like her while I was walking through MY neighborhoods as a younger man.

FORGOTTEN MOVIE STARS OF THE 30's, 40's, and 50's

Randolph Scott – 1898-1987

Everything you need to know about Randolph Scott can be learned by watching Mel Brooks' *Blazing Saddles*. There is a scene where Sheriff Bart and his deputy, The Ringo Kid, are trying to convince the townspeople to do something – I believe to accept black people into the town. The townsfolk are completely balking at the idea until Sheriff Bart says, "You'd do it for Randolph Scott, wouldn't you?" In unison, the townsfolk let out a hail-mary chorus of "RANDOLPH SCOTT!" in reverence to Scott, and immediately accept the Sheriff's plan. This mixture of past and present was no accident.

Randolph Scott was simply the ultimate Hollywood western hero, probably more so than even John Wayne or Gary Cooper. Unlike Wayne and Cooper, almost all of Scott's films were westerns. He was the consummate man of few words and great action. In his westerns, there were always clear heroes and obvious villains, and Scott was always the hero. While he was in many good movies, he was also in many B westerns in the 1940's through 1960's.

FORGOTTEN MOVIE STARS OF THE 30's, 40's, and 50's

> The line from *Blazing Saddles* is a truly great reference and Mel Brooks' tribute to a great Western star. That pretty much tells you the stature of Randolph Scott in the ranks of Western heroes. And as you can guess, I am a big fan of westerns.

My favorite Randolph Scott films include:

- *Ride the High Country*
- *Ride Lonesome*
- *The Tall T*
- *Western Union*
- *Pittsburgh*
- *The Spoilers*
- *The Last of the Mohicans*

Biography

Randolph Scott was a handsome leading man who developed into one of Hollywood's greatest and most popular western stars. Born George Randolph Scott, on January 23, 1898, to George and Lucy Crane Scott. Scott was raised in Charlotte, North Carolina in a wealthy family. He attended Georgia Institute of Technology but, after being injured playing football, transferred to the University of North Carolina, where he graduated with a degree in textile engineering and manufacturing. Not typical for a future Hollywood star.

> Scott served in France as an artillery observer during WWI. His wartime experience would give him training that would be put to use in his later film career, including how to ride a horse.

FORGOTTEN MOVIE STARS OF THE 30's, 40's, and 50's

While in College, Scott discovered acting in school plays and developed a love for the stage that took him to California, in 1928, with a letter of introduction from his wealthy father to millionaire filmmaker Howard Hughes. Hughes read the letter and obtained an audition for him for Cecil B. DeMille's *Dynamite* (1929), a role which went instead to Joel McCrea. Scott and McCrea would go on to become friends and star in one film together, Scott's last motion picture.

Because of his background, Scott was hired to coach Gary Cooper in a Virginia dialect for *The Virginian* (1929) and also played a bit part in the film. After that, Paramount scouts saw him in a play and offered him a contract.

Scott met Cary Grant, another Paramount contract player, on the set of *Hot Saturday* (1932) and immediately the two became friends and roommates. Their on-and-off living arrangement would last until 1942, including some speculation – never proven – that they were homosexual lovers.[13] Scott married and divorced wealthy heiress Marion DuPont in the late 1930's. During this time, he moved into leading roles at Paramount with his easygoing personality.

> Scott remained close friends with Cary Grant until the day Grant died. When he heard of his old friend's death, Scott reportedly put his head in his hands and wept.

---

[13] In *Hollywood Gays* (1996), **Boze Hadleigh**, author of numerous books purporting to "out" the sexual orientation of celebrities, makes various claims for Scott's homosexuality

FORGOTTEN MOVIE STARS OF THE 30's, 40's, and 50's

A pleasant enough personality in comedies, dramas and the occasional adventure, it was not until he began focusing on westerns in the late 1940s that he reached the stardom that he was ultimately known for. His screen persona altered into that of a stoic, craggy, man-of-few-words type, an uncompromising figure, often a tough, hard-bitten man completely different from the light comedy leads he had played in the 1930's. This personality became what we think of when we envision western heroes. He became one of the top ten box-office stars of the 1950's in westerns mostly directed by Budd Boetticher for Ranown Productions, which Scott owned.

> During the 1950's, Scott also produced several films, beginning with *Man in the Saddle* in 1951.

In the 50's, Scott worked almost exclusively in Ranown westerns, in which he was partnered with veteran producer Harry Joe Brown. This trio, including Boetticher, produced many of the finest medium-budgeted westerns ever made – nothing on the order of *High Noon, Shane, Red River,* or *The Searchers*, but still pretty darn good western flicks.

While Scott was still in top physical condition, his face had become weary and weather beaten (perfect for the roles he was playing); this facial appearance, combined with his deliberate characterizations of soft-spoken, fatalistic, yet supremely self-reliant "Western Tough Guys," brought a new dimension to Scott's performances that, sadly, has been much ignored until recent years when his films started showing up consistently on Turner Classic Movies and Encore's Western Channel, where you can regularly find a Randolph Scott flick.

FORGOTTEN MOVIE STARS OF THE 30's, 40's, and 50's

Not only was he one of the top box office stars of the 1950's, but Scott was also a critically important figure in the western film as an art form. Following a critically acclaimed, less-heroic-than-usual role (rare for Scott) in one of the classics of the genre, *Ride the High Country* (1962), Scott retired from films at the age of 64.

A multimillionaire as a result of many shrewd investments and reportedly worth several hundred million dollars, Scott spent his remaining years playing golf and avoiding film industry affairs, stating that he didn't like publicity. He supported both Barry Goldwater and Ronald Reagan in their presidential bids and attended the 1964 Republican convention that nominated Goldwater for the presidency. After a series of illnesses in his later years, Scott died in 1987 at the age of 89, survived by his second wife, Patricia Stillman, and his two adopted children, Christopher and Sandra. He is buried in his home town of Charlotte, North Carolina.

> According to the International Movie Data Base (IMDB), Scott's theory on publicity was, "Never let yourself be seen in public unless they pay for it. The most glamorous, the most fascinating star our business ever had was Garbo. Why? Because she kept herself from the public. Each member of the audience had his own idea of what she was really like. But take the other stars of today. There is no mystery about them. The public knows what kind of toothpaste they use, whether they sleep in men's pajamas, and every intimate fact of their lives."
>
> Truer words were never spoken, if you think of today's stars. Overexposed is a word that quickly comes to mind.

FORGOTTEN MOVIE STARS OF THE 30's, 40's, and 50's

Recognition

Randolph Scott has a star on the Hollywood Walk of Fame at 6243-6245 Hollywood Boulevard. He was also nominated for a Laurel Award in 1958. Scott won a Golden Boot award in 1997 posthumously.

> The Golden Boot awards are given to movie people – actors, directors, writers, and stunt people – who had significant involvement in the western genre in movies and television. Scott was certainly worthy of that award for his contribution to western films. He would have been proud to receive this award, I am sure.

My Favorite Randolph Scott Films

1. Ride the High Country – 1962

Aging gunfighters Randolph Scott and Joel McCrea ride together again in *Ride the High Country*.

FORGOTTEN MOVIE STARS OF THE 30's, 40's, and 50's

Directed by Sam Peckinpah, many serious movie fans believe that *Ride the High Country*, not *The Wild Bunch*, is Peckinpah's best western. It is the story of two aging gunfighters trying to find redemption and peace, set in the early 1900's when the Old West was slowly giving way to the New West. Aging ex-marshal Steve Judd (Joel McCrea), an honest but poor lawman, is hired by a bank to transport a gold shipment through dangerous territory.

He hires an old partner, Gil Westrum (Randolph Scott), and Westrum's young friend Heck Longtree to assist him. Unfortunately, Steve doesn't realize that Gil does not possess his integrity but is instead looking for a quick buck. Gil and Heck plan to steal the gold, with or without Steve's help.

On the trail, the three get involved in a young woman's desire to escape from her father, a religious fanatic, so that she can join her fiancé. Unfortunately, her fiancé and his brothers turn out to be dangerous psychos.

This union leads to several complications, including a final shootout that pits a reunited McCrea and Scott, along with Scott's young partner and the woman, against the three psychotic brothers and their father.

This film was released and virtually discarded by MGM but has grown to be considered a western classic, and rightly so. It also serves as the end of the careers of both McCrea (virtually his swan song), and Scott (his actual last film.) While McCrea is his usual stalwart self, Scott steals the film as the former lawman who has become an outlaw but who switches back to the side of law and order to help his pal when it counts most. The scenery is beautiful, and Scott and McCrea play off each other extremely well as McCrea attempts to understand why his old pal has switched to the dark side, and Scott is torn between stealing the gold and helping his old buddy.

An unusually strong supporting cast includes Mariette Hartley in her film debut as the young woman, R.G. Armstrong as her religious fanatic father, James Drury before starring in "The Virginian" as her fiancé, character actor John Anderson as his father, L.Q. Jones as one of his brothers, Warren Oates as the other brother, and Edgar Buchanan – remember him from "Petticoat Junction"? as a judge – a virtual who's who of top-notch supporting players in westerns of that era. A must see for those who like westerns!

> The last scene of the film – in which Scott and McCrea side by side face the bad guys – is one of the classic western endings and a great tribute to the careers of both Scott and McCrea.

2. Ride Lonesome - 1959

Randolph Scott and a young pre-Bonanza Pernell Roberts in a scene from *Ride Lonesome*.

FORGOTTEN MOVIE STARS OF THE 30's, 40's, and 50's

Ben Brigade (Randolph Scott), a bounty hunter, captures a wanted murderer, Billy John. Brigade intends to take him to Santa Cruz to be hanged. Brigade stops at a supply station, where he saves the late manager's wife, Carrie Lane (Karen Steele) from an Indian attack, and enlists the help of two outlaws to continue the journey to safety. However, the Indian attacks persist, and the outlaws plan to take Billy for themselves as their bounty because they are tempted by the offer of amnesty for his captors – it seems they are wanted by the authorities, and returning Billy will get them off the hook.

Meanwhile, Billy's brother Frank is determined to rescue his younger brother before he can be tried for murder. But Brigade has plans of his own. It seems that Brigade and Frank have an old score to settle, and Billy is the bait. Through it all, Brigade has to make sure that no harm comes to Carrie Lane as he also escorts her back to civilization.

This is yet another Scott western directed by the venerable Budd Boetticher in which an older and wizened Scott (61 in real life) vies with the elements, the bad guys, and maybe the men on his side as the group treks across the rugged terrain to reach civilization. I like the fact that Scott is his typical man of few words but rugged action, and you can't see how he is going to get out of this mess with villains chasing him and enemies in his own ranks.

While the drop-dead-gorgeous Karen Steele serves as a pleasant distraction throughout the film, the villains include James Best and Lee Van Cleef as Billy and Frank, and the fellows on Scott's side – maybe – are Pernell Roberts before his "Bonanza" days as Adam Cartwright, and James Coburn, before his days as *Our Man Flint*. Plus, the action scenes in *Ride Lonesome* are impressive, and it is noteworthy to see Scott's riding skills at the age of 61.

FORGOTTEN MOVIE STARS OF THE 30's, 40's, and 50's

Coburn, by the way, played a lot of villains in westerns before his breakthrough role in *The Magnificent Seven* in 1960.

> Karen Steele starred in many westerns and was also the brother-in-law's wife in the film classic, *Marty*, with Ernest Borgnine. Karen grew up in Hawaii and was living in Honolulu as a young girl when Pearl Harbor was attacked on December 7, 1941. She was one of the most beautiful actresses ever to work in Hollywood. I am sure that not many supply station managers' wives in the Old West really looked like Karen Steele. Western expansion might have been faster if more of them looked like her.

FORGOTTEN MOVIE STARS OF THE 30's, 40's, and 50's

3. The Tall T - 1957

Randolph Scott in a publicity photo from *The Tall T*.

Having lost his horse in a bet, former ranch foreman Pat Brennan (Randolph Scott) hitches a ride with a stagecoach carrying newlyweds Willard and Doretta Mims. At the next station the coach and its passengers fall into the hands of a trio of outlaws headed by a man named Usher (Richard Boone) with Skip Homeier and Henry Silva as his two partners. Unlike in *Ride Lonesome*, these varmints are three of the meanest you will ever see in a western.

You quickly come to the realization that Mrs. Mims was a wealthy spinster and Willard Mims has married her strictly for her money. When Usher learns that Doretta is the daughter of a rich copper-mine owner, he decides to hold her for ransom. Tension builds over the next 24 hours as Usher awaits a response to his demands, Scott nobly serves as the protector for Mrs. Mims even though he is himself powerless, and a romantic attachment grows between the two.

FORGOTTEN MOVIE STARS OF THE 30's, 40's, and 50's

This movie is yet another classy western directed by Budd Boetticher. *The Tall T* is definitely a darker, more adult western than *Ride Lonesome* – it features three really surly villains, two of whom – Homeier and Silva – may snap at any time. Further, you know that the villains plan to kill Brennan, and rape and kill Mrs. Mims rather than merely letting them go when they get the ransom money. As a result, there is real tension throughout this movie.

> An aging Randolph Scott was first offered the role of a Knight of the Old West. Richard Boone ended up with the part of Paladin, in the TV show "Have Gun Will Travel"; which became Boone's signature role.

A superlative cast is headed by man-of-few-words but lots of action Scott, and an older Maureen O'Sullivan, almost 20 years after her last Tarzan movie as Jane. She plays the role of spinster who married because of her money perfectly. Richard Boone is Frank Usher, the head of the outlaws who must constantly be watchful of Scott but has an equally difficult time keeping his two younger partners under control. Homeier and Silva are excellent as the two younger, vicious bad guys. And Arthur Hunnicutt has a small role as Scott's friend, killed by the outlaws near the beginning of the film.

Arthur Hunnicutt played in tons of westerns. His many western roles included playing Davy Crockett. I have seen pictures of Crockett, and the real Davy Crockett looked a lot more like Arthur Hunnicutt than John Wayne or Fess Parker. In non-western roles, Hunnicutt popped up a couple of times on episodes of "Perry Mason."

FORGOTTEN MOVIE STARS OF THE 30's, 40's, and 50's

Arthur Hunnicutt in one of his many western roles. Now here is a guy who looks like someone you might have found in the Old West.

4. Western Union – 1941

Dean Jagger, a rather miscast Robert Young, and Randolph Scott discuss where to lay railroad tracks in a scene from *Western Union*.

FORGOTTEN MOVIE STARS OF THE 30's, 40's, and 50's

This early Randolph Scott western serves as a fitting contrast with later Scott westerns like *Ride the High Country, Ride Lonesome,* and *The Tall T.* Twentieth Century-Fox's *Western Union* was actually loosely based on a story by western author Zane Grey. The basic historical facts behind the connecting of telegraph wires between Omaha and Salt Lake City serve as a backdrop for a fictional story which is more a melodrama than historically accurate.

Randolph Scott and Barton MacLane are cast as brothers who pursue wildly divergent paths in adulthood: Vance Shaw (Scott), an ex-outlaw, goes to work for Western Union and its boss, Edward Creighton (Dean Jagger) after saving Creighton's life, while Jack Slade (MacLane – almost always the villain in movies, and that is certainly the case here) - remains a criminal. Slade leads a concerted effort to sabotage the telegraph company. Robert Young, who for some strange reason receives top billing in this western, is the young engineer from back East, Richard Blake (Robert Young); he and Scott vie for the affections of Creighton's daughter, played by Virginia Gilmore.

The Indians, too often merely villains in westerns, are treated with relative sympathy in this movie. When they do attack the whites, it is principally because they have been falsely accused of crimes that were actually committed by MacLane and his cronies. The rest of the film consists of Shaw and Blake attempting to absolve the Indians of any blame for trying to scuttle the telegraph while attempting to find the real culprits trying to sabotage the building of this new means of communication.

> This flick was directed by Fritz Lang, who was born in that legendary old western town, Vienna, Austria.

FORGOTTEN MOVIE STARS OF THE 30's, 40's, and 50's

Western Union was the second Technicolor western from German director Fritz Lang; the first was the equally popular *The Return of Frank James*, starring Henry Fonda and Gene Tierney. An excellent supporting case includes Slim Summerville, John Carradine as the company doctor, Chill Wills, Victor Killian, and Chief Thundercloud as the Native American leader. But it is Scott who is the hero and moves the story along; he is outstanding as the reformed outlaw bound and determined to connect the telegraph wires between the Great Plains and the West.

> Robert Young was successful mainly in romantic comedies before moving on to his two famous television roles – *Father Knows Best* in the 1950's and *Marcus Welby* in the 1970's.

5. The Spoilers/Pittsburgh - 1942

John Wayne supporting his best buddy, Randolph Scott, in a scene from *Pittsburgh*. They are trying to raise money for Wayne's business ventures. Looks like Wayne got the easy part here.

FORGOTTEN MOVIE STARS OF THE 30's, 40's, and 50's

I have included these two films together for the following reasons:

- They were both made in 1942
- They both had the same three stars – John Wayne, Marlene Dietrich, and Randolph Scott
- In both cases, the two men vie for the affections of Dietrich. In *Pittsburgh*, Scott is the hero and Wayne is someone who loses his way but redeems himself. In *The Spoilers*, Wayne is the good guy and Scott clearly the baddie.

The Spoilers takes place in Nome, Alaska, during the Alaskan gold rush. Miner Roy Glennister (John Wayne) and his partner Dextry (Harry Carey), financed by saloon entertainer Cherry Malotte (Marlene Dietrich), fight to save their gold claim from crooked commissioner Alexander McNamara (Randolph Scott). *The Spoilers* has a fairly conventional plot about prospectors, claim-jumpers, and the various hangers-on, honest and crooked, that made mining towns like Nome so exciting,--and also very dangerous! Just like earlier versions of the film, this one features a famous fight between Wayne and Scott that begins in a saloon and ends several blocks down the street. Windows get shattered, tables and chairs fly through the air, and people are aghast.

The actors are fine, particularly Dietrich as the tough dance hall queen who really has a heart of gold, a specialty of Dietrich's. She played virtually the same role in *Destry Rides Again* with James Stewart three years earlier. Scott is actually a bit more convincing as the villain than is Wayne as the hero. Another good supporting cast in addition to Harry Carey includes Richard Barthelmess, Margaret Lindsay, and Samuel S. Hinds as the judge. (It seems like Samuel S. Hinds always played a judge).

FORGOTTEN MOVIE STARS OF THE 30's, 40's, and 50's

> Gary Cooper starred in a 1930 version of *The Spoilers*. This was the only time that Cooper and Wayne played the same part in their illustrious careers.

Pittsburgh, also 1942, has nothing to do with either the Pirates or the Steelers, but basically deals with the emergence of the steel industry with cities like Pittsburgh as the hub. Charles 'Pittsburgh' Markham (Wayne) is a coal miner with ambition – He rides roughshod over and uses his friends, his girlfriend, and his ideals in his trek toward financial success in the Pittsburgh steel industry, only to find himself deserted and lonely at the top. He doublecrosses his best friend (Scott), and dumps his girlfriend (Dietrich) in order to marry the daughter of the boss of the steel mill where he works, for personal gain rather than love.

When his crash finally comes, he finds that fate has dealt him a second chance. With World War II approaching and the need for steel increasing, he goes to work under an assumed name for a steel company owned by his old pal Scott. The redeemed Markham becomes a new man and strives for positive outcomes in the steel industry rather than greed.

Popular at the box office, the film received a lukewarm reception by critics because of its heavy handed and obvious message. But the three stars – Wayne, Scott, and Dietrich – work well together. The supporting cast includes Thomas Gomez, Louise Albritton, Paul Fix, and Shemp Howard of The Three Stooges as Shorty the Tailor. (Nyuk, Nyuk – oops! That was Curly. Shemp did not actually return to the Stooges until his younger brother Curly suffered a career-ending stroke in 1947.)

FORGOTTEN MOVIE STARS OF THE 30's, 40's, and 50's

> Ironically, Scott was billed over Wayne in both of these films, even though Wayne had the bigger part in both films. Wayne was not yet the iconic star in 1942 that he would become a few years later.

6. The Last of the Mohicans – 1936

Randolph Scott as Hawkeye in *The Last of the Mohicans*

In the year 1756, The English and French are fighting for control of what is now New York State – at that time the West - in the French and Indian War. Fort William Henry on Lake George is under siege by the French and the Huron Indian tribe under French General Montcalm. Alice and Cora Munro, young daughters of the British Commander, Colonel Munro, set out from Albany to join their father at the fort.

FORGOTTEN MOVIE STARS OF THE 30's, 40's, and 50's

They are accompanied by Major Duncan Heyward, who has loved Alice for a long time, and by a renegade Huron named Magua. Magua leads the party astray with the view of betraying them into the hands of a wandering party of Hurons. His plans are foiled by Hawkeye, a Colonial scout, when he and his Mohican comrades, Chingachgook and his son Uncas, rescue the party and conduct them safely to the fort; Chingachgook and Uncas are the last two survivors of the Mohican tribe.

During their travels to the fort, Alice falls in love with Hawkeye, while younger sister Cora falls in love with Uncas. Shortly afterwards, Munro surrenders on honorable terms to Montcalm and is permitted to march out of the fort under arms and colors. However, Munro is then mortally wounded by Magua during a massacre by the Indians as the fort is being evacuated. Cora and Alice are carried off by Magua, and Heyward, Hawkeye, Chingachgook and Uncas set out in search of them. During the rescue, Magua is responsible for the deaths of Cora and Uncas. As revenge, Chingachgook finally disposes of the evil Magua. Hawkeye is also taken prisoner by the brutal Hurons, and Maj. Heyward must organize a band to rescue Hawkeye before he is tortured to death.

Randolph Scott is an excellent hero as Hawkeye is this early movie version of the James Fenimore Cooper novel. The film features an outstanding plot, romance, and lots of action, as well as excellent performances throughout. Scott's performance as Hawkeye compares favorably with that of Daniel Day Lewis in the 1995 version.

Also included in the cast are Binnie Barnes as Alice, Heather Angel as Cora, Henry Wilcoxon as Major Heyward, Bruce Cabot as Magua, Robert Barrat as Chingachgook, and Phillip Reed as Uncas.

FORGOTTEN MOVIE STARS OF THE 30's, 40's, and 50's

> You might be wondering where you have heard of Bruce Cabot before. Cabot played the part of the hero, Jack Driscoll, in the original 1933 version of *King Kong* with Fay Wray and Robert Armstrong.

> The *Last of the Mohicans* refers to a quote from Chingachgook, who calls Uncas the last of the Mohican tribe after the death of his son, Uncas. But technically, Chingachgook is the Last of the Mohicans, since he outlives his son.

As you can see, Randolph Scott was a real Hollywood star and one of the great western stars of all time. While he ventured occasionally into romantic comedies, dramas, and other types of movies, it is in westerns that Scott will be most remembered. Mel Brooks got it right when he had the townspeople shout out praises to this western movie icon.

FORGOTTEN MOVIE STARS OF THE 30's, 40's, and 50's

Marlene Dietrich – 1901-1992

Marlene Dietrich was a star in her native Germany who became an even bigger star in the United States. After she became an icon in her own country, she was offered and accepted a contract from Hollywood. Marlene became a U.S. citizen in 1939 and remained a star in the United States from that time onward. She also displayed a nice singing voice in several films, which led to a singing career in her 50's. Her moniker was her deep, sensuous voice, glamorous appearance, and relatively thick German accent, which was often mimicked in later comedy films. Fashion wise, she was known for wearing men's wear - tuxedos, hats, and tailored suits.

> Another *Blazing Saddles* reference: The character played by Madeline Kahn – Lily Von Shtupp – was basically an impersonation of Dietrich, right down to the thick German accent and singing style. And we all know what "Shtupp" means in German, right?

FORGOTTEN MOVIE STARS OF THE 30's, 40's, and 50's

My favorite Marlene Dietrich films are the following:

- ➢ *Witness for the Prosecution*
- ➢ *Destry Rides Again*
- ➢ *Judgment at Nuremberg*
- ➢ *Touch of Evil*
- ➢ *Pittsburgh/The Spoilers*
- ➢ *Stage Fright*

Biography

Marlene Dietrich (Maria Magdalene Dietrich) was born on December 27, 1901 in Berlin, Germany, the daughter of a police lieutenant. Marlene was known in school for her "bedroom eyes" and her first affairs were as a teenager – in fact, a professor at her school was terminated as a result of their involvement. After failing an audition with the famous German theatre director Max Reinhardt in 1921, she joined the chorus line of a touring musical revue. She entered the cabaret scene in 1920s Germany, first as a spectator then as a singer. In 1924, Dietrich married director Rudolf Sieber and, although they lived together for only five years, they remained married until his death in 1976.

In 1922, she re-auditioned for Reinhardt and this time was accepted in his drama school. She began playing small roles on the stage and in German films, never getting anything more substantial than supporting roles. However, by the late 20's she had risen to playing leads with moderate success.

Her big break came when she was spotted onstage by American director Josef Von Sternberg, who cast her to play a sexy, seductive vamp in 1930's *The Blue Angel,* filmed in Germany. Von Sternberg soon became her mentor (and lover, I should add), molding her into a glamorous, sensuous star. She got a Hollywood contract and left her husband and daughter behind, going on to star in six films for Von

FORGOTTEN MOVIE STARS OF THE 30's, 40's, and 50's

Sternberg. Their collaboration made her a star equal in magnitude to Greta Garbo.

A series of successes followed, and Marlene became the highest paid actress of her time, but many of her films in the mid 1930's were critical and popular failures. She returned to Europe at the end of the decade, after a series of affairs with former leading men (she had a reputation of romancing her co-stars like Gary Cooper and James Stewart), as well as other prominent artistic figures like writer Erich Maria Remarque.

Because of her affection for the United States and hatred of Nazi Germany, Dietrich became an American citizen in 1939; meanwhile, her films were banned in Germany because she had refused a lucrative offer from the Nazis to return and star in German films. During World War II she entertained U.S. troops, participated in war bond drives, and made anti-Nazi broadcasts in German. She was awarded the Medal of Freedom for her efforts to help the United States win the war.

In the 50's, as her film career slowed, Dietrich began a second career as a recording star, cabaret performer, and even Broadway star. She sang to packed houses in major cities all over the world. Her last movie role of any substance was *Judgment at Nuremberg* in 1961. Late in her life, she was rarely seen in public, but she agreed to provide the voice-over for Maximilian Schell's screen biography of her, *Marlene* (1984). Spending the last 11 years of her life mostly bed-ridden, Marlene Dietrich died on May 6, 1992 in Paris, France of natural causes at the age of 90. During those last 12 years, however, she remained a prolific letter writer and did not lose touch with her friends.

> Dietrich was probably more of an internationally-known star than anyone else in this book. The fact that she made only 54 movies is not really relevant.

FORGOTTEN MOVIE STARS OF THE 30's, 40's, and 50's

Recognition

Marlene Dietrich was nominated for an Oscar for Best Actress in a Leading Role for her performance in *Morocco* (1930). She received a David di Donatello special award for her performance in *Judgment at Nuremberg* (1961) and a German Film Award in 1980 for continued outstanding individual contributions to the German film industry. She was nominated for a Golden Globe for Best Actress in a Drama for her performance in *Witness for the Prosecution* in 1957.

In 1999, the American Film Institute named Dietrich the ninth-greatest female star of all time. I am not surprised by that vote. She has a star on the Hollywood Walk of Fame at 6400 Hollywood Boulevard.

> Marlene Dietrich should have won an Academy Award for her performance in *Witness for the Prosecution*, in my opinion. Her performance in that movie was simply riveting. If you are looking for one Marlene Dietrich flick to watch, I suggest *Witness for the Prosecution*. She is simply amazing in this movie.

My Favorite Marlene Dietrich Films include the following:

1. Witness for the Prosecution – 1957

(Next Page) Marlene Dietrich as the loyal wife – or is she? – in *Witness for the Prosecution*.

FORGOTTEN MOVIE STARS OF THE 30's, 40's, and 50's

This film is simply one of my two favorite courtroom dramas of all time – the other being the original *Twelve Angry Men* with Henry Fonda as the holdout juror. It features outstanding performances from three stars – Marlene Dietrich, Tyrone Power, and Charles Laughton – as well as a number of plot twists and a real surprise ending. The film takes place in London in the early 1950's, with a flashback to Germany in World War II.

Upon his return to work following a heart attack, outstanding but irrepressible barrister Sir Wilfrid Robarts (Charles Laughton), a defense attorney who often works on seemingly hopeless cases, takes on a murder case, much to the exasperation of his medical team, led by his overly dictatorial private nurse, Miss Plimsoll (Elsa Lanchester).

FORGOTTEN MOVIE STARS OF THE 30's, 40's, and 50's

She tries her best to ensure that he not return to his hard living ways - primarily excessive cigar smoking and drinking - while he takes his medication and gets his much needed rest, including an upcoming cruise. However, to her chagrin, he accepts a case defending American war veteran Leonard Vole (Tyrone Power), a poor, out of work, struggling inventor living in London who is accused of murdering his fifty-six year old lonely and wealthy widowed friend, Emily French.

The initial evidence is circumstantial but points to Leonard being at the scene of the crime and therefore the likely murderer. Despite being happily married to East German former beer hall performer Christine Vole (Marlene Dietrich), Vole clearly fostered that friendship with Mrs. French in the hopes that she would finance one of his many inventions to the tune of a few hundred pounds. But is he capable of murder? Only his German-born wife can provide the facts needed to clear him.

There are several reasons why this film is one of my all time favorite courtroom dramas. First, the cast is outstanding – Laughton is the prickly, irascible defense attorney looking for his next great case, Power is very believable as the seemingly harmless weak and timid Leonard Vole, and Dietrich is just simply amazing as the loyal wife; her performance clearly carries the film. And there are several plot twists that will keep you on the edge of your seat, especially during the last 30 minutes of the flick.

As usual, an outstanding supporting cast includes veteran performers such as Henry Daniell, Torin Thatcher, Una O'Connor, Ruta Lee, and of course Elsa Lanchester. The great Billy Wilder directs, and Dietrich even sings in the flashback sequence where she meets her future husband Power as the American soldiers are invading Germany during WWII.

FORGOTTEN MOVIE STARS OF THE 30's, 40's, and 50's

> Dietrich issues one of the great movie lines of all time – "I'll give ya somethin' to dream about, Mister. Wanna kiss me, ducky?" At that point, you will go, "Ah ha!" because this line explains everything. Why is a German woman speaking in a cockney accent? See the film.

2. Destry Rides Again – 1939

James Stewart and Marlene Dietrich in a scene from *Destry Rides Again*. James Stewart plays a non-violent sheriff and Dietrich the dance hall queen who at first dismisses him as a fool but then realizes otherwise.

FORGOTTEN MOVIE STARS OF THE 30's, 40's, and 50's

Kent, the unscrupulous boss of the Western town of Bottleneck, who clearly runs the town, has reliable, old Sheriff Keogh killed when Keogh asks one too many questions about a rigged poker game. The mayor, who is in cahoots with Kent, appoints the town drunk, Washington Dimsdale, as the new sheriff assuming that he'll be easy to control and that Kent will continue to run the town without any interference. But what the mayor doesn't know is that Dimsdale was a deputy under famous lawman Tom Destry, and is able to call upon the equally formidable Tom Destry Jr. (James Stewart) to be his deputy.

Unfortunately, when Destry appears, he seems to be the antithesis of a law enforcement officer – he is gentle rather than intimidating and he actually refuses to wear a gun. After a difficult debut, the town comes to realize that there are some things that might actually be mightier than a gun – such as strength of character and being in the right. And if Destry can get bar singer Frenchy (Marlene Dietrich) on his side, he will only strengthen his case for settling disputes in a non-violent manner.

Destry Rides Again features a solid performance from James Stewart as Destry coupled with a career reviving performance from Marlene Dietrich as bar singer Frenchy. Brian Donlevy is very good as the villain, Kent, with Charles Winninger as Sheriff Dimsdale. A stalwart supporting case includes reliables such as Una Merkel, Mischa Auer, Irene Hervey, Jack Carson, Billy Gilbert, and Samuel S. Hinds (naturally playing a judge who is also the mayor.) Dietrich gets to sing three splashy dance hall numbers: "Little Joe," "You've Got That Look" and, most famously, "See What the Boys In the Back Room Will Have." That last song is the one that served as the basis for the Mel Brooks takeoff in *Blazing Saddles,* and Dietrich gives it all the gusto she can muster in her performance.

FORGOTTEN MOVIE STARS OF THE 30's, 40's, and 50's

3. Judgment at Nuremberg – 1961

Marlene Dietrich tries to convince Spencer Tracy that Ernst Janning (Burt Lancaster) is different from the other German judges who are on trial.

Richard Widmark, Spencer Tracy, Montgomery Clift, and Burt Lancaster between takes in *Judgment at Nuremberg*. What a cast that also included Dietrich, Maximilian Schell, Judy Garland, and even a young William Shatner!

FORGOTTEN MOVIE STARS OF THE 30's, 40's, and 50's

Judge Dan Haywood (Spencer Tracy) arrives in Nuremberg in 1948 – three years after the end of World War II - to preside over the trial of four Nazi judges allegedly guilty of war crimes. Each was charged with having abused the court system to help cleanse Germany of the politically and socially undesirable. The opening statement of the prosecuting attorney (Richard Widmark) is a vicious one, depicting the defendants as willing, evil accomplices in Nazi atrocities, but American Judge Haywood wonders if it is really that simple.

> The film clips that the prosecution shows of what took place in the Nazi concentration camps are hard to watch but very compelling.

Confounded at how one defendant, a renowned German champion of justice named Ernst Janning (Burt Lancaster) appears to have played the greatest role in molding Germany's Ministry of Justice into a destructive instrument of Nazism, Judge Haywood resolves to gain some personal perspective outside the courtroom on the period in which the German legal system strayed from a course of entirely objective justice.

Probing for the truth proves difficult, though, as nobody who lived in Germany during the Nazi years seems willing to admit to having much inside knowledge. Haywood befriends Mrs. Bertholt (Marlene Dietrich) the widow of an executed Nazi army officer, but she offers few insights, more consumed by her personal experiences than the broader matters of Nazism.

Mrs. Bertholt is focusing on being a catalyst for the cultural rebirth of Nuremberg, keen on remolding the image of a city that had become notorious as the site of the Nazi rallies and training sessions for Hitler youth. She attempts to convince the judge that Janning is a symbol of virtue to Germany.

FORGOTTEN MOVIE STARS OF THE 30's, 40's, and 50's

In the climactic scene, Janning (Lancaster) speaks of how economically-stricken Germany had become a nation of fearful, desperate people, and how only such a people could submit to Nazism. Hitler's promises, Janning explained, in which he openly vowed the elimination of those accountable for Germany's hardships were, at first, soothing and reassuring to the German people.

Janning then noted that, even once those in power realized the inhumanity of Hitler's approach, they stayed at their posts to help things from getting even worse, but, predictably, failed to derail the atrocities of the times. He explained that national allegiance had motivated most of them to the point that they sacrificed their own personal senses of morality. In a deeply personal, yet self-damning statement, he conceded that most of them should have known better, and that those that had gone along had in highsight betrayed Germany. At long last, the issue at the heart of the case becomes clear to Judge Haywood, and he takes the action he believes is right.

The entire movie is outstanding and very meaningful – trying to understand how the people living in Nazi Germany could live with themselves knowing full well of the inhumane actions taken by Hitler and his cohorts. The performances of all – particularly Tracy, Lancaster, Widmark, Dietrich, and Judy Garland and Montgomery Clift in supporting roles – are just outstanding.

> NOTE: My wife and I were on a European river cruise that included Nuremberg in 2010. We visited the training site for Hitler youth during the early and mid 1930's while we were there. It definitely left an impression on us, I can say that.

FORGOTTEN MOVIE STARS OF THE 30's, 40's, and 50's

Maximilian Schell won a Best Actor Oscar for his performance as the defense attorney opposite prosecuting attorney Widmark, but I actually thought he was guilty of overacting. In a relatively small but key and effective role, Dietrich is impressive in conveying the atmosphere of Germany toward the Nazi years and contrasting that with the rebuilding Germany of the post-WWII era. She tries her best to convince Tracy of the difficult choices that a judge such as Ernst Janning had to make at that time. Whether the judges buy it or not is key to the decision.

4. Touch of Evil - 1958

Marlene Dietrich as a fortune teller in *Touch of Evil*.

Mexican Narcotics officer Ramon Miguel "Mike" Vargas – believe it or not, Charlton Heston as a Mexican law enforcement officer - has to interrupt his honeymoon on the Mexican-U.S. border when an American building contractor is killed by a car bomb explosion. He is killed on the U.S. side of the border but it is clear that the bomb was planted on the Mexican side.

FORGOTTEN MOVIE STARS OF THE 30's, 40's, and 50's

As a result, Vargas delays his return to Mexico City where he has been mounting a case against the Grandi family crime and narcotics syndicate. Police Captain Hank Quinlan (a very heavy Orson Welles) is in charge on the U.S. side and he soon has a suspect, a Mexican named Manolo Sanchez.

Vargas is quickly distrustful of Quinlan and his sergeant when he catches them planting evidence to convict Sanchez. With his new American wife, Susie (Janet Leigh), safely tucked away in a hotel on the U.S. side of the border - or so he thinks - Vargas starts to review Quinlan's earlier cases. While he is concentrating on the corrupt policeman, however, the Grandis have their own plans for Vargas, and they start by kidnapping his wife. Vargas must deal with this issue while attempting to find the real killer.

Dietrich, in a brunette wig, has a small but important role as the jaded, fortune-telling madam. She delivers a classic line when Welles asks her to tell him his future? "What future? You haven't got any. Your future is all used up!" And what a fortune teller she was! Although Welles was a truly great and innovative director, this was the last Hollywood film that Welles would ever direct. An outstanding supporting cast includes Akim Tamiroff, Joseph Calleia, Ray Collins, Mercedes McCambridge, and Dennis Weaver.

5. Pittsburgh/The Spoilers – 1942

I have already reviewed these two films in the section on Randolph Scott. Suffice it to say that the actors are fine, particularly Dietrich as the tough dance hall queen who really has a heart of gold, a specialty of Dietrich's in *The Spoilers*.

Dietrich played virtually the same role in *Destry Rides Again* with James Stewart three years later.

FORGOTTEN MOVIE STARS OF THE 30's, 40's, and 50's

The Duke – John Wayne – and Marlene Dietrich in a scene from *The Spoilers*. They join forces against bad guy Randolph Scott.

6. Stage Fright - 1950

Lovers Marlene Dietrich and Richard Todd in *Stage Fright*. Did they plot to kill her husband?

FORGOTTEN MOVIE STARS OF THE 30's, 40's, and 50's

Not one of Alfred Hitchcock's more famous films, *Stage Fright* is a very good one, just the same. Unlike most of his films, which feature a man wrongly accused of a murder and trying to find the real killer to prove himself innocent – *North By Northwest, Vertigo, Saboteur, Strangers on a Train* - in this film a female plays the lead role as she hides the man accused of murder while attempting to find the real killer.

Stage actor Jonathan Cooper (Richard Todd) is wanted by the police, who suspect him of killing his lover's husband. His aspiring stage actress friend Eve Gill (Jane Wyman) offers to hide him, and Jonathan explains to her that his lover, actress Charlotte Inwood (Marlene Dietrich) is the real murderer. Eve decides to investigate for herself, but when she meets the detective in charge of the case (Michael Wilding), she starts to fall in love with the policeman.

Posing as a reporter, she bribes Charlotte's theater maid to pretend that she is ill and cannot work for Charlotte for a while. Eve then utilizes her acting skills to affect the false identity and accent of a Cockney maid, claiming to be the maid's cousin, "Doris Tinsdale," and takes the temporary job of replacing "her cousin" in order to infiltrate Charlotte's household and do some investigating on her own. The remainder of the film consists of Eve trying to hide Jonathan while being courted by the detective and trying to find the real murderer on her own. In the style fitting of Hitchcock, the real murderer is revealed in a way that places our heroine Eve in great danger.

Dietrich is again at her best as the leading lady who may or may not be the real killer but is certainly not going to let any mere detective trick her into confessing. Richard Todd is excellent as the man being hunted, and Jane Wyman is outstanding as the leading lady. The supporting cast includes

FORGOTTEN MOVIE STARS OF THE 30's, 40's, and 50's

Michael Wilding as the detective and Alistair Sim as Wyman's uncle.

Featured in this film is an original Cole Porter song, "The Laziest Gal in Town," performed by Dietrich in a sultry fashion. One of her trademarks was singing sultry songs in movies.

In the biography of Dietrich by her daughter Maria, she recounts how Dietrich did not particularly like Jane Wyman, perhaps because they were such opposites. Hitchcock, however, may have utilized this animosity to the film's advantage. At one point in the film, Dietrich compliments Wyman for a change in the way she dresses, when Wyman appears at the garden party. [14]

> At this time, Jane Wyman was recently divorced from a journeyman actor turned politician who was beginning to make a name for himself. His name – Ronald Reagan.
>
> They were married from 1940 to 1948. Their children were Maureen Reagan and Michael Reagan.

You may be asking yourself – Where have I heard of Richard Todd? Well, Todd was the star of the 1952 Walt Disney film, *The Story of Robin Hood*, playing the title character. Here is a picture of Todd and also one other fellow you may recognize who also played the legendary outlaw some 15 or so years earlier.

---

[14] From Wikipedia article on *Stage Fright*

FORGOTTEN MOVIE STARS OF THE 30's, 40's, and 50's

Errol Flynn and Richard Todd

As far as I am concerned, this quote, from Ernest Hemingway, sums it all up on Marlene Dietrich.

> "If she had nothing more than her voice she could break your heart with it. But she has that beautiful body and the timeless loveliness of her face. It makes no difference how she breaks your heart if she is there to mend it."

FORGOTTEN MOVIE STARS OF THE 30's, 40's, and 50's

And this one from John Wayne himself, who was in several films with Dietrich:

> "The most intriguing woman I've ever known."

The more I learn about Marlene Dietrich, the more I like her. She had a great many talents – including acting and singing – and was a huge star in both Europe and the United States. She is yet another star who should never be forgotten.

FORGOTTEN MOVIE STARS OF THE 30's, 40's, and 50's

A Few Key Terms

Character actor or actress - an actor in support of the leading man or woman, synonymous with "supporting actor."

Costume Drama - a period piece film with lavish costumes, often but not always also called swashbuckler films.

Film Noir - stylish, cynical black-and-white crime drama featuring heroes who often get duped by duplicitous women.

Golden Boot Award - The Golden Boot awards are given to movie people – actors, directors, writers, and stunt people – who had significant involvement in the western genre in movies and television.

Hollywood Canteen - a social club offering food and entertainment for American servicemen. This outstanding organization was universally heralded for its treatment of the armed forces especially during World War II.

Laurel Award - The Laurel Award is given to those who, through their efforts, advanced the art of film.

Method acting - a form of acting where the actor mystically 'becomes' the character or tries to somehow literally live the character in life.

Nebbish – what we would today call a nerd.

Pixilated – another word for slightly mad or loony, made famous in *Mr. Deeds Goes To Town*. The official definition is "somewhat unbalanced mentally."

FORGOTTEN MOVIE STARS OF THE 30's, 40's, and 50's

Sent up the river - an old movie term for "in jail." The term originates from the fact that convicts from New York City would be sent up the Hudson River to Ossining State Prison ("Sing Sing").

Swashbuckler – an adventure film that typically features lots of swordfights.

Talkies – talking pictures (movies with sound) which came into existence with *The Jazz Singer* in 1927. Until then, all motion pictures were silent films. Silent films and talkies went toe to toe for a couple of years before talkies took over completely around 1930. A number of silent film stars who either spoke very little English or had very poor speaking voices could not make the transition to talkies.

TCM – Turner Classic Movies, the cable TV channel that shows classic films from the 1930's and on WITHOUT commercial interruption. The key host as of this writing is Robert Osborne.

FORGOTTEN MOVIE STARS OF THE 30's, 40's, and 50's

Website Acknowledgements

1. Biographical information was extracted from several places, including **www.imdb.com** and **www.wikipedia.com** . Those two sites were also a big help in supplementing my knowledge on certain films. The vast majority of photos are taken from two sites where the pictures are in the public domain – **www.commons.wikimedia.org**, and **www.classicmoviefavorites.com**.
2. Robert Taylor's pictures are from **www.fanpix.net**. In fact, many of the pictures in this book were from that site. Also, pictures were taken from **www.acertaincinema.com**.
3. Louis Hayward's pictures are from various sites, including **www.imdb.com**, **www.commons.wikimedia.org**, and Louis Hayward's Facebook page.
4. Dana Andrews' pictures are from **www.fanpix.net** and **www.acertaincinema.com** .
5. Gene Tierney's pictures are from various sites, including **www.commonswikipedia.org**, **www.cmgww.com/stars/tierney**, and **www.fanpix.net**.
6. Teresa Wright's pictures are from various sites, including **www.IMDB.com**, **http://people.famouswhy.com**. **www.acertaincinema.com**, and **http://www.reelclassics.com/Actresses/Teresa/teresa2.htm**.
7. Victor Mature's pictures are from the Victor Mature gallery at **www.victormature.net** and also from **www.commonswikimedia.org**.
8. Paulette Goddard photos are from the Paulette Goddard gallery at **http://www.fanpix.net/picture-**

FORGOTTEN MOVIE STARS OF THE 30's, 40's, and 50's

gallery/paulette-goddard-picture-14309539.htm, www.commons.wikimedia,org, and **www.acertaincinema.com**
9. Glenn Ford's pictures are from the Glenn Ford gallery at **http://www.fanpix.net/gallery/glenn-ford-pictures.htm** Thanks to the following site - **http://www.classichollywoodbios.com/glennford.htm** - for contributions on his biographical information.
10. Barbara Stanwyck's pictures are taken from the following sites: **www.commons.wikimedia.org** and **http://www.classicmoviefavorites.com/stanwyck/** .
11. Ray Milland's pictures are taken from **www.fanpix.net. www.dvdbeaver.com** and from **http://www.briansdriveintheater.com/raymilland.html** .
12. Joseph Cotten's pictures are taken from **www.fanpix.net**, from **http://hiwaay.net/~oliver/duel.html** and from **http://movieimages.tripod.com/citizenkane**. .
13. John Garfield's pictures are taken from **www.TheMave.com**, **www.commons.wikimedia.org** , and **www.flixter.com**. Information is taken from **www.mademan.com**.
14. Susan Hayward's pictures are taken from **www.fanpix.net**, **www.commons.wikimedia.org**, and **www.meredy.com**.
15. William Powell's pictures are taken from **www.themave.com** and **www.fanpix.net**.
16. Myrna Loy's pictures are taken from **www.classicmoviefavorites.com/Loy**
17. Ronald Colman's pictures are taken from **www.classicmoviefavorites.com/Colman**

FORGOTTEN MOVIE STARS OF THE 30's, 40's, and 50's

18. Kathryn Grayson's pictures are taken from **www.fanpix.net** and **www.commons.wikimedia.org**.
19. Howard Keel's pictures are taken from **www.fanpix.net** and **www.commons.wikimedia.org**.
20. Tyrone Power's pictures are taken from **www.fanpix.net**., from **www.classicmoviefavorites.com**, and from **www.Tyrone-Power.com**.
21. Jean Simmons' pictures are taken from **www.fanpix.net** and **www.allmovie.com**
22. Jean Arthur's pictures are taken from **www.fanpix.net**, **www.commons.wikimedia.org**, **www.acertaincinema.com**, **www.allmovie.com** and **www.flixter.com** .
23. Gail Russell's pictures are taken from **www.acertaincinema.com** and **www.findadeath.com**.
24. Lizabeth Scott's pictures are taken from **http://www.briansdriveintheater.com/lizabeth scott.html**, **www.commons.wikimedia.org**, and **www.acertaincinema.com**.
25. Randolph Scott's pictures are taken from **www.acertaincinema.com**
26. Marlene Dietrich's pictures are taken from **www.commons.wikimedia.org**, **www.acertaincinema.com** and **www.classicmoviefavorites.com**

Acknowledgments

I wish to thank my family and friends for their support in writing this book and for their encouragement in actually finally getting started instead of just talking about it.

I would also like to thank the Writers' Club in the community where I live for assisting me with their encouragement and positive feedback. This includes the suggestion that I personalize the book by bringing in my witty and sparkling personality on occasion. A special thanks to my neighbor and friend, who wishes to remain anonymous, for assisting me greatly with the self-publishing aspects of this work and also for the graphics on the front and back covers. Also thanks to my proofreaders, Jack Schroeder, Bill Kolasinski, and my daughter Karen Schmidt. A special thanks also to Joanne Kenealy, who helped me with some of the Microsoft Word issues. Sometimes, Word seems to just have a mind of its own!

Finally, I wish to thank Chicago sports talk show host Mike North for his unknowing assistance. As I indicated in the introduction, the day after Glenn Ford died – August 31, 2006 – he was discussing what a huge western star Glenn Ford was, on his daily morning show. Half the callers were over 45 and were calling him to agree with his statement, and the other half were people – mainly guys under 40 – calling in to ask him, "Who the hell is Glenn Ford?" That bit of information started me thinking that maybe it was time for a book on some of these forgotten stars who should be remembered.

This is the result. I hope you liked it.

About the Author

Gary Koca has had a love of classic movies from the 30's, 40's, and 50's for as far back as he can remember. He is a devoted fan of Turner Classic Movies and got many of his ideas from films shown on that network. Professionally, he worked in human resources for 42 years, either as a Federal government employee or contractor. He wrote hundreds of position papers, proposals, articles for journals, letters, and many other written products during that time. Now retired and able to devote more time to his love of classic movies, his major character flaw is being a life-long fan of the Chicago Cubs.

Gary is married with two daughters and four grandchildren, and lives in suburban Chicago.

Printed in Great Britain
by Amazon

14151308R00241